THE MASTERS

The Masters

A Hole-by-Hole History of America's Golf Classic

THIRD EDITION

David Sowell

University of Nebraska Press
Lincoln

Library of Congress Cataloging-in-Publication Data
Names: Sowell, David, 1948– author.
Title: The Masters: a hole-by-hole history of
America's golf classic / David Sowell.
Description: Third Edition. | Lincoln, Nebraska:
University of Nebraska Press, [2019] | Includes index.
Identifiers: LCCN 2018037065
ISBN 9781496212832 (cloth: alk. paper)
ISBN 9781496215017 (epub)
ISBN 9781496215024 (mobi)
ISBN 9781496215031 (pdf)
Subjects: LCSH: Masters Golf Tournament—History.
| Golf—United States—History.
Classification: LCC GV970.3.M37 S69 2019 | DDC
796.352/66—dc23 LC record available at
https://lccn.loc.gov/2018037065

Set in Linotype Sabon Next by E. Cuddy.

To all those who love the Masters

CONTENTS

ACKNOWLEDGMENTS

I would like to first thank my wife, Susan, whose steadfast support and encouragement made this undertaking possible. I would also like to express my deep gratitude to our sons, Brett and Brandon, who are both stretched thin in their own careers but always managed to find the time to provide support and assistance when Dad needed it.

Also, many thanks to Robert Taylor at the University of Nebraska Press and to my agent, Robert Wilson, at Wilson Media.

Last but certainly not least, I will always be indebted to my best friend since high school, Dr. Cordell Scott, who infected me with the golf bug and despite my erratic play has put up with me as his partner in tournaments for more than thirty years.

Six days before Christmas in 1933, it was announced that a new golf tournament would take place in the spring. The tournament would be held on a new course in Georgia, the Augusta National Golf Club, and it would be hosted by the club's founder, who happened to be the greatest golfer of all time, Bobby Jones. The game of golf has never been so enriched and has never been the same.

Bobby Jones was one of the most celebrated figures in what was called the golden age of sports. From 1923 through 1929 he won nine major golf titles. In 1930 he captured that era's Grand Slam by winning the British Amateur, the British Open, the United States Open, and the United States Amateur. Up until this incredible feat, no golfer had ever won more than two of these prestigious tournaments in a single year.

In the fall of that year, after announcing his retirement from competition at the age of twenty-eight, Jones remained very much in the public eye. He signed on with Warner Bros. studios to make golf instructional films that were shown in movie theaters across the country. The films were a huge success, allowing a whole generation of golfers to see his beautiful swing at actual speed and in slow motion.

Jones had another endeavor he wanted to pursue, and that was to build what he called his "dream course." In the spring of 1931 friends of Jones in Augusta, Georgia, suggested that he drive over from Atlanta, his hometown. The friends wanted him to look at a property, Fruitlands Nurseries, which was for sale. This 365-acre tract was once the site of an indigo plantation that had been purchased in 1857 by a Belgian baron named Louis Mathieu Edouard Berckmans. The baron, who was a horticulturist, and his son Prosper, a professional agronomist and horticulturist, had turned the old plantation into one of the South's finest commercial nurseries.

When Jones came to the property to inspect it, he was driven down the impressive entranceway, Magnolia Lane, to the stately pre–Civil War manor house. He then walked around to the rear of the house and saw before him a beautiful canvas upon which to create his masterpiece: stands of tall pines with flowers and shrubs and vast stretches of open ground that ran down a long hillside toward a stream, Rae's Creek. A deal for the property was struck, and soon afterward the Augusta National Golf Club was formed.

Jones was an exceptional achiever off the golf course as well. After he earned a degree in mechanical engineering at Georgia Tech in just three years, he received a BS degree from Harvard, where he had spent two years studying English literature. The son of a lawyer, Jones subsequently entered Emory University law school in Atlanta. During his second year at Emory, he passed the Georgia Bar Exam and became a lawyer.

What made Jones a truly exceptional man, in addition to his academic accomplishments, was that he had also been blessed with an attribute often in short supply in the population—the gift of common sense. While he had an abundance of knowledge about what was required to make a golf hole truly outstanding, he knew that he would need first-rate support if he was to make his "dream course" the great layout he wanted it to be.

One of the first steps Jones took after the Augusta National Golf Club was organized and he had been named its president was to engage the services of renowned Scottish golf course architect Alister MacKenzie. Jones had played Cypress Point on the Monterey Peninsula, one of the courses in the United States that MacKenzie had designed, and he had been deeply impressed.

Another factor in Jones's selection of MacKenzie was that he wanted Augusta National to have the playing characteristics of the Scottish courses he had come to admire so much. Jones wanted the natural contours of the land to dictate the strategy of the holes.

The fairways would be wide and quick, the fairway and greenside bunkers would be kept to a minimum, and the greens would be large, undulating, and fast.

Another key player in the founding of Augusta National was Clifford Roberts, a Wall Street investment banker who handled the financing and operational details of the club. In a few short years Roberts would display an as yet untapped talent, which was showing the world how to put on a first-class golf tournament.

The course formally opened for play in January 1933. Later that year, the inner circle of the club decided that beginning in the spring of 1934, the club would play host to an annual invitational tournament in which the top players in golf would participate. Cliff Roberts wanted the event to be called the Masters, but Jones thought the name too presumptuous, so the event took the official name of the Augusta National Invitational. But a large number of sportswriters had picked up on Roberts's preferred name, and they referred to the tournament as the Masters from the very beginning. In 1938 Jones finally agreed to change the tournament's name to the Masters.

The rise of the Masters, the youngest by far of golf's four major tournaments, is one of the great stories in American sports. The game's other three major events—the British Open, the United States Open, and the Professional Golfers' Association of America Championship—were first played in 1860, 1895, and 1916, respectively. During the first full week in April when the tournament annually takes place, millions of Americans who ordinarily can go right on living, even if they confuse a nine-iron with scrap iron, suddenly become consumed with golf, golfers, and Augusta National. As for the millions of golfers and golf fans, it has been said there is a consciousness of the Masters in the air every day of the year.

Because the Masters is the only one of professional golf's four major tournaments with a permanent home, the game's greatest players have played more holes of major championship golf at Augusta National than at any other course in the world. In the process they have executed some of the game's greatest shots and have also on many occasions been humbled beyond belief.

Each of the eighteen holes on Bobby Jones's masterpiece is named for a plant or tree that adorns it, and they have all made their mark on what has been so aptly called "the tournament like no other." This book will chronicle each of the individual holes' contributions to the excitement, pressure, heartbreak, and exhilaration that is the Masters.

THE MASTERS

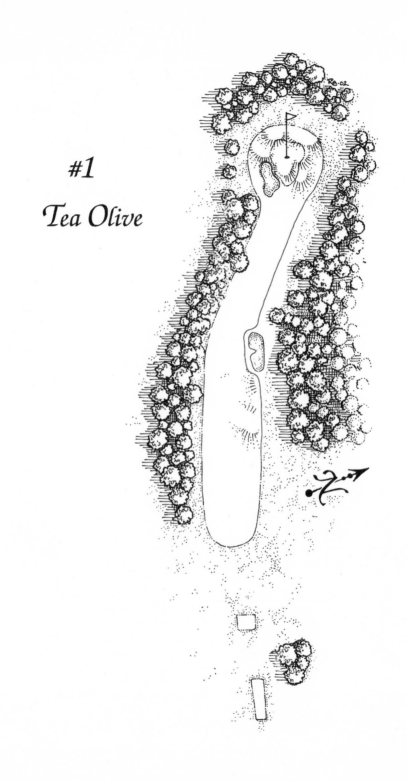

#1

Tea Olive

Hole No. 1

| PAR FOUR—445 YARDS | TEA OLIVE |

For fifty-one weeks of the year, the first tee at Augusta National is a serene and idyllic setting, but Thursday of Masters week, and for the following three days, it becomes the center of the golf universe. Whether you are playing in your first Masters or your twenty-first, the first-tee jitters here are like the tournament itself, as big as they get.

When the players arrived for the 2006 Masters, they had to make an adjustment for the fact that the center of the golf universe had shifted slightly. The first tee had been moved back 10 yards, increasing the hole's distance from 435 to 445 yards. The change at the first hole was part of a package of changes made at Augusta National that also involved the lengthening and toughening of five other holes: 4, 7, 11, 15, and 17.

This was the second time in four years there had been a host of changes at Augusta National. Before the 2002 Masters three of the holes that were updated for the 2006 Masters—1, 7, and 11—along with 8, 9, 10, 13, 14, and 18 had their tees pushed back in addition to other modifications.

These changes were dictated by the increased length achieved by today's golfers, assisted greatly by their high-tech clubs and improved long-distance golf balls. As in 2002 the 2006 changes stirred up quite a bit of discussion and debate in the media, among the players, and among golf fans. Many believed this wonderful national treasure was being defiled. Others thought the changes were long overdue.

As each hole's history will chronicle, the fact is the Augusta National course has always been a work in progress, from the day it opened in 1933. Bobby Jones designed and oversaw a number of changes before his death in 1971. Masters champions Ben Hogan, Byron Nelson, and Jack Nicklaus are just a few of the professionals who have also participated in making changes to the course. In addition to the players, noted golf course architects Perry Maxwell, George Fazio, Robert Trent Jones, and Tom Fazio (who oversaw the 2002 and 2006 changes) have assisted in designing and implementing improvements to Jones and MacKenzie's original masterpiece.

There was another change at the Masters in 2002 that was universally hailed, and it was one for which millions of golf fans had been clamoring for years—televising the play on the front nine during the final two rounds. Masters officials had long feared that televising the front nine would dilute the quality of the telecast, but the demands from the Masters faithful were too great to be ignored. The change called for almost all of the leaders' play to be covered on Saturday. On Sunday coverage would start an hour earlier and show the leaders teeing off at the first hole.

The first hole is a very demanding dogleg-right uphill par four, and it has experienced its share of changes over the years. For starters, it was originally the tenth hole when the club opened in 1933. The original layout posed a problem in winter, because the first three holes were set on the lowest part of the course. In colder months these holes were often covered by frost during the early-morning hours, which delayed play. To alleviate this problem, the nines were reversed after the first Masters in 1934. Right off the bat, the first shot at the first hole presents the player with the risk-versus-reward scenario Jones loved to have on a hole. On this hole the reward has always been for a drive that clears the large bunker on the right side of the fairway at the bend of the dogleg. If the shot is successful, the player has an ideal approach to the green with a short iron. If the shot comes up short, the player has what can be a very challenging second shot from the sand.

The hole's distance has been lengthened over the years from its original four hundred yards to keep the fairway bunker in play. In 1982 Masters officials decided to lengthen the hole by ten yards and not tell the players about the increased length. The players picked up on the covert change in the practice round, when their drives began filling up the fairway bunker. The added distance certainly affected the scoring on the hole that year. The number of birdies dropped by almost 40 percent, and bogeys increased by more than 30 percent.

There has always been one element that can make this shot a very risky proposition or a breeze, and that is the wind conditions. If the wind is at the player's back, he can really let one ride. But if it is in his face, he generally opts to take the safe route and play to the left center of the fairway to avoid the bunker.

It used to be that if a player pulled his tee shot too far to the left, he was not overly concerned. Even if the ball rolled into the adjacent fairway of the ninth hole, he would still have a clear approach to the green. However, this avenue to the green has been taken away with the addition of more pine trees up that side of the fairway.

The green is protected by a bunker on the left side, which was a 1951 addition. The putting surface is very undulating. It has a ridge on the back section that can make things very interesting if a player is long with his approach and has a lengthy putt or chip back down to the hole. This green has an abundance of subtle breaks that have always produced a very high number of missed putts from the four- and five-foot range. The pin is usually tucked behind the bunker once in an early round and in the final round. The locations of the pin in the other two rounds are typically right center and front right. In the 2001 Masters the first had ranked as the second most difficult hole on the course. Its Tiger Woods ranking was also pretty high. Before the 2002 Masters, Woods had made only one birdie in twenty-six attempts at the hole. The changes made to the first prior to the 2002 Masters were increasing the length from a listed 410 to 435 yards and extending the fairway bunker an additional 25 yards toward the green. These changes added an additional 50 yards to the carry a drive would need to clear the fairway bunker.

Many players have encountered problems before they have even had a chance to place a tee in the ground at the first hole. In one of the Masters in the late 1960s, Bert Yancey got to the course with plenty of time to warm up and get ready for his opening round, but his caddie was nowhere to be found. Yancey had made what was, in hindsight, a big mistake. He had allowed the young man who had been assigned to him by the Augusta National caddie master to borrow his car the previous evening. And to make matters worse, his clubs were in the trunk. Yancey was practically hysterical. The assistant caddie master was hurriedly dispatched to locate the missing young man. He played a hunch and soon found the caddie and the vehicle at a brothel just a few miles from the club. He was able to get the clubs to Yancey in time for him to make his appointment at the first tee with a new caddie.

In 1937 Harry Cooper, whose nickname was Hard Luck, was tied with the eventual winner, Byron Nelson, after the third round. The caddie who had worked so effectively with Cooper for fifty-four holes did not show up for the final round. Forced to use a replacement, Hard Luck shot his worst round of the tournament, a 74, to finish in third place, four strokes off the pace.

Herman Keiser, the surprise leader after the first two rounds in 1946 and the eventual winner, was enjoying a relaxing lunch in the clubhouse an hour before what he thought was his scheduled tee time, until Henry Picard charged into the dining area. Picard, the 1938 Masters champion, frantically told Keiser that he had just been called to the first tee. Keiser raced out to the first tee without the benefit of any practice. Keiser parred the hole and went on to post his third straight subpar round.

Jimmy Demaret held the lead after the first three rounds in 1947, and he opted not to go to the practice range before the final round—not because he didn't want to or need to; he just wasn't in any condition to swing a club. Demaret had been out partying the night before, and he was still feeling the effects of overconsumption of alcohol. Instead of practicing, he found a quiet, shady spot off the tenth fairway to use as his personal detoxification area until he was called to the tee. Demaret's tee shot at the first that day was far from spectacular. He slapped it out into some brush on the right side of the fairway. On his second shot he managed to slice his ball around a group of pines onto the front of the green and then two-putted for his par. After a bogey at the second, Demaret settled down and finished the round at a one-under-par 71 and won the tournament by two strokes.

Before Sam Snead reached the first tee in his first Masters in 1937, he was advised he was being assessed a penalty. It wasn't a stroke penalty but a financial one. His employer, the Greenbrier Resort at White Sulphur Springs, West Virginia, had advised him that he would be docked ten dollars (a week's pay) for being away from his duties as the resort's golf professional to play in the Masters. Snead's first appearance at Augusta did not get off to a good start, as he made bogey on his first hole. Snead finished the day at four over par, 76. He played the second round at even par and the third round at one under. Snead stood the chance of easily recouping his financial penalty, but he ballooned to a seven-over-par 79 in the last round and finished five strokes out of the money, which in that year's tournament was paid to only the top ten finishers.

In spite of the fact that this was his twenty-second Masters, Snead was a little too eager when it came time for him to tee off in the first round in 1961. He did not allow enough time for the pairing that had teed off ahead of him to clear the landing area. Snead's tee shot almost struck one of them, and it was not just anyone. It was an individual who at that time probably had the most nicknames of any player in the field. Those that can be printed are "Tantrum Tommy," "Terrible Tommy," and "Tempestuous Tommy." Snead had nearly struck the living legend of short fuses, Tommy Bolt. Bolt let loose with a verbal tirade back at Snead that almost peeled the bark off some of the pines lining the fairway. Bolt's verbal wrath must have still been ringing in Snead's ears when he got to the green, because he missed a two-footer for his par.

Arnold Palmer received a rousing welcoming ovation from the gallery when he walked on the first tee for the opening round in 1968. A few moments later, Masters officials told him that the ball he was playing was not welcome and he would have to use another brand. This was particularly stinging to Palmer because the brand of the ball he was playing was the "Arnold Palmer." Prior to the tournament, the United States Golf Association had ruled that the ball was illegal because it did not meet its specifications. After that ruling, Palmer's company had made the changes required for compliance and had been advised by the USGA the balls were now legal. When Palmer showed up at the first tee, however, his ball was one of nineteen on a list of banned balls Masters officials had prepared. Palmer played his round with balls from two competing brands, Titleist and Maxfli, and shot an even-par 72. By the start of the second day, the Masters officials were made aware that Palmer's ball was, in fact, now legal, and he used it in the second round. He may have wished he had played with the other two brands again because he shot a 79 and missed the cut for the first time in his Masters career.

Two competitors who had to tee off at the first hole under very difficult personal situations were Byron Nelson and Jack Nicklaus. And both went on to win the tournament. In Nelson's case he had arrived at the first tee for his playoff with Ben Hogan in 1942 after a night of virtually no sleep.

Nelson had a long history of chronic stomach trouble. During the night before, he had experienced one of his worst bouts ever with the problem, describing his stomach as "churning like a washing machine." When Hogan saw how ill Nelson looked that morning, he offered to delay the playoff until the afternoon, but Nelson insisted they tee off that morning as originally scheduled. Nelson's tee shot at the first was probably the worst of his career. It could almost be defined as a shank. The ball shot out to the extreme right, flew over a concession stand, ricocheted off a pine tree, and came to rest under a little evergreen tree. His ball's position prevented him from addressing his ball as a right-handed player. He had to become a switch hitter and execute his next stroke with a left-handed stance. He used a putter and punched it back into play. His next shot flew over the green, and he took three more strokes to get down and started the day with a double-bogey six. Nelson would take several holes to recover from his stomach problem and then make a remarkable comeback to defeat Hogan.

Nelson's physical problem would have to be considered mild in comparison to the emotional issues Jack Nicklaus was dealing with when he stepped onto the first tee for the first round in 1966. The day before, four of Nicklaus's Columbus, Ohio, friends were killed when their private plane crashed in Tennessee while en route to Augusta.

After a woefully hooked tee shot that ended up in the ninth fairway and an approach shot that left him almost forty feet from the pin, Nicklaus somehow managed to find a way to deal with the tragic events of the previous twenty-four hours. He drained the putt for an opening birdie. It would take him an extra day, but Nicklaus would go on to claim the third of his six Masters titles in an eighteen-hole, three-way playoff with Gay Brewer and Tommy Jacobs.

Unlike golf's other three major championships, the Masters is strictly an invitation tournament sponsored by a private organization, the Augusta National Club. The club sets the qualifications for receiving an invitation. Doug Sanders probably put it best from a player's perspective about being invited to Augusta when he said, "If you don't get an invitation to the Masters, it is like being out of the world for a week."

Like the course itself, the criteria for qualifying for an invitation have gone through many changes over the years. Being a winner or a top finisher in a major championship has always been a means of qualifying. For a number of years, winning a Professional Golfers' Association (PGA) Tour event has automatically qualified a player. Also, at one time, the prior Masters champions selected one player by ballot from a list of players who were not otherwise qualified.

The best way for a player to ensure he is in the field each year is to win the Masters, because prior champions are granted a lifetime invitation. Besides being a former Masters champion or qualifying through a major championship, the other two primary means of qualifying are by being in the top fifty in the World Golf Rankings or being in the top forty money winners on the PGA Tour from the previous year. Also, the top sixteen finishers from the previous year's Masters are invited back the next year. The qualifications used by the Invitation Committee for the 2018 Masters are listed in appendix 2.

To give the tournament an international flavor, the Invitation Committee has often issued special invitations to foreign players. In 1957 Cliff Roberts received a letter from a man in Johannesburg, South Africa, seeking an invitation for his twenty-two-year-old son. The man stated that his son was a great admirer of Bobby Jones and always had an ambition to play in the Masters. He said his son did not have the money for the trip, but if he were extended an invitation, he would pass the hat around among friends to get the necessary funds. The letter moved Roberts, although the man's son did not have an especially strong record. Roberts took up the matter with the committee, and it voted to extend the young man an invitation. Roberts then wired the father and advised him to go ahead and pass the hat because an invitation was on the way. Gary Player was the young man they were passing the hat for in Johannesburg, and in that 1957 Masters, he would finish in a very respectable twenty-fifth place. In 1961 Player would win his first of three green jackets. The first hole was crucial for Player in that one-stroke victory, as he made birdies here in three out of the four rounds.

Since the incorporation of the World Rankings into the invitation criteria, these special invitations have become less numerous. Recent recipients of a special invitation have been Ryo Ishikawa of Japan in 2013 and Shubhankar Sharmar of India in 2018. The most interest in a player making his first appearance at the first tee was in 1975, when Lee Elder became the first black athlete to play in the Masters. In the late 1960s a controversy began brewing over the fact that a black player had never qualified for the Masters, and there were increasing calls that a special invitation be issued. In March 1973 a group of eighteen congressmen wrote Cliff Roberts and requested that a special invitation be extended to Elder. This was two years after the death of Bobby Jones. Roberts was now solely in charge of Augusta National and the Masters. Roberts declined the calls for a special invitation, stating that when a black player did qualify, he would by all means be extended an invitation. The calls for the special invitation continued after the 1973 Masters, but Roberts remained fixed on his position. The controversy ended when Elder qualified for the 1975 Masters by winning a PGA Tour event and received his invitation as Roberts had stated he would.

When Elder stepped onto the first tee that morning, a light rain was falling, but the fairway was lined with spectators from tee to green. Elder seemed very relaxed on the tee. He teed up his ball and smoothly launched his first drive. It split the fairway; he put his second shot safely on the green and two-putted for a routine par. He picked up his first Masters birdie on the second hole and finished the day with a 74. He didn't make the cut that year, but he would play in six more Masters. His best finish would be seventeenth place in 1979.

It is often hard to judge what kind of round a player is going to have by his score at the first hole. In the third round in 1986, Nick Price's drive did not clear the bunker. His shot from the sand still left him almost eighty yards to the green. He hit a wedge to within about twenty feet and two-putted for bogey. Price then went on a tear, recording ten birdies over the remaining seventeen holes to shoot a nine-under-par 63. This broke the single-round record for the Masters of 64, which had been established by Lloyd Mangrum in 1940.

When he started his last round in 1990, Nick Faldo had probably pushed far back in his memory the double-bogey six he had had at the first hole in the third round in 1989. Faldo had eventually fought his way back from that disaster. He was never in the lead outright in that tournament, but by the time he had putted out on the seventy-second hole, he had a share of it. Faldo went on to win his first green jacket in a sudden-death playoff with Scott Hoch. Now a year and one day later, Faldo was coming off a splendid third round of 66 and was just two strokes behind leader Raymond Floyd. Faldo would have normally played a draw from right to left. On this day there was a crosswind blowing from left to right, however, which made him reluctant to attempt that shot. He decided instead to play his shot to the left center of the fairway and let the wind bring it back to the landing area. The shot did not come off as he had planned, and he pushed his drive into the fairway bunker. Faldo's seven-iron second shot from the trap was more the type you would expect from an eighteen-handicapper than the defending Masters champion. He got it out of the bunker but advanced his ball only about fifty yards. His wedge to the green was of the high-handicapper variety as well, and he left himself thirty-five feet to the right of the hole. The green here is no place to be lying that distance from the pin in two, much less in three. His nightmarish start continued as he three-putted from that distance and walked off the green with an opening double bogey.

Faldo may have not looked a Masters champion on the first hole, but he played the remaining seventeen holes like one. For the second straight year, he battled his way into a first-place tie and then won a sudden-death playoff. This time his playoff victim would be Raymond Floyd.

In 1996 the first hole did provide a preview to what would be the most unexpected final-round finish in Masters history. Greg Norman had dominated the tournament since the first round, when he birdied nine of the last twelve holes to shoot a 63 and tie Price's record for a low-round score. After the second round, Norman was in the lead and Faldo in second place, four strokes behind him. The two were paired for the third round, and Norman extended his lead to six strokes.

It truly looked as if it was finally going to be Norman's year and that the final round would be a coronation ceremony for him. Norman, who was again paired with Faldo, pulled his opening drive and missed the fairway to the left. He came up short with his approach shot, and it fell in the greenside bunker. Faldo drove the ball perfectly to the center of the fairway. His nine-iron approach landed in the center of the green about twenty feet from the hole.

Norman's bunker shot was a solid one, finishing four feet to the right of the hole. Faldo's putt for birdie missed by two feet, and he tapped in for his par. Norman's putt was one of those in that dreaded four-to five-foot range that the first is notorious for in the number of misses it generates from that distance. Norman became another one of its victims, as he missed his effort on the high side. The day would only get worse for Norman. After starting the day six in front of Faldo, he would end it five strokes behind him in second place.

The all-time best start of a contender in the Masters in the final round would have to be by Roberto De Vicenzo in 1968. De Vicenzo hailed from Buenos Aires, Argentina, and had been part of the international contingent of players at the Masters for many years. He had won 140 tournaments worldwide but had just claimed his first major the previous July, when he won the British Open. He made his first appearance at Augusta in the 1950 Masters and never had any real success until 1967, when he finished tied for tenth. At the start of play in the final round in 1968, he was just two strokes behind the leader, Gary Player, and one stroke behind four other players, who were tied for second.

At the first tee he uncorked a big drive and had a nine-iron left to the green. The pin was positioned on the front-left side, tucked in behind the bunker. De Vicenzo hit a splendid-looking approach shot with a nine-iron. The shot cleared the bunker by about ten feet, hopped once, and then rolled into the hole for an eagle two.

It was already a special day. It was De Vicenzo's forty-fifth birthday, and now he was tied for the lead in the final round of the Masters. The gallery sang "Happy Birthday" to him as he walked to the second tee. In about three and half hours, what had started out as the greatest day of his career would turn into the most tragic ever experienced at a major championship. De Vicenzo would shoot the round of his life only to be knocked out of a playoff for the green jacket by an errant stroke, not with a golf club, but with a pencil. The events of that dark day will be covered in greater detail in chapters 10, 17, and 18.

Strange things go on at Augusta National. Million-to-one shots go in the hole, golf balls disappear before the eyes of the television audience, the wind sometimes seems to be blowing in two different directions at the same time, a pimento cheese sandwich tastes out of this world, and patrons are not gouged on beer prices. To further establish this point, here are two prime examples from the first hole.

In the 2016 opening round, Ernie Els, a four-time major winner, played a good drive off the tee. His approach shot was a little off, leaving him with a chip shot of sixty feet. Ernie's chip finished three feet from the hole. As he took his putter from his caddie and prepared for what he hoped would be a one-putt par, no one in the throng surrounding the green could have fathomed what they were about to witness.

Els's par attempt from three feet went two feet by the hole. His bogey putt rolled past the hole and again stopped in the two-foot range. His double-bogey effort finished four feet past the hole. Ernie's next putt left him a foot away. From this tap-in range, he putted one-handed and missed. He had about the same distance remaining. Using the one-handed stroke again, he finally got it in the hole for a nine, the highest score ever recorded at the first hole in the tournament's history. The Masters staffers doing the electronic scoring gave Ernie a ten. Their error was corrected after the round.

Els finished the round with an eight-over-par score of 80. He had a chance at a 79, but he missed a two-footer at 18 for par. When asked in the press room how he was able to carry on after his opening-hole debacle, Ernie said, "I don't know how I stayed out there. But you love the game, and you got to have respect for the tournament."

In the second round in 1979, Mac McClendon's approach shot missed the green and flew into the gallery, striking a woman in the head. The dazed woman was taken to the first-aid station and then on to the hospital for X-rays. After the woman checked out all right at the hospital, she returned to the course and started following Mac McClendon again. It wasn't because she now felt she had a special bond with him. She already had that, for she was Mrs. Mac McClendon.

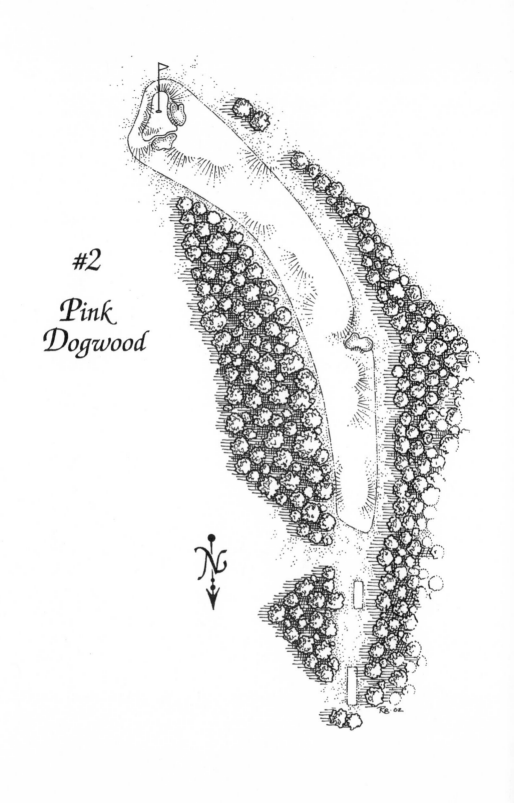

#2

Pink
Dogwood

Hole No. 2

PAR FIVE—575 YARDS	PINK DOGWOOD

Every player who steps onto the tee at the second hole is thinking birdie at this dogleg-left par five, although it is the longest hole on the course. From the tee the fairway slides gradually down until, approximately 300 yards out, it takes a left turn at the crest of a very steep slope. The elevation drops some 90 feet from tee to green, but most of that descent occurs in the last 275 yards. This hole originally measured 525 yards. Its distance has been increased several times over the years. The last lengthening came before the 1999 Masters, when it was stretched from 550 to 575 yards.

If a player opts to take the short route down the left side on his tee shot, he must guard against getting into the woods, which are just off the fairway. Also he must be aware of the ravine that is concealed behind the trees that has swallowed up the hopes of many a Masters participant.

In 1985 amateur John Inman was off to a great start. Inman had shot a two-under-par 70 in the first round, and he had parred the first hole to start his second round. Inman had birdied the second in the first round, and he was undoubtedly thinking birdie again, but he hooked his drive into the woods on the left side. His ball came to rest against an azalea bush. Inman's next swing failed to move the ball, so he then elected to take a drop. His next stroke got him out into the fairway, and two shots later he was in a greenside bunker. Inman's blast from the sand still left him six feet from the hole, and he two-putted for a nine. To his credit Inman fought off the effects of his visit to the left-side woods, and he played the rest of the round at even par.

The highest score ever at the second hole occurred after a drive visited the left-side woods in the first round in 1948. Sammy Byrd was the guilty party. Byrd was a former Major League Baseball player who had played on Augusta's minor league team while working his way up to the big leagues. Byrd had spent most of his time in the majors with the New York Yankees, where he was tagged with the nickname "Babe Ruth's caddie." Ruth was in the latter stages of his career with the Yankees at that time, and Byrd's chief duties were to pinch run for Ruth and take over for him defensively in the late innings. Byrd also took a good deal of money out of Ruth's pocket on the golf course. After retiring from baseball, he decided to become a professional golfer, and he had a very successful career. His best finish at Augusta was third in 1941. The 1948 Masters was his last appearance at Augusta, and it is one he would undoubtedly like to have forgotten. After opening with a par at number 1, he paid a visit to the woods on the left with his drive at the second, and when it was all said and done, he had recorded a ten.

Fifty-eight years later in 2006, David Duval tied Byrd's mark at the second. Duval, who was coming off a double bogey at the first hole, duck-hooked his drive at the second deep into the pines on the left side. It was four strokes and two penalty strokes later before he could reach a greenside bunker. He then blasted out and two-putted for his record-equaling quintuple bogey.

In the final round in 2003 Phil Mickelson made a remarkable recovery after pushing his drive into the pines on the left side. The errant shot left him with an unplayable lie. After taking a drop, he took out his driver with the hope of reaching one of the bunkers in front of the green. With his ball sitting on pine straw, Phil hit a perfect cut shot, and to his own surprise the ball reached the front edge of the green. He was still ninety feet from the pin, but after studying the putt at length, he followed up his remarkable recovery shot with a remarkable putt that did a little ring around the lip of cup before falling in. Mickelson, who was 0 for 42 in majors for his career, was now just three strokes off the lead at that point. When that putt dropped for a birdie, he looked skyward as if to ask is this going to be my year? But he would have to wait twelve more months for that first major title and a green jacket, as he would finish the day in third place, two strokes out of first.

Driving down the right side of the fairway was originally a relatively safe play on this hole. In 1966 a bunker was added there at the suggestion of golfing legend Gene Sarazen. Sarazen made "the shot heard 'round the world" at the par-five fifteenth in the 1935 Masters, which will be detailed later in chapter 15. He did not play in the first Masters owing to previous commitments, but the first time he played the course in 1935, he was not impressed because he believed several holes were too weak. Sarazen was impressed with the way Bobby Jones accepted criticisms of the course and the way he sought suggestions from players on ways to improve it. But it is hard to please everyone. Another golfing legend, Ben Hogan, disapproved of Sarazen's site selection for the bunker. Hogan thought the bunker should have been on the left side of the fairway. It should be noted that Hogan played a left-to-right fade on his drives, and the new trap put a ball with that type of flight path in jeopardy.

Even before the last lengthening, the second hole gave up eagles sparingly, as evidenced by the fact that Tiger Woods is still seeking his first eagle at this hole.

In the 1976 Masters three eagles were recorded at the second hole. Two of those were by the pairing of Ben Crenshaw and Jack Nicklaus in the second round, and both were set up by outstanding second shots. Crenshaw brought a four-wood in from 260 yards, and it rolled to within 8 feet of the pin. Nicklaus followed with one of his patented high three-iron shots from 220 yards. It nestled down 10 feet from the hole. It was Crenshaw's first career eagle at the second in his Masters career that began in 1972, and it was only Nicklaus's second in a Masters career that began in 1959.

An eagle at the second hole in the first round was a key part of Sam Snead's first Masters win in 1949. It helped propel him to a three-stroke victory. The 1949 Masters was the first year a green jacket was presented to the winner. Snead slipped on the first one, and it soon became the most coveted garment in golf.

Eagles were more plentiful in the early Masters, but this green's defenses have been substantially bolstered over the years. Originally, there was a bunker only on the right side of the green. In 1946 a second bunker was added on the left side, but there was still a wide opening in front of the green, which allowed players to run their shots onto it. Over the years these bunkers have been deepened and expanded significantly and the distance between them greatly reduced. The opening between the two that would allow a player to run a shot onto the green is now only about 50 feet wide. Ken Venturi proved in 1960, however, that landing in the greenside bunkers in two was not necessarily a bad thing. In each of the four rounds he was in one of the bunkers and ended up playing the hole five under par for the tournament. In the first round he holed out from the sand for eagle, and in the other three rounds he got up and down for birdie.

The green is approximately 120 feet across. It is very narrow on both the left and the right sides and features a ridge running across the back section. It has a wide middle, which is the safe play, but the surface is usually rather firm and can be hard to hold. The green slants from the rear to the front and slopes from left to right.

One of Bobby Jones's guiding principles for par fives was that they be reachable with two excellently hit shots. Getting on the green is just half the battle at Augusta, however. For a number of years the head professional at Augusta National automatically qualified to play in the Masters. Ed Dudley was the head professional at Augusta from 1933 to 1957. In the opening round of the 1935 Masters, Dudley reached the second hole in two shots but three-putted for par. Dudley would also reach the other three par fives in two that day and three-putted them as well.

The second hole was the last of the par fives at Augusta National to surrender a double eagle. It came in the seventy-sixth edition of the Masters in 2012. In the previous seventy-five editions, there had been a number of close calls. The two players who had come the closest were Cary Middlecoff and Jack Nicklaus.

The second shot that found the bottom of the cup at the second was by twenty-nine-year-old Louis Oosthuizen of South Africa. It came in the final round and was the fourth double eagle in Masters history.

Besides the three other double eagles, there have been many shots holed for eagles on par fours and a number of holes in one on par threes. Louis's double eagle from 253 yards outdistanced them all, making it the longest shot ever holed in the Masters.

Louis had laced a long drive from the tee and selected a four-iron for his second shot. Although the shot was a good one, it initially appeared as if its result would leave him with a long putt for eagle. Its flight ended at about 210 yards at the opening between the bunkers at the front of the green, but its journey would continue for a good while.

The hole was cut on the far-right side of the green and 129 feet from where Louis's ball landed. From there it took a hard right turn. At what could best be described as an unhurried pace, it rolled and rolled until it fell into the hole.

The shot took Louis from two strokes behind to a shot in the lead. He would ultimately finish in a tie with Bubba Watson. He would lose the playoff as a result of Watson pulling off a phenomenal shot that would join Louis's double eagle of several hours earlier as one of the greatest shots ever in the Masters. It will be detailed later in chapter 10.

As stated at the end of chapter 1, strange things happen at Augusta National. One of the second hole's contributions to this realm happened to Phil Mickelson in the final round in 2010. Phil was in a battle with Lee Westwood for the top spot. Phil had a delicate downhill birdie putt from six feet. Just as Phil was taking his putter back, a bud from one of Augusta National's pines landed, as though laser guided, directly in his line. Given the circumstances of the putt, his ball was traveling at a slow pace.

When it struck the bud, it tumbled off line to the left, and he had to settle for a tap-in par.

With that kind of bad fortune, one would have had to wonder at that point if this wasn't going to be Phil's day. But he turned in a stellar performance over the rest of the round to win his third green jacket.

In another example from this category at the second is what happened to Gene Sarazen in the first round in 1953. Sarazen was assessed a two-stroke penalty when his drive struck his caddie. No explanation has been unearthed about how this exactly happened. If there had been a wait at the tee, the caddie could have walked on ahead, so he could signal back to the tee when the group ahead of them was out of the way. Or perhaps he was intending to keep an eye on Sarazen's drive in case it strayed out of the fairway and into the woods. In any event he was definitely in the wrong place at the wrong time, and Sarazen picked up a double bogey as a result.

Since there will be a number of stories about the actions of caddies in the chapters that follow, now would be a good time to provide some background on the two different caddying periods in the Masters. From the first Masters in 1934 through the rain-plagued 1982 version, a Masters participant had to use a black caddie provided by Augusta National. Most of this caddie corps were known by their colorful nicknames such as "Reindeer," "Stovepipe," "First Baseman," and "Cemetery."

Two of the most famous caddies to emerge from the Augusta National caddie shack were Nathaniel Avery and Willie Peterson.

In 1955 nineteen-year-old Nathaniel Avery reported to the caddie master at Augusta National looking for a bag for the Masters. Jackie Burke, Gene Littler, and Mike Souchak were the players who were thought by the caddie corps to have the most heat and were the most coveted assignments. Avery was fortunate enough not to be given one of the hot bags. He received one that was about as cold as it could get because it belonged to one of the first-timers in the field. The caddie master told Avery that if he gave him this bag, he would have to keep it. Avery said he would. He kept the bag for the next fourteen years and became the best-known caddie in the country, since that cold bag belonged to Arnold Palmer.

Avery was nicknamed "Iron Man." Masters lore tells us that he got the name because he could always pick out the right iron for his player to hit, but in a 1974 interview he told a reporter that a fellow caddie called "Charlie Boy" gave him the name because he was like an iron man on the course. Charlie must have witnessed Iron Man with Palmer's bag during a practice round, which has been said to look as if it contained forty-one clubs instead of the usual fourteen.

Avery was with Palmer for all of his four Masters victories, and during Masters week he came to be interviewed and photographed nearly as much as his famous boss.

Willie Peterson started caddying in the Masters as a sixteen-year-old in 1949, but he never caddied for the same golfer for more than one year. In 1959 his string of one-year stands ended when he picked up the bag of a young amateur by the name of Jack Nicklaus, who was making his first Masters appearance. Peterson would carry clubs for Nicklaus for the next twenty-three Masters. Nicklaus would pick up five of his six Masters wins with Peterson on his bag. These five caddie victories tied Peterson with Pappy Stokes for bringing home the most winners. Stokes's victories took place in three different decades and for four different players: 1938 (Henry Picard), 1948 (Claude Harmon), 1951 (Ben Hogan), 1953 (Hogan again), and 1956 (Jack Burke Jr.).

Peterson was probably the most animated caddie in Augusta history. He was always trying to coax Nicklaus's ball into the hole when he was tending the pin—twisting his body, waving his arms, and yelling. He would jump up and down and dance when Nicklaus holed a long putt.

With Augusta National open only six months out of the year and almost all the membership residing elsewhere, the amount of play the course receives is very light, and the number of caddies it can support is actually very small. The caddie pool was never large enough to cover the entire Masters field, so caddies were brought in from other Georgia and South Carolina country clubs to lend a hand. Even with the out-of-town reinforcements, the caddie master had trouble meeting the demand, and a player could end up being assigned a very young and inexperienced caddie or one whose breath indicated he was caddying while impaired. As the purses grew and the caddying profession evolved, there were growing calls from players that they be allowed to use their own caddies.

The pressure continued to build and came to a head in 1982. The first round was played in an almost steady rain. By early afternoon the gallery at the thirteenth hole was paying more attention to the caddies than the players because nearly half of them were slipping and falling into the mud trying to negotiate the rain-slickened fairway with their heavy bags. This was an ironic foreshadowing of the Augusta caddie corps' demise.

By 4:00 p.m. that day, with half the field still on the course, play had to be suspended because the back nine had become unplayable. The golfers who had not finished their round were told that play would resume at 7:30 the next morning. The players showed up at the appointed hour, but a large number of caddies did not. To compound an already bad situation, many golfers discovered that their equipment had been put away wet the night before. This was one of the biggest embarrassments Masters officials had ever experienced.

Tom Watson spearheaded a renewed call by the players that they be allowed to use their regular caddies. Watson pleaded their case to the tournament chairman at that time, Hord Hardin, who was a retired lawyer. "Suppose you had to go into your biggest trial and you were told you couldn't use your own legal secretary? That's what it's like for us at Augusta." Hardin's answer wasn't long coming. It was soon announced that in 1983 the players would be allowed to use their own caddies in the Masters.

From 1934 through 1975, if a tie occurred in the Masters, it would be settled by a playoff the day after the final round. The first playoff occurred in 1935 between Gene Sarazen and Craig Wood, which Sarazen won, and was contested over thirty-six holes. Subsequent playoffs were eighteen holes in length, until the format was changed to sudden death in 1976.

The last eighteen-hole playoff occurred in 1970 between Billy Casper and Gene Littler, and it was all but decided at the second hole. Both players were heavyweights: Casper had won two United States Opens, and Littler had United States Open and the United States Amateur championships to his credit. To add a little more spice to the playoff, they were both from San Diego and had competed regularly against each other as teenagers.

Casper jumped out into the lead with a birdie at the first hole but then hooked his tee shot at the second into the woods on the left side. Littler's drive was solid and in the fairway.

Casper's lie in the woods was terrible. He was barely able to get his club on the ball, and his swing was going to be hampered by the Augusta National foliage that virtually surrounded him. Also, he had to get the shot up quickly because there was a fallen tree limb just in front of his ball. Casper was going to need some luck just to get the ball back in the fairway. He took a big cut with a lofted club, and a cloud of pine needles, grass, and small limbs sprayed into the air along with his ball, which came out cleanly and landed safely in the fairway.

Littler almost reached the green with his second shot, leaving it just a few yards behind the bunker on the right side of the green. Casper's third shot just missed the green. It looked as if Littler was going to leave the second hole at least even with Casper and possibly one stroke ahead. All he had to do was pitch his third ball over the bunker and onto the green. Littler was known as "Gene the Machine," but he stripped a gear on this shot. He flubbed it, and the shot flew only a few feet and landed in the bunker. Littler collected himself and then blasted his ball out of the sand and two-putted for a bogey. Casper got down from the fringe in two for a par and moved two strokes ahead.

Casper carried his momentum from the second hole to the third, as he picked up a birdie there to Littler's par, and moved to a three-stroke lead. Casper was in control for the rest of the round. By the eleventh hole he was seven strokes ahead, and then he practically coasted home from there and ultimately won by five strokes.

Nick Faldo had become interested in golf at the age of thirteen. During his Easter vacation from school, he watched something on his family's new color television set that he found captivating. It was a golf telecast, beamed from the United States to the United Kingdom, of a tournament called the Masters. Faldo was fascinated by a player by the name of Jack Nicklaus. Almost immediately after the telecast, he began to hound his parents to take him to the local course, and they soon obliged. His parents signed him up for lessons with the local pro, and after six sessions he was hopelessly hooked on golf.

Two of the biggest shots in Nick Faldo's first Masters win in 1989 occurred at the second hole in the third round. Faldo had begun the day tied for the lead, but the double-bogey six he made on the first hole had all the makings of a Masters meltdown. Then his tee shot strayed on the second hole out of the fairway to the right and parked itself very close to the side of a pine tree. Faldo could not address the ball in his normal right-handed position and faced either hitting it like a left-hander or using a one-handed backhand stroke with his right hand. All he wanted to do was to get the ball back on the fairway, so he chose the backhand shot. Faldo took out an eight-iron and stood with his back to the fairway. He held the club in his right hand by his side with the clubface turned around toward his body and aimed back toward the fairway. He then made a pendulum swing with his right arm. The shot came off as well as he could have possibly hoped for; the ball darted back into the fairway and ran about seventy yards toward the green.

Faldo's third shot landed on the extreme right-hand side of the green. Unfortunately for him, the hole was cut on the far left side of the green. It was a definite putt-it-and-hope situation. Faldo did put a fine stroke on the ball with his gooseneck-style putter. It had plenty of speed, and the line looked great. At about the ten-foot mark, the crowd began to stir and soon broke out into a loud roar when the ball dropped into the hole for a birdie. Nick's playing partner, Lee Trevino, walked off the putt, and it took him thirty-two paces, which put the putt in the one-hundred-foot range and made it one of the longest putts, if not the longest, ever made in the Masters.

In the final round, after draining a fifty-footer for birdie on the first hole, Faldo made another birdie at the second hole from twelve feet. If you are thinking his gooseneck putter was putting its way toward the Flat Stick Hall of Fame, you would be mistaken. It was in Faldo's locker in the clubhouse.

It must have been spent after the hundred-footer, since Faldo's putting went in the tank after the second hole in the third round. Play was suspended in that round because of rain and darkness, after Faldo had completed twelve holes. He completed the round on Sunday morning, and his putting was still ice cold. Faldo was five strokes off the lead and decided to switch putters before the final round started in the afternoon. The gooseneck was benched, and a blade-style putter was put in his bag.

It was one of the best decisions Faldo ever made in his life. Beside the fifty-footer at the first and the twelve-footer at the second, he made six other birdie putts in the final round. He ended regulation play in a tie with Scott Hoch, whom he then defeated in a sudden-death playoff with another long birdie putt.

In the first round of his first Masters in 1995, nineteen-year-old amateur Tiger Woods strayed into the same woods that Faldo had used his creative backhand shot to escape. Tiger was in better shape because he could take a normal swing. He took a big rip with his three-iron, and his ball tore through an azalea bush and still had enough power behind it to carry 230 yards to the front of the green. Tiger then two-putted from there to pick up the first birdie of his Masters career.

In 1955 Furman Bisher, sports editor of the *Atlanta Constitution*, was out strolling on the course during the first round and witnessed what he thought was an extremely peculiar sight. A twosome was at the second green, and there was not a single other spectator anywhere around. The only other persons present were the officials for the hole and the two caddies. It was by no means an undistinguished pair of players. One was Ed Furgol, who was the defending United States Open champion, and the other was Arnold Palmer, the recent United States Amateur champion, who had recently turned professional. Each made par and continued on their lonely journey. Furgol never became a household name, but Palmer, seemingly overnight, developed a connection with the sports fan that had not been equaled in America since the days of Babe Ruth.

In just a few short years Palmer would be surrounded by crowds, not just on the golf course but everywhere he went. At Augusta National there was born a particular large and vocal group of Palmer partisans—"Arnie's Army." A definitive electricity ran through this corps. They would trek along with their leader with unabashed admiration and zeal. The salvos they unleashed when Palmer made a birdie or pulled off an outstanding shot were enough to make the most steel-nerved competitor wonder if he should lay down his clubs.

After their colors were unfurled at the Masters, these detachments began forming at every tournament Palmer played in from Pebble Beach to St. Andrews, but like the Eighty-Second Airborne to Fort Bragg, Arnie's Army's home base was always Augusta National. They actually had a military beginning. Cliff Roberts obtained the services of soldiers stationed at nearby Fort Gordon to assist in crowd control and to man the leaderboards. In his book *A Golfer's Life*, Palmer said the first time he believes he saw the term was when he looked up at a leaderboard during the 1959 Masters and saw one of the Fort Gordon soldiers proudly holding a sign that said "Arnie's Army."

The army may have violated the rules of engagement at the second hole during the second round in 1965. On his second shot to the green Palmer considered two options for his attack on the right-side pin placement: either be pin high to the left or be long and let the ball be stopped by the massive gallery behind the green. He chose the latter and hit a hard two-iron with a slight draw. The shot hit the green hard and bounded some fifteen yards into the crowd. It possibly could have been clean living, or Palmer's ball could have received some assistance from some overzealous members of his army. Suddenly there was a stir in the crowd, a sort of ripple effect, and Palmer's ball suddenly reappeared at the fringe of the green. When Palmer reached the green, he asked what had happened, and someone yelled out, "Didn't hit a thing." Palmer then took his putter and rolled the ball within a foot of the hole for a birdie.

One of the most endearing aspects about Arnie's Army was their undying devotion, even after Palmer had passed his prime. They were like D-Day veterans ready to answer another call to duty at a moment's notice. One of the most memorable first rounds in Masters history was in 1983, when at the second hole the bugler sounded the charge one last time. When a fifty-two-year-old Palmer rolled in a birdie, the army immediately mobilized and was on the move in the same fashion that had seen it sweep over the hills of Augusta in its glory days. Palmer made the turn at two under. He slipped a bit at the tenth with a bogey, but he proceeded to lay down a birdie barrage at the fourteenth, fifteenth, and sixteenth that was truly a joy for his legion to behold. When the dust had finally settled at the end of the day, Palmer was tied for the lead at four under.

He gave the army a rousing opening in the second round when he started with a birdie at the first hole. Palmer's attempt to turn back the clock ended where it had begun the previous day. He bogeyed the second hole and began to slip down the leaderboard. He did, however, easily make the cut for what turned out to be the last time.

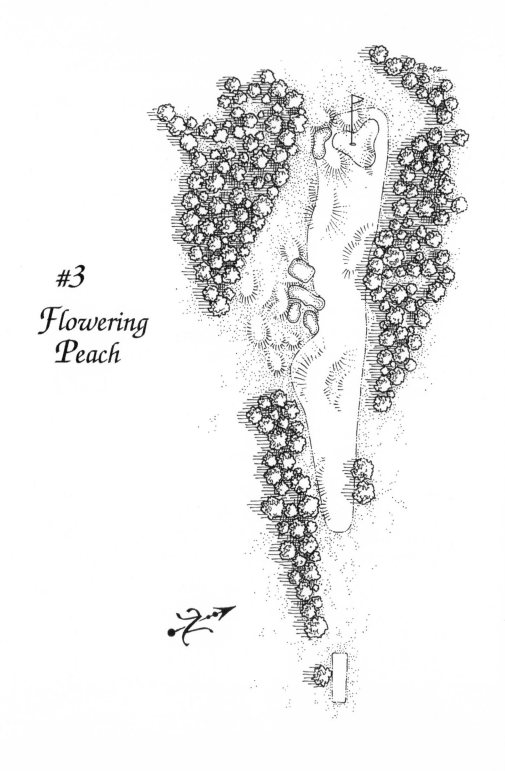

#3
Flowering
Peach

Hole No. 3

PAR FOUR—350 YARDS	FLOWERING PEACH

The shortest par four on the course, this hole has undergone few changes over the years. It is still at the same length it was for the very first Masters in 1934: 350 yards.

What club a player elects to use off the tee will be dictated by the location of the pin on the green. If it is on the right side, many players will chose to go with a driver and carry the cluster of sand traps on the left side of the fairway. If the pin is on the very narrow left side, the play off the tee is to use a long iron and lay back from the fairway bunkers. This sets up a short iron to the green, which will allow the player to apply the backspin he will need for his approach to hold the green.

Whether the player cleared the bunkers and has a little three-quarter sand-wedge shot or has laid back behind the bunkers and has a full shot, this will be one of the most demanding approach shots he will have on the course.

The green is protected in the front by a swell that can send a shot hit short thirty to forty yards back down the fairway. If this happens, the player faces very long odds on being able to get up and down for par. The green sits up on a plateau and slopes significantly from right to left and features a huge bunker on the left side. The green is eighty-five feet deep on the right side but narrows dramatically as it flows to the left. The traditional final-round pin placement is on the left side at a point where the green is barely ten paces across.

On the way to his third green jacket in 2002, Tiger Woods birdied the hole in three out of the four rounds. In the first three rounds, he elected to hit his drive over the bunkers and picked up birdies in rounds one and three and a par in round two. In the final round with the pin tucked on the left side, Woods elected to lay back from the bunkers on his drive, and then he stuck a wedge shot twenty feet above the hole and then rolled in the putt for another three.

In 1940 Lloyd Mangrum birdied the third on his way to shooting a new course record of 64, breaking the old mark of 66, coheld by Byron Nelson and Henry Picard. In just a few years Mangrum was still shooting, but he was getting shot at as well as a soldier in General Patton's Third Army in Europe. The 1942 Masters, which took place just four months after Pearl Harbor, was the last tournament held until World War II was over. Bobby Jones, Ben Hogan, and Sam Snead joined Mangrum in uniform, along with many other players on the professional circuit.

Jones served as an intelligence officer for the Army Air Corps. By the spring of 1944 he had been promoted to the rank of lieutenant colonel and was assisting in the preparation for the D-Day invasion. Shortly before the Allied invasion, Jones's unit was converted to infantry, and they went ashore at Normandy on D-Day plus one.

Some six months later, Lloyd Mangrum, while serving under General George S. Patton's command, was wounded in the Battle of the Bulge and was awarded the Purple Heart. He was also awarded four Battle Stars. It was during the Battle of the Bulge that General Dwight D. Eisenhower met the man who would be responsible for introducing him to the Augusta National Golf Club, making him the club's most famous member.

William E. "Bill" Robinson was an executive for the *New York Herald Tribune* and a member of Augusta National. Robinson was sent to France by his newspaper, shortly after the Allies liberated Paris. He was attempting to conduct some business for his employer and ran up against some regulations that General Eisenhower had imposed concerning the dos and don'ts of engaging in commerce in Allied-occupied territory. Robinson requested a meeting with the general to seek relief from a few of these regulations. The arrangements were worked out for the meeting to take place at Eisenhower's headquarters, which appropriately enough were in the clubhouse of what was left of a French country club.

A couple of days before the meeting, the surprise German offensive that became known as the Battle of the Bulge began, and Robinson had expected the appointment to be canceled. When he inquired about the status of the meeting, he was told it was still on. When the meeting started, Robinson apologized to Eisenhower for troubling him over his problem while a big battle was taking place. Eisenhower told him not to worry about it. He was confident that his forces would deal effectively with the German offensive, and he was now developing plans for actions weeks after the current battle. Robinson and Eisenhower hit it off during the meeting, and they became good friends.

Ike left the service in early 1948 to become the president of Columbia University. There was a period of several months before he took on his new position, and during that period he wrote his World War II memoir, and Robinson assisted him in getting the book published. It was after the manuscript was completed that Robinson invited Eisenhower down to Augusta for a golf vacation.

On this vacation two things happened that would affect the remainder of Eisenhower's life profoundly. First, this trip triggered his conversion from a casual golfer to a golf fanatic. Second, he made two new acquaintances as a result of this trip. These acquaintances, Bobby Jones and Cliff Roberts, would become two of his closest friends for the rest of his life.

Eisenhower was an honorary member of hundreds of country clubs across the country, but he was a dues-paying member at Augusta National. He greatly enjoyed taking part in the club's activities. He served on the Board of Governors twice during the eight years he was president of the United States. He looked forward to receiving his monthly newsletter at the White House, so he could keep up to date with the goings-on at the club.

There was one aspect of Augusta National life, however, that Eisenhower could not enjoy, and that was the Masters. After World

War II and before being elected president, Ike had tried to attend several golf tournaments, but he found his presence created too much of a distraction to the gallery and the golfers. He knew if he were ever present during Masters Week, it would create too many problems. Since this was long before all four rounds were televised, Cliff Roberts arranged for Eisenhower to be given Masters updates every thirty minutes at the White House.

After he became president of the United States, Eisenhower always started his annual spring vacation at Augusta National the day after the Masters was over. He typically played a round with the tournament winner immediately upon his arrival. This caused much dismay among the Senators—not the ones on Capitol Hill, but the ones over at Griffith Stadium, the home of the American League's Washington Senators. The early Masters tournaments benefited from baseball in that a large number of newspaper sportswriters would stop by and cover the Masters on their way back north after spring training. Now with Eisenhower in the White House, the tournament suddenly found itself controlling when the American League started its season.

During the eight years Ike was in office, the baseball season was eight games shorter than it is now, and the season started much deeper into April. This put Eisenhower's golf vacation in direct odds with one of the great traditions of that day: the president of the United States throwing out the first ball at the American League opener in the nation's capital.

Eisenhower was probably the biggest baseball fan ever to occupy the Oval Office. While growing up in rural Kansas, Eisenhower idolized Honus Wagner of the Pittsburgh Pirates, and he played a season or two of semipro baseball before heading off to West Point. He even played a key part in getting the White House doorkeeper's son a contract with the Pirates. There was one game that Eisenhower loved more than baseball, however, and that was golf, particularly golf at Augusta National.

In 1953, the first year Eisenhower was president, he agreed to return to Washington and then fly back to Augusta. The day before, he played golf with Ben Hogan and played a game of catch behind the clubhouse to make sure he was ready for his first-pitch duties. Eisenhower performed his first-pitch duties flawlessly. He ducked out of Griffith Stadium after the second inning to give a speech and then head back to Augusta. During the speech he took ill with a stomach problem, and when he returned to Augusta he spent the rest of his vacation recovering from the problem.

The 1954 and 1955 season openers did not conflict with Eisenhower's Augusta trip, but the 1956 opener collided head-on with it. The White House sent word to the Senators that the president would not be available and that Vice President Richard Nixon would pinch hit. This caused great turmoil for the Senators and the American League. The season opener with Eisenhower would be one of their biggest games of the year, and they did not want to lose it.

The Senators' front office worked extremely hard with the league office and the White House staff and rescheduled the opener on a date that would occur after the war hero/president/golfer had returned from Augusta National.

Many people thought it was fitting that the first Masters after the war was won by a war veteran, Herman Keiser. Keiser had played on tour with some moderate success before the war, but his name was anything but a household word. He had joined the navy shortly after Pearl Harbor and spent the war patrolling the Atlantic and the Mediterranean on a light cruiser. After the war was over, he spent the last months of his hitch running the navy's driving range in Norfolk, Virginia.

In January 1946 Keiser rejoined the professional golf tour and had some strong finishes. He lost to Ben Hogan in a playoff in Phoenix and finished in second place behind Sam Snead in the Greater Greensboro Open. Keiser's play that winter earned him an invitation to the Masters. Keiser grabbed the lead on the third hole of the first round, and at the end of the round, he was sharing first place with Chick Harbert at three-under-par 69.

Everyone thought Keiser was going to be a one-round wonder, but he shot a 68 in the second round and moved out to a commanding five-stroke lead. He posted a third-round score of one-under-par 71 and retained his five-stroke advantage. Keiser stumbled during the last round and shot 74. His chief pursuer that day was Ben Hogan. Hogan could have won with a birdie at the seventy-second hole and forced a playoff with a par, but he three-putted for a bogey to give Keiser a one-stroke win.

From the first Masters until the early 1950s, one of the big goings-on during tournament week would be "the Calcutta." On an evening before the start of the tournament, there would be gatherings of Augusta National members, players, and numerous other interested parties at one of Augusta's resort hotels. Each member of the Masters field would be placed up for auction to the highest bidder. The name players went for big dollars, while some of the lesser-known players had to be grouped and auctioned off in blocks. The auction of the field generated quite a sizable pool of cash. The person who had the good fortune to have bought the winner of the tournament would take home the lion's share of the pool, with smaller cuts going to those whose selection finished from second to fourth place.

Besides the publicly held Calcutta, there were numerous other gambling opportunities available, some just for members and others that were nonexclusive.

Some events that week led Keiser, who was auctioned off in a block of seven other dark horses for $1,250, to believe that there were some parties at Augusta National who did not want to see him win. These parties had big money wagered on other players, and Keiser believed they had worked behind the scenes to derail his chances.

Keiser thought that the tee-time mix-up detailed in chapter 1 was a prime example of the deck being stacked against him. As another example, he cited the fact that when he got to the course that day, he found he had been assigned a thirteen-year-old caddie who could hardly carry his bag. In the case of the tee-time problem, it is hard to say that was not just an unfortunate mix-up, either on Keiser's part or the club's. As to the caddie situation, it appears that the Augusta National caddie corps was in a postwar rebuilding phase in 1946, since Keiser was not the only player to draw a rookie. Cary Middlecoff was playing in his first Masters that year, and he had a similar experience. Middlecoff knew he was in deep trouble at the first tee when his caddie, also about thirteen years old, handed him a seven-iron instead of a driver.

Joe Kirkwood Jr. was two strokes off the lead going into the last round in 1949, despite playing only one round of golf in the four months before the Masters. His father had been a professional golfer and one of the great golf trick-shot performers of all time. Kirkwood had also tried the life of a full-time golf professional but had switched to part-time status to be a performer of another kind: an actor.

Kirkwood had worked his way up the actor's leaderboard and was now playing Joe Palooka—the boxer/crime fighter character from one of the most successful comic strips of all time—in a series of movies on the silver screen. He had qualified for the Masters by a high finish in the United States Open the year before, but his movie production schedule and the romancing of his costar had allowed him little time for golf. His last round of golf before arriving in Augusta had been in the first week in January.

Despite his lack of play, Kirkwood moved into serious contention in the third round with his second birdie in three days at the third hole. He ended the round in a tie for second place with Sam Snead and Lloyd Mangrum, one stroke behind leader Johnny Palmer. Sunday did not follow a Hollywood-type script, however, as Joe's play faltered in the last round, when he shot a 75 and finished eight strokes behind winner Sam Snead in seventh place. His high finish that year and in the next three years earned him four more sequels in the Masters.

In 1973, at the age of thirteen, Augusta resident Larry Mize, the winner of the 1987 Masters, worked the scoreboard at the third hole. Mize obviously did not pick up any tips on how to play the hole because he was already a Masters champion before he recorded his first birdie at the third hole. His first three at the hole came in the 1989 Masters on his twenty-first attempt.

As evidenced by Larry Mize's record, it can take a while for a player to get comfortable playing the third. Tiger Woods bogeyed the hole in the first round of his Masters debut in 1995. It was still giving him problems when he won his first green jacket in 1997. In the second round that year, Woods pounded his drive 335 yards, and had only 15 yards left to the green. His little pitch shot would not hold the green, and it ran off the backside. Woods chipped back onto the green to within about 6 feet, but he missed that putt and made bogey. Arnold Palmer and Jack Nicklaus also bogeyed the third the first time they played it in competition. Ben Crenshaw must have felt very comfortable at the hole, however, as he made birdies on the hole in rounds one through three in his Masters debut in 1972.

Nobody has ever played the hole any better than Ken Venturi did in the 1960 Masters; he birdied the hole in all four rounds.

It was a long time before the third hole gave up its first eagle. Roberto De Vicenzo almost became the first player to accomplish this feat in the final round in 1968. After already having recorded an eagle at the first hole, his nine-iron second shot stopped just inches from the cup. Bruce Crampton finally picked up the first eagle at the third hole in the final round in 1974.

An eagle at three in 1985 triggered quite a turnaround. Curtis Strange started the opening round as one of the favorites. He was the leading money winner on tour for the year, and his game appeared to be rock solid. To make things even better, he had drawn one of the best possible pairings in the field: Jay Haas. Haas was one of Strange's teammates at Wake Forest University and was one of the most respected and likable players on tour.

Strange started out with two routine pars, but at the third hole he made a bogey. That started a string of three in a row, and his game went downhill from there. When the round was finally over, he was humbled, distraught, embarrassed, and everything else a player could have felt after shooting an eight-over-par 80.

Only two other players in the field shot worse: an amateur from Spain and a future green-jacket winner, José María Olazábal. He had an 81. And bringing up the rear was another Wake Forest alum, four-time green-jacket winner Arnold Palmer, who had shot an 83, at the time his worst round in a Masters.

Strange did not think there was any way he could make the cut after his disastrous opening score. So as soon as he could after the round, he got to a telephone and made a plane reservation out of Augusta for 2:50 Friday afternoon. His tee time the next day was at 9:07 in the morning, so he would hopefully have just enough time to finish his round and get to the airport.

Strange's get-out-of-town-quick plan hit a snag early. It looked as if the first twosome off was going to be slow playing. The field was an odd number, and Arnold Palmer, with the highest score from Thursday's round, had to be paired with a "noncompeting marker," which in golf language means someone to play along with you and keep your score. Augusta National member Charlie Coe was asked to play with Palmer. He had competed in the Masters as an amateur nineteen times and finished in a tie for second with Palmer in the 1961 Masters. Coe's game was no longer anywhere near that level, however. He had large numbers of Arnie's Army running for cover, as he sprayed several shots off the fairway and spent a lot of time in the woods.

The pace-of-play problem soon disappeared. Coe pulled a muscle after a few holes and retired to the clubhouse. Another Augusta National member kept Palmer's score but did not play along with him. Playing alone, Palmer was soon long gone.

Strange's thought about making an afternoon flight was soon long gone as well, and he began to focus on what he thought the night before was virtually impossible: making the cut. Whereas his fortunes had begun that rapid trip south on the third hole the day before, they made an abrupt about-face there on this second day, and Strange came roaring back in an almost unbelievable fashion.

Strange made a birdie at the second and then exploded at the third hole. He laid back with his drive and had 137 yards to the pin. He drew out an eight-iron and let it fly, and a few seconds later his ball was settling into the bottom of the cup for an eagle. Strange then made birdie at the fourth, and he parred the remaining holes on the front nine for a 32. He then ran off four straight birdies on the back nine, beginning at the eleventh hole, before bogeying the fifteenth, and then parred in for 33 and a round of 65.

Strange ended up making the cut by five strokes, and by the end of the third round he was just one stroke off the lead. He blitzed the front nine in the final round with a four-under-par 32 and bolted into the lead by four strokes, but he stumbled hard on the back nine's par fives and finished in second place.

Charl Schwartzel's eagle at 3 was a huge part in his charge to victory in the final round in 2011. The round was like a set of bookends. His start was spectacular. He had chipped in from 75 feet at the first hole and made a two from 114 yards here at the third. Charl, who was four strokes off the lead when the day began, used a sand wedge for his eagle. The shot landed in the left center of the green 10 feet above and to the left of the hole, which was cut on the far left, and then spun back. The right-to-left slope of the green took it right into the hole.

Charl played the next eleven holes one over par and then closed his round in astonishing fashion, holing four consecutive clutch birdie putts to grab the top spot by two strokes over runners-up Jason Day and Adam Scott.

In 1995 Jay Haas was vying to become the second member of his family to win a green jacket. His uncle Bob Goalby had won the 1968 Masters. Haas got an up-close-and-personal look at Augusta National when he was fifteen years old. He came to Augusta with his uncle and was on the course with him for some early practice rounds and took the opportunity to play some shots with his uncle's clubs on the back nine.

Haas qualified for his first Masters in 1976 and had had four top-ten finishes at Augusta. The 1995 tournament was his fifteenth appearance, and he opened the tournament with a respectable one-under-par 71.

As Haas was leaving the house he was renting for the week to head to the course for his second round, he got quite a shock. On the hood of the courtesy Cadillac that had been provided by the tournament was a dead beaver. From the amount of blood present, it appeared a car had hit the animal, and then someone had thrown it up on the hood of Haas's Cadillac. Dealing with the beaver's remains took some time, but it didn't seem to have any impact on Haas's play that day, as he shot a 64 and vaulted into the lead.

The next morning when Haas went to his car, he found three stuffed animals on the hood. Having heard about the beaver, some friends had placed them there. They were hoping the stuffed animals would bring Haas as much luck on the course as it seemed the beaver had, but they certainly did not.

Haas's fortunes took a bad turn at the third hole. His tee shot landed in one of the fairway bunkers. His shot from the sand nicked the lip of the bunker on the way out and dropped short of the green. Haas chipped on and had a testy eight-footer to save his par. After he had addressed his ball, it moved about a quarter of an inch, and Haas had to call a penalty stroke on himself. Haas then two-putted for a 6. By his own admission, he was never able to shake off the effects of his misfortunes at the third hole. He finished the tournament in third place, three strokes behind Ben Crenshaw.

Haas is not alone in suffering a bad break at the third hole. In the 1935 Masters Henry Picard took the lead with an opening round of 67. He followed that up with a 68 in the second round, and his lead expanded to four shots. Picard had not recorded a stroke over par on any of those thirty-six holes. In the third round he parred the first and second holes, extending his bogeyless streak to thirty-eight holes.

At the third hole he pulled his approach shot into the bunker on the left side of the green. It was going to be tough to extend his streak from that spot. When Picard reached his ball and requested his sand wedge, the situation got a lot tougher. At that time, there was no fourteen-club limit. A player could have in his bag as many clubs as his caddie could carry, so it wasn't too easy to detect when one was missing. Picard and his caddie discovered they were missing a club, his sand wedge. Without it, Picard had to improvise with another high-lofted club. The results from the improvisation were four more strokes to get down and a double-bogey six. There was collateral damage from his experience at the third hole. His psyche was rattled from such an uncalled-for circumstance. He bogeyed the fourth and the fifth before he could get reconnected with his confidence. He finished the day with a four-over-par 76 and dropped from the lead.

The missing club was found later at the clubhouse. It is believed that someone had taken it out of his bag to admire it and had failed to return it to Picard's bag. Picard shot a 75 in the final round and finished in fourth place, four strokes behind Craig Wood and Gene Sarazen, who finished in a tie, thanks to Sarazen's double eagle at the fifteenth, "the shot heard 'round the world." If Picard had had his sand wedge at the third hole in the third round, he would most likely have not experienced the disaster and its side effects, and Sarazen's double eagle possibly would have been just a noteworthy footnote to the tournament instead of the most famous shot in golf.

Three years later, in 1938, Picard would win the Masters by two strokes. His win that year was the first year the margin of victory in the tournament had been greater than one stroke.

During the 2003 Masters the highest scores recorded at the third hole were five double bogeys and a triple bogey. One of the double bogeys and the triple bogey were made in a span of twenty minutes in the final round, staggering two of the top contenders: Tiger Woods and Jeff Maggert.

Woods had stepped onto the tee box fresh from a birdie at the second hole. The roar that had gone up when that birdie was posted on the leaderboard had extremely grave overtones for the rest of the contenders.

Tiger had gotten off to a rotten start with a 76 in the opening round. In the second round he had to get up and down from a bunker at 18 just to make the cut. On Saturday he had surged back into contention with a blistering six-under-par 66. His birdie at the second in the final round had moved him within three strokes of the leader, Jeff Maggert, and everyone on the grounds of Augusta National was taking notice.

Tiger and his caddie, Stevie Williams, had a lengthy conference at the tee about what club to use. Tiger was leaning toward laying back with a two-iron; Williams wanted him to use a driver and rip it as close to the green as possible. Tiger departed the conference with a driver in his hand, a club that he had not controlled well during his previous three rounds.

The wind conditions dictated that Tiger play his tee shot a little to the right and let the wind bring it back to left. But his shot flew way right into the pines and into big trouble.

When Tiger reached his ball he found it nestled just below an azalea bush on a bed of pine needles. The ball's position would not allow Tiger to take his normal right-handed stance, so he had to play the shot as a left-hander, using a pitching wedge with the blade turned upside down. Tiger played the shot as well as any left-hander could have, slipping it through an opening in the pines and landing it short and to the left of the green.

After such a splendid recovery, Tiger should have perhaps continued to play left-handed, as his next shot from his right side was a dismal effort. He semi-bladed his chip shot, and it ran across the green into the back fringe. From there he took three more shots to get down for a double-bogey six. He never got back in sync during the remainder of his round and ended the day with a 75, his worst score to that date in the final round of a major.

Twenty minutes later the hopes of Jeff Maggert for a green jacket, the tournament leader, were dealt a crushing blow at the third hole. Electing to lay back so he would have a full shot into the green, Maggert used a two-iron off the tee, but the shot was too far left and landed in a fairway bunker near its front lip. Maggert had 106 yards left to the hole and elected to go with a sand wedge, but the shot caught the lip of the bunker and ricocheted directly back at Maggert, striking him in the chest.

Rule 19-2b states: "If a competitor's ball is accidentally deflected or stopped by himself . . . [he] shall incur a penalty of two strokes."

After conferring briefly with an official, Maggert stepped back into the bunker and played what would now be his fifth stroke to the green. This shot was long and ran into the back fringe. He hit his next shot too firmly, and it ran eighteen feet by the hole. Maggert then rattled that putt into the hole for a triple-bogey seven. To his credit, Maggert gallantly tried to recover from his disaster at the third, going two under par for the next eight holes, but another disaster at the dangerous par-three twelfth would drive a stake through his green-jacket hopes.

#4
Flowering
Crab Apple

Hole No. 4

PAR THREE—240 YARDS	FLOWERING CRAB APPLE

From the first Masters in 1934 through 1959, there were several different preliminary events staged prior to the first round on Thursday. The events ranged from a two-man best ball to a long-drive contest. During the summer of 1959, a nine-hole, par-three course was added to the Augusta National landscape by Cliff Roberts. Starting in 1960 the new little course became the home of the Par 3 Contest, held on Wednesday afternoon prior to the start of the tournament. This quickly proved to be the perfect prelude to the main event. It is a lighthearted event, with plenty of banter among the players and between the players and the fans. This event does have a downside for the winner, because since its inception, no winner of the event has gone on to win that year's Masters.

In 2001 David Toms collected his first major, and it was on a Georgia course, but it wasn't the Masters at Augusta. It was the PGA Championship played at the Atlanta Athletic Club. Earlier that year at the Masters, Toms had fallen victim to the Par 3 Contest jinx. He won the Wednesday-afternoon event but finished well back in the pack in the tournament. In addition to his mastering the Par 3 Course, Toms had a very successful week at the par-three fourth. He became only the second player ever to record three birdies there during the tournament. The other player to birdie the hole in three of the tournament's four rounds had pulled it off during the inaugural Masters in 1934. His name was Bobby Jones.

The announcement in December 1933 about the new tournament to be held at the Augusta National Golf Club contained an early Christmas present for golf fans. Not only was Bobby Jones going to host the tournament, but also he was going to end a four-year retirement from competition and play in the event as well.

The Second Coming of Bobby Jones gave the tournament an unbelievable amount of press coverage. Jones had been a darling of golf fans and the media since he burst onto the scene in 1916, when at the age of fourteen he reached the quarterfinals of the United States Amateur championship. His remarkable performance in his Grand Slam year in 1930 moved his exploits off the sports page and onto the front page of newspapers. Jones was one of four finalists for *Time* magazine's Man of the Year in 1930. His other three competitors for the award were Adolf Hitler, Joseph Stalin, and Mohandas K. Gandhi. Gandhi won.

Jones's departure from the game had left an incredible void in the American sports scene. It was widely believed that Jones would pick up right where he had left off in 1930, and to a degree this belief was not unfounded. It had been reported that Jones had shot a 69 in his first round on the Augusta National course when it was officially opened in January 1933. It had also been reported several weeks before the tournament that he had recently shot a 65 on his new course. These reports had an effect on another group of very interested followers, the oddsmakers, and they made Jones the cofavorite, along with Paul Runyan, at eight to one.

The touring professionals had a different view of his chances. They knew that a four-year absence from competition would be tough to overcome, even for the great Bobby Jones, and they were right. Although he was striking the ball as well as ever, his short game, particularly his putting stroke, could not be found. In a warm-up match against Runyan and Horton Smith, Jones and Augusta National pro Ed Dudley were beaten handily. On Wednesday a two-man best ball was played as the final warm-up for the tournament, and Bobby and his partner, Ross Sommerville, finished well back in the pack.

In the opening round Jones played his full shots as strong as anyone. His short game was still nowhere to be found, however. At the end of the day, he had posted a very un–Bobby Jones–like score of 76. The next day he spent a full hour on the practice green and raised his followers' hopes by rolling in putts from every angle. As Bobby left for the first tee, he joked that he hoped he was not leaving his putting stroke on the practice green, but he did. His play on his full shots was even stronger than the day before, but his putting went further south. Jones missed six putts from four feet or less. The shortest miss was from a foot. The only putt he made all day was on the par-three thirteenth hole, which, of course, is now the fourth, after the reversing of nines following the first Masters. At this hole he laced a long iron to about ten feet from the hole and somehow made the putt.

In his glory days Jones had used his famous putter, Calamity Jane, named after the famous female trick-shot artist from Buffalo Bill Cody's Wild West Show, with deadly accuracy. He needed her now, but she was on a shelf at the Spalding factory in Massachusetts where she had been used as a model for the putter in the Bobby Jones line of clubs. After his poor putting in the second round, he recalled that years earlier he had given his mother a Calamity Jane–style putter. Jones placed a call to an Atlanta golf professional, Chuck Ridley. He dispatched Ridley out to the bag room at East Lake Country Club in Atlanta, where his mother's clubs were stored, to get that putter and bring it to him in Augusta.

The night before, Walter Hagen, whose stature in golf was surpassed only by Jones's, requested that he be paired with Jones in the third round. Hagen was also having a dismal tournament and hoped that he and Jones could find some inspiration in each other. Whether it was the arrival of Calamity Jane's cousin or the pairing with his old rival, Jones's game finally clicked on the green, and he used eight fewer putts than he had needed the day before. Although he and Hagen were not in contention, they had most of the gallery following them. The highlight of the day for the gallery was when both legends drilled in putts at the thirteenth hole for birdie. Hagen would shoot a two-under-par 70, while Bobby would finish with an even-par 72.

The two were paired together for the final round as well. Jones took the measure of Hagen by five strokes, 72 to 77. They both finished the tournament with seventy-two-hole totals of six-over-par 294, for a share of thirteenth place. The highlight of the day for Jones was again the thirteenth hole, as he almost holed his tee shot and tapped in a putt of about a foot for his third consecutive birdie at the hole.

The fourth hole is considered to be one of the top par threes in golf. It is believed that Jones and Alister MacKenzie fashioned the hole after the eleventh hole at St. Andrews, the Old Course, which is considered by many to be the finest par-three hole in the game. The green at Augusta has the same shape as its Scottish cousin and almost possesses the same ultraquick speed. It also has bunkers in similar positions, one on the front right and one on the left side. It is from the left-side bunker of number 11 at St. Andrews that Bobby Jones had perhaps his darkest moment in his career. He took four strokes to escape the hellish sand in the third round of his first appearance in the British Open in 1921. After his ball was finally on the green, Jones picked it up and then tore up his scorecard and walked off the course.

The fourth hole has had two major changes since 1934. In 1964 the tee was moved to the right and back 15 yards, increasing the distance from 190 to 205. The tees stayed at that length until 2006, when they were backed up an additional 35 yards to increase the hole's distance to 240 yards. Since the 1964 increase in distance, the members' tee, which measures 180 yards, has often been used for one round during the tournament.

Since the fourth played as the third-toughest hole on the course in the 2005 Masters, many players, including Tiger Woods, voiced dissatisfaction in the 2006 lengthening. The change prompted Woods and Ernie Els to place five-woods in their bags to deal with the increased yardage at the hole. Some of the short hitters in the field would elect to go with three woods on their tee shots.

Due to the numerous pin locations that are available on the huge green and the unpredictability of wind conditions, selecting the right club on the tee was a problem even at the fourth's previous distances. Once for Ken Venturi, his club selection at this tee resulted in his receiving a brand-new set of clubs.

At the eighteenth Masters in 1954 amateur Venturi was making his first appearance at Augusta. Since seeing the great Ben Hogan play in the 1953 United States Open, Venturi had become a huge admirer. As a result, Venturi began to study Hogan's swing and the way he managed his game on the course. Venturi became somewhat of a Ben Hogan clone. He began wearing the same style of cap as Hogan and even began emulating some of his gestures and mannerisms.

After his first round in the Masters, Venturi was asked by an Augusta National member whom he would like to be paired with the next day, and Venturi replied, "Hogan!" Evidently, the member had some real firepower because at 1:30 Friday afternoon, Venturi was standing on the first tee with Hogan.

After the first three holes, Venturi was one up on his idol. Hogan had taken a shine to Venturi and had told him to call him Ben after Venturi had addressed him as Mr. Hogan. When they arrived at the fourth tee, Venturi had the honor, and he hit his tee shot to within twelve feet of the pin. Hogan had evidently taken a shine to Venturi's swing as well. He had noticed that Venturi used his three-iron for the shot. When he saw the outcome of Venturi's tee shot, he decided to go with a three-iron as well. Hogan took his classic swing and made perfect contact. His shot was dead on line with the flag, but it fell just short of the green into the front bunker.

By this time in his career Hogan had started his own golf club company and was an expert on the performance of clubs. He was also as analytical as they come in every aspect of the game. He knew there had to be a logical reason for what had just occurred. As he and Venturi were walking toward the green, he asked Venturi if he could take a look at his three-iron. Once he had given it a quick inspection, he shook his head in disgust. He could tell that the loft on Venturi's club was off. It might have had three-iron imprinted on the sole of the club, but it was a one-iron in its distance capability. He told Venturi what his inspection had concluded and then in disgust with himself said, "It serves me right for looking into an amateur's bag."

Venturi struggled for words to say to his idol and finally told him that he was in the army and his clubs were the best he could afford. Hogan then told him to give him his address at the end of the round, and he would send him a set of clubs. When Venturi returned home after the tournament, a set of Ben Hogan clubs was waiting for him.

Venturi, still playing as an amateur, returned to the Masters in 1956 and came very close to winning it all. He started the first round with a heavy birdie barrage, recording one-under-par scores at the first four holes. Here at the fourth, his tee shot stopped just a couple of feet from the pin. His tap-in birdie would be only one of ten made at the hole during the entire tournament. His fantastic start propelled him into the lead, and he was still in the lead when the third round concluded.

The 1956 Masters was played in the most brutal wind conditions in Masters history. This is evidenced by the cumulative statistics for the eighteen holes, as five of the holes' record for highest average score are from the 1956 tournament. The fourth is one of those five, and its scoring average for that week was 3.497.

Venturi experienced tough going in the final round in 1956 and shot 80. He finished in second place, one stroke behind Jackie Burke. The wind put Burke's club selection to the test at the fourth tee on that final day. It was blustering so fiercely into his face he had to use the biggest stick he had in his bag, the driver. Burke still did not come close to reaching the green. He had to pitch on with his second shot and then one-putted to save his par.

In 1962 Arnold Palmer hit one of the worst tee shots in his career at the fourth in the final round. He had begun the day two strokes in the lead, but the wheels were wobbling on his game. He missed a 20-inch birdie putt at the second hole. At the third hole he drove his ball into the woods and had to scramble for a par. Then the wheels came completely off at the fourth tee; his one-iron shot ballooned high into the air and fell to the ground, just 120 yards from the tee. He used a wedge to cover the remaining yardage and two-putted for bogey. Palmer would shoot a 75 that day, but it could have been much worse. Thanks to one of his patented late charges, he birdied two of the last three holes to get into a three-way eighteen-hole playoff, which he won the next day.

In the opening round in 1977, Tom Weiskopf picked up a unique par. He hooked his tee shot, and it was heading for trouble off to the left of the green, but it struck a spectator in the head and ricocheted back onto the green, where Weiskopf two-putted for his par.

Phil Mickelson had a ricochet with his tee shot at the fourth in the final round in 2012. It was not one of good fortune like Weiskopf's. Phil's wayward tee shot ricocheted off the grandstand on the left side of the green and ended up in the trees, nestled down in weeds.

Phil could have could have gone back to the tee and played his third shot. Instead, he elected to try to hack it out. Given his ball's position, he could not use his normal left-handed swing. He had to play it as a right-hander. His first effort advanced it only a few feet. Still playing as a right-hander, his next swing moved the ball about twenty feet to an area of hardpan.

From the hardpan, Phil had to carry a bunker to reach the green, which he failed to do. From the bunker, he played a splendid shot and almost holed it. From eighteen inches, he tapped in for a triple bogey.

Phil had started the round alone in second place, one shot out of the lead at eight under. Thanks to his six at the fourth, he would finish in a tie for third, two strokes out of first.

Forty-five players made the thirty-six-hole cut in 1998 and teed off in the third round. Of that number, only one would make birdie that day at the fourth hole: nineteen-year-old amateur Matt Kuchar. The Georgia Tech sophomore brought a five-iron just over the left edge of the right-front bunker, and it stopped within two feet of the pin.

Sixteen years later in 2014, Matt Kuchar, a professional since 2000 and the winner of seven PGA events and millions in prize money, had a major meltdown at the fourth. He had just grabbed a share of the lead with Jordan Spieth, when he chipped in for birdie at the third. But his putter let him down; he four-putted the fourth for a double bogey and never recovered. He would finish six strokes behind the eventual winner, Bubba Watson.

Watson was matched up in the final pairing that day with Spieth, who was vying to become the youngest player ever to win the Masters. This pairing put on quite a show at the fourth. Watson dropped his tee shot four feet from the pin.

Spieth had the lead by himself at that point by a stroke over Watson, thanks to Kuchar's putting woes a few minutes earlier. After his tee shot, his sole possession of the lead looked like it was in serious jeopardy. It landed in the middle of the front bunker. With Watson in excellent birdie range, it looked like Spieth would need an up-and-down from the bunker to maintain a share of the lead. He did better than that. His blast from the sand landed ten feet short of the pin and rolled into the cup for a birdie.

Watson, who would be the eventual winner, dropped his putt for birdie to stay one back at that juncture.

In 1983 Seve Ballesteros took control in the final round in his duel with other former Masters winners Raymond Floyd, Craig Stadler, and Tom Watson with an opening burst that concluded at the fourth. Ballesteros had started the day one stroke behind Stadler and Floyd, who were tied for the lead and one stroke ahead of Watson. Ballesteros birdied the first, eagled the second, and parred the third. When he reached the fourth tee, the wind was blowing stiffly into his face, and the pin was set fifteen feet behind the front bunker. He took a two-iron and hit it hard. The ball fought the wind all the way and then dropped softly down by the hole for a tap-in birdie. The birdie here put him three strokes in the lead; he never looked back and went on to win by four.

In 1953 Ben Hogan had set a new seventy-two-hole scoring record of 274, shattering the old mark of 279 set by Ralph Guldahl in 1939. After the tournament Hogan said it was the finest seventy-two holes he had ever played. The fourth hole had contributed significantly to Hogan's success that week. In the third round, he birdied from six feet. In the final round he picked up another birdie, when his tee shot stopped just ten inches from the hole.

A shot from off the green played a huge part in deciding the winner in 1988. Players trying to make sure they clear the front bunker can often overdo it and go over the green. This happened to Sandy Lyle in the final round in 1988. His tee shot here was long and ran into some fairly deep rough behind the green. From his location, with the green running away from him, saving par would be a very difficult proposition, but Lyle played the shot splendidly. He hit a sweet-running pitch with his sand wedge, and it rolled into the hole for a birdie. This shot would have a huge outcome on the finish, because Lyle would have a very wild up-and-down day. He would be required to make one more miraculous birdie at the eighteenth to win by one stroke.

As previously mentioned, the putting surface is huge and heavily contoured. It flows from left to right and can produce more than its share of three-putts. In the third round in 1965 Jack Nicklaus broke away from the field with a record-tying round of 64. At the fourth he picked up his second birdie of the day. From the tee he hit a four-iron to within about twelve feet and then rolled in a touchy left-to-right putt for his two. In the final round he recorded another birdie by dropping a testy sixteen-footer and finished the tournament seventeen under par, which shattered Hogan's mark set in 1953 by three shots.

Nicklaus certainly appeared to have the fourth green mastered, but like practically all the greens at Augusta, the fourth can reach up and grab you at any time. In the first round in 1984 it gave Nicklaus his worst putting experience ever at Augusta. After he placed his tee shot twenty-five feet from the hole, his birdie attempt broke off line to the left and finished about four feet from the hole. His par putt from that distance wasn't even close and cruised by on the left side. His bogey putt from two feet caught the left lip and spun out. He then tapped in for a five. It was the first time Nicklaus had four-putted a green at Augusta in twenty-six years.

Billy Casper was leading the tournament when he walked on the fourth green in the final round in 1969. He made the mistake of hitting his tee shot too long. He was just in the fringe about sixty-five feet from the hole. His putt down the slope to the pin was much too strong and almost ran into the front bunker. Casper had a fifteen-footer coming back for his par that he just missed on the low side. In the first three rounds Casper had made only two bogeys. This one here at the fourth started a slide that would result in four more bogeys over the next six holes, which wrecked his chances for a green jacket that year.

In the final round in 1998 the day after Matt Kuchar, in the field as an amateur, made the field's only birdie at the fourth, there were only three birdies recorded at the hole. Fred Couples and Mark O'Meara, the last pairing of the day, were responsible for two of them. O'Meara rolled in a sixty-foot snake to briefly claim the lead outright, but his lead lasted for only about two minutes, as Couples calmly rolled in a ten-footer to regain a share of the lead. The two would battle down to the wire, with O'Meara claiming a one-stroke win.

The best shot ever at this hole belongs to Jeff Sluman. In the first round in 1992, Sluman accomplished what no other Masters participant had ever done before: he made a hole in one at the fourth. Sluman had been in professional golf for nine years, and this was his first ace in competition. It was not his first ace at Augusta National, however. He had aced the sixteenth in a practice round in 1991.

Sluman used a four-iron, and when he struck the ball it looked pretty good to him, but he never dreamed it would go in the hole. The shot landed about twenty feet short of the pin and began to track for the hole. Sluman didn't think it was going to be that close because there was no reaction from the gallery, but they may have been holding their collective breath. The ball was virtually crawling toward the hole, but when it dropped, they really let loose. Longtime Masters statistician Bill Inglish calculated that it was a one-in-eleven-thousand shot. His basis for the calculation was that there had been eleven thousand previous tee shots in Masters competition at the fourth hole, since the inaugural event in 1934. The ace helped propel Sluman to an opening round of 65 and a share of the lead. He would finish the week in fourth place.

As Sluman walked from the green to the fifth tee, a woman in the crowd called out that she wanted the ball as a souvenir, and Sluman obeyed and gave it to her. The woman was his mother.

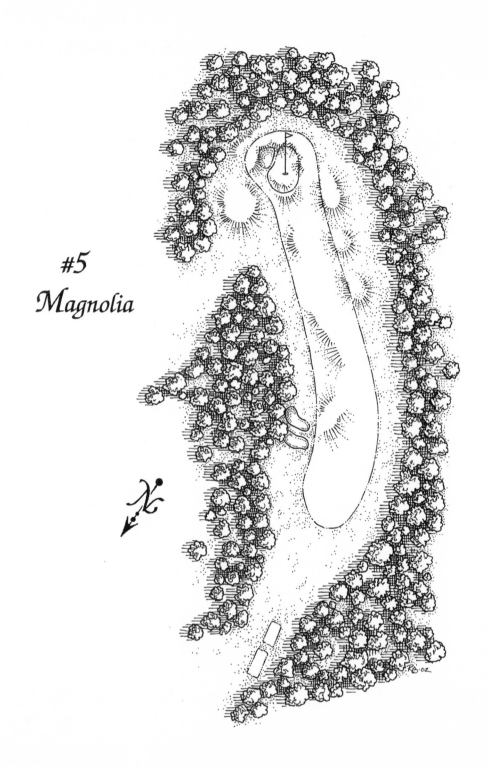

#5
Magnolia

Hole No. 5

| PAR FOUR—455 YARDS | MAGNOLIA |

Prior to the expansion of television coverage in 2002 to include the entire front nine, the fifth hole was the most unseen and unknown hole at Augusta National. Located on the southeast side of the course, it is off the beaten path. It is about as difficult for the gallery to get to as it is difficult for the players to play.

This hole has consistently been ranked as one of the toughest par-fours at Augusta National. It is a dogleg left with a very intimidating green. Before the 2003 Masters it measured 425 yards. The play off the tee here was to try to cut as much off the dogleg as possible. This route featured two bunkers that were in the bend of the dogleg. But at 240 yards from the tee, they had ceased to be a factor because of the increased driving distance achieved by the field over the years. The stand of trees alongside and well past the bunkers, however, were very much a factor, as Ian Woosnam can readily attest.

The fifth hole played a huge part in Woosnam's 1991 win, when he made birdie in the final round on his way to a one-stroke victory. In 1992 Woosnam was making a very strong run at repeating as Masters champion. He opened with a 69, and then he followed that up with his best Masters round ever of 66, which included a birdie at the fifth. Woosnam's tee shot on the fifth, however, was his undoing in the third round. He hooked his drive into a thick section of bushes in the woods on the left side. Woosnam waded into the thicket and gave some thought to hitting the ball left-handed. He decided against it and made that long walk back to the tee to play another ball. Woosnam would end up with a double-bogey six on the hole, which began his steady drop down the leaderboard. He would shoot a one-over-par 73 that day, and he followed up that score with a three-over-par 75 in the final round to finish in nineteenth place.

One of the few bumps in the road during Tiger Woods's march to victory in the final round in 2002 occurred at the fifth hole. Woods, like Woosnam, lost his drive to the left, and it flew into the trees. Woods received a tremendous break, however, because his ball hit one of the trunks of the pines squarely and caromed backward. It landed in an open area in the rough, where Woods could at least hit it again. Woods then played a great recovery shot. He hit a big hook to get around a stand of trees in front of him, and the shot made it to the very front right side of the green.

This green is one of the most formidable on the course. It is so undulating that from the fairway it looks like a section of billowing ocean. It has two tiers, and it has been said that there is not a level spot on it. Its lower part is almost a continuation of the fairway for about twenty feet. And then there are two large camel-type humps—one on the left front and one on the right front. Once a player is on the second level, the green runs away from him.

The humps in front will repel a weak approach shot and throw others to the left or right, depending on which hump the ball encounters. Having to putt up over the humps is definitely a challenge. After his great recovery shot in 2002, Woods still walked off the green with a bogey in the final round. His putt over the hump on the right side was short and thrown off to the right, and he missed his next effort from ten feet.

There is a bunker behind the green that actually serves as a safety net to keep shots from running down the steep slope into even deeper trouble on the wooded hillside located behind it.

The pin locations are always on the upper level, but generally they are in positions that make firing at them too much of a risk to take. Most players will opt to play for the center of the green and then will try to hole a long putt for birdie.

The fifth, which had had just a few minor changes over the years, received a significant overhaul before the 2003 Masters. The tee was moved back 30 yards, bringing its distance to 455 yards. The fairway and the fairway bunkers on the left side were shifted to the right, making the dogleg more pronounced. These bunkers were also extended 80 yards and now require a drive in excess of 315 yards to carry them. Also, the bunkers were deepened so much, that when a player takes his stance in one, the only things he can see are the lip of the bunker and the sky.

In the first round in 1974, 1959 Masters winner Art Wall was just trying to make sure he would make the cut. He was 220 yards out and hit a four-wood. The ball struck a mound in front of the green, which kicked it onto a line with the pin. The ball then ran over one of the camel humps and disappeared from view. A few seconds later, the gallery erupted with shouts and cheers when the ball ran into the cup for the first eagle ever at the fifth.

The fifth hole had never been that kind to Nicklaus. In the ten Masters preceding the 1995 edition, he had birdied the hole only once, but his fortunes at the hole made a remarkable turnaround that year. In the first round he had strung together four straight pars, and his drive at the fifth had left him with approximately 185 yards to the pin. He went with a five-iron, and the ball went into the hole on the fly. He went on to post an opening round of 67, which put him in third place.

The fifth hole (which he bogeyed) as well as several other holes were not kind to Nicklaus in round two. He shot eleven strokes higher than he did the first day. He barely made the cut and was in last place. Nicklaus had the dubious honor of being the first person off in the third round.

Nicklaus again started with all pars on the first four holes. His drive at the fifth left him about 20 yards closer than he had been in the first round, and he elected to go with a seven-iron. The pin was in one of its most difficult locations on the top right. Nicklaus thought he could not get anywhere near it, but he thought wrong.

He was actually aiming for the center of the green, but his aim was off by about 15 feet to the right. The ball landed just a few feet short of the flag and then rolled into the hole.

Nicklaus became the tenth player in Masters history to eagle a hole twice in the same tournament and the first to do so on a par four. The other nine all accomplished the feat on par fives.

In the final round of the 2017 Masters, Russell Henley's eagle from 185 yards at the fifth turned out to be quite a showstopper.

Henley, who made the Masters field by winning the previous week's Shell Houston Open, slam-dunked his second shot for the first eagle at the fifth hole in fourteen years. The shot, however, was not truly the slam dunk that it had appeared to be. On the way into the hole, it took out a portion of the cup.

The Augusta National grounds crew responded with dispatch. The crew plugged the original hole and cut a new one as close to the old one as possible. They sprayed the new cup with white paint and meticulously tamped down the old hole's location.

CBS opted to stay live with the five-minute repair process at 5 instead of following the action on the course, which included two former Masters champions teeing off on number 1, prompting a number of complaints from viewers.

In the first Masters in 1934, the fifth hole played as the fourteenth hole. On the first day of the tournament, Bobby Jones teed off at 10:35 in the morning. Horton Smith had been the last man to defeat Bobby Jones in a tournament, and that had occurred four years before in the 1930 Savannah Open. Shortly after that tournament, Bobby Jones won a tournament in Augusta by fourteen strokes and then went on to claim the Grand Slam later that same year. Smith did not tee off until 1:41, so he decided to follow Jones around the course. He watched him play through the fourteenth hole (now number 5), and then he headed back to the first hole to start his own round.

Although Jones's putting was awful, the way he attacked his own course with his drives and approaches was classic Jones. Smith obviously benefited from his walk with the man who built the course, since he posted a two-under-par 70 for a three-way share of the lead.

Smith had the lead by himself by one shot at the end of the second round, and he maintained that margin at the conclusion of the third round. In the fourth round Smith had added a stroke to his lead by the time he reached the fourteenth hole. Smith's approach shot barely reached the front part of the green, and he still had to go over a hump to the second tier. He elected to chip the ball instead of putting, and his chip got him to within four feet of the hole. He could not convert the putt, and his lead slipped back to one. This miss would cause him some anxious moments down the stretch, but he would manage to claim a one-stroke victory.

For a number of years the fairway at the fifth was far from ideal. It had an abundance of rocks just below the playing surface. The rocks kept working their way to the top and wreaking havoc on golf clubs and golf course equipment. In the early 1960s the fairway was reworked with new topsoil. As a test to see if it was now smooth, a club employee was ordered to drive up and down the fairway in a golf cart at full throttle to make sure no bumps were detected. This means of testing was ordered by Cliff Roberts, a one-man gang if there ever was one.

It seems that everyone who had any type of association with the Masters in the period from 1934 until his death in 1977, or knew somebody who did, has a Cliff Roberts story to tell. Many are not very flattering. Roberts had a personality that made it easy for people to dislike him, but one certainly had to admire his accomplishments. Coming from humble beginnings, he went from men's clothing salesman to oilman, to soldier, to Wall Street guru, to confidant of the president of the United States, and into the World Golf Hall of Fame.

Roberts was born in the small town of Morning Sun, Iowa, in 1894. His mother was a distant cousin of Francis Scott Key (of "Star-Spangled Banner" fame). His father was a real estate salesman who always wanted to see what was on the other side of the hill, so the family moved frequently and eventually ended up in Texas.

The frequent moves made Roberts's family life a constant struggle. He never finished high school. Instead, he took to the road selling men's clothing when he was about sixteen, and he did quite well at it. After several years in that line of work, he tried his hand in the oil business. Roberts ultimately decided New York City was where he needed to go to really make money. After one failed assault on the Big Apple, Roberts recouped and tried again, but World War I got in the way.

Roberts entered the army and received his first exposure to Augusta, Georgia, at government expense as he was sent for training to Fort Hancock, which was located just outside the city. After his training was completed, he shipped over to France and spent approximately a year rushing the wounded back from the front lines as an ambulance driver.

Following the war Roberts was able to get a foothold in the New York financial scene, despite his lack of formal education. He endured many ups and downs, including taking a beating in the crash of the stock market in 1929. He persevered, however, and forged a very successful career on Wall Street, eventually becoming a partner with the Reynolds and Company brokerage firm.

In the mid-1920s Roberts took up the game of golf. He soon made it his practice to spend part of the winter in Augusta, Georgia, which at that time was still a celebrated retreat for northerners wishing to escape the doldrums of winter and a good place to make business contacts. During those junkets he played golf at the Augusta Country Club and became acquainted with most of the Augusta regulars. When he was introduced to Bobby Jones by a mutual acquaintance, the two hit it off quite well, and their long and successful association began.

Roberts became aware of Jones's desire to build his dream course, and while they were both in Augusta during a winter holiday, Roberts put this question to Jones: "Why don't you build that golf course you have been thinking about here in Augusta?" Jones replied, "I will if you will finance it," and a superb partnership was formed.

When it was decided that their new club would stage an invitational tournament in the spring of 1934, Roberts's thoroughness and his skill at threading his way through mounds of detail made him the natural choice for the post of tournament chairman. He would hold this post for the next forty-four years.

Roberts had an extremely reserved disposition. Slight in build and stone-faced, he said no more on any subject than he had to. He lived for Augusta National and the Masters, and he earned a lasting place in golf history as the man who showed the world how to stage a golf tournament. He was the first to construct spectator mounds and to install permanent bleachers. He started the handing out of daily pairing sheets. He also wanted the course to be kept spotless during tournament week, so he put a small army into the field from dawn to dusk that speared spectator trash as soon as it hit the ground. Roberts's leaderboards became the standard for all golf tournaments. They were mammoth and positioned throughout the course, so spectators could easily keep informed of the action. His leaderboards also introduced a unique method of scoring. A green number beside a player's name denoted how many strokes over par he stood through the last hole he had played. A green zero indicated that he stood at even par, and a red number denoted how many strokes a player was under par.

Roberts ran Augusta National with the iron hand of a dictator. Although members were captains of both industry and finance, and not usually bashful about expressing their opinions, whenever an issue arose at Augusta National, what Roberts said went.

In Bernhard Langer's first Masters victory in 1985, the fifth was a critical hole for him in the final round. He had to figure he had given away one stroke and possibly two to the field, when he had made bogey at the very birdieable second hole. He got back on track with a birdie at the third and a par at the fourth. His confidence-level warning light had to be flashing on the fifth tee, because he had bogeyed the hole in the three previous rounds.

Langer was only twenty-seven at the time, but he had had a serious bout with what is typically an older player's malady: the yips, a condition that can best be described as the inability to execute a smooth putting stroke. Ben Hogan had it in his later years and would seemingly stand over putts for what seemed like an eternity before finally getting off his stroke. Sam Snead contracted the yips later in his career as well. Snead first used a croquet-style stroke as a remedy, but it was soon banned. He then developed a side-saddle stroke he could live with.

Langer had developed his own method for dealing with the problem. From outside twenty feet he putted with a conventional stroke, and from inside twenty feet he putted cross-handed. His approach at the fifth hole in the final round came to rest eighteen feet from the hole, which put him in cross-handed range. Although he would have some shaky moments with his method later in the round, here at the fifth it worked to perfection as he drained the putt with his cross-hand stroke. It turned out to be a huge stroke in his one-shot victory.

Cary Middlecoff opened his defense of his Masters title in 1956 with a fine first round of five-under-par 67. He came back the second day with an even-par 72 and was one under at the turn in the third round. After completing the ninth hole in that round, Middlecoff ducked into the clubhouse. He was a chronic hay-fever sufferer and was in need of his medication, which he had left in the pocket of his jacket. He could find neither jacket nor pills. A friend had decided to borrow the jacket. Red-eyed and suffering, Middlecoff headed for the tenth tee. He would shoot a four-over-par 40 on the backside to fall four strokes off the lead.

Middlecoff got off to a fast start in the fourth round, picking up birdies at the first and second holes. He gave back a stroke with a bogey at the fourth hole, and then the roof caved in on him at the fifth. His second shot barely got to the front of the green, and he had to putt over one of the humps up to the upper-level pin. His first putt died just about five feet from the hole. Unfortunately, his second putt left him three feet away from the hole on the other side, and he missed that putt coming back and then tapped in for a four-putt, double-bogey six.

Middlecoff's woes seemed to carry over from the fifth hole. On the next hole, the par-three sixth, he placed his tee shot just three feet from the hole, but his birdie putt rimmed out. On the par-four seventh, instead of chipping over a bunker, he chipped his ball into it and took another double bogey. At the seventeenth hole, he made another double bogey. The three double bogeys really cost him, for at the end of the day he was in third place, just three strokes behind the winner.

Dow Finsterwald had had some tough holes and used a lot of strokes at Augusta during his early Masters career. In his first Masters, in 1951, he made an eleven at the par-three twelfth, and in his second Masters, in 1952, he made a nine at the par-four eleventh.

His most costly stroke ever at Augusta, however, came in the 1960 Masters when he was in his prime and considered to be one of the best players in the game. To make matters worse, this stroke was actually a practice stroke. In the first round that year Finsterwald made a routine par at the fifth hole on his way to an opening-round 71 that placed him in a four-way tie for second place. After that par at the fifth hole, Finsterwald had dropped his ball back onto the green and putted it off the green in the direction of the sixth tee.

In the second round, after putting out at the first hole, Finsterwald dropped his ball and was about to stroke it across the green toward the second tee when his playing partner, Billy Casper, yelled at him and told him not to do it. It was against the rules. It was a Masters rule, and it was printed on the back of the scorecard. Finsterwald then sought out an official to report the infraction he had made the day before at the fifth hole. He was told that the Rules Committee would make a decision as soon as possible and that he was most likely looking at being disqualified from the tournament.

Finsterwald continued to play while officials gathered and deliberated on his fate. Despite the likelihood that a tournament death sentence was going to be imposed on him, Finsterwald played very steadily, and when the sentence finally came down when he was on the fourteenth hole, he was one under par on his round.

The ruling by the Rules Committee turned out to somewhat of a surprise and was a landmark case in that it was thought to be the first time a penalty was assessed the day after an infraction had occurred. The committee chose not to disqualify Finsterwald, because the breach of the rules had not occurred while his ball was actually in play, but they did impose a two-stroke penalty.

After hearing the news, Finsterwald played out his remaining holes at one under par and finished the round at two under for the day. Two strokes were added to his total score, and he stood at 141, three under par. Finsterwald shot even par on Saturday and one under on Sunday. He finished the tournament at four-under-par 284, which was two strokes behind the winner, Arnold Palmer. If it had not been for the penalty for the practice putt at the fifth hole, Finsterwald would have been playing Palmer for the green jacket in an eighteen-hole playoff the next day.

In the early 1970s Lee Trevino did the unthinkable. To many golf fans and members of the media, it was the ultimate golf travesty. He started declining Masters invitations.

Trevino had played in his first Masters in 1969 and had finished in fortieth place. In 1970 he improved considerably and finished nineteenth, but for the next two years he declined to play in the tournament. He cited the fact that the course did not suit his game. His primary shot pattern was left to right, and the Augusta National was a course that favored players who worked the ball from right to left. Also, there were reports that Trevino had some problems with some of the officials at the Masters, which may have added to his anti-Masters feelings.

When asked why he was giving up on winning the Masters, which was every other golfer's dream, without a try, Trevino replied,

"Everybody has their own idea of what the [Grand] Slam ought to be. Mine is just different from most. I would put the Tournament of Champions in place of the Masters. In my mind, if I could win the Champions, U.S. Open, British Open, and PGA, I would have won the 'Slam.'"

After he had expounded this golfing heresy, it was initially thought that Trevino would never be invited back to the Masters. When Roberts was quizzed about Trevino before the start of the 1970 Masters, his tone was conciliatory: "All I have to say about this is that I have a higher opinion of Lee's ability than he seems to have. He has played here twice, and I would like to point out that he scored better those two years than either Palmer or Nicklaus did their first two times here. It is always a cause for concern to us when a player of Lee's stature fails to make an appearance here. I am sorry because I think he would have added much to the tournament."

During the two years he chose not to play at Augusta, Trevino won two British Opens and the United States Open. Adding a Masters title to his record seemed to take on more importance to him, and he accepted his invitation and returned to Augusta with much media fanfare in 1972.

It can hardly be said that Trevino went back to Augusta entirely at peace with the course or Masters officials. He chose not to use the clubhouse, opting to change his shoes in the parking lot, and he turned down an invitation to have tea with Cliff Roberts.

His performance was lackluster, as he failed to break par in any round, and he finished in the thirty-third spot. After the third round Cliff Roberts sought him out, and they had about a thirty-minute meeting where they appeared at least partially to bury the hatchet concerning any ill will between the Masters and Trevino and vice versa.

Trevino continued to struggle with the course. The following year he shot a two-over-par 74 in the first round. In the middle of his second round, he ran off three straight bogeys and was getting ready to hit an approach shot to the par-four tenth hole when he put his club back in his bag and then walked over to the gallery. Some thought a camera had clicked, and others thought a remark from behind the ropes had ticked him off, but actually it was Trevino who wanted to make some remarks.

Trevino walked over to the ropes and did not direct his remarks at anyone in particular but wanted to get something off his chest. He told the surprised gallery members, "I can play in graveyards, on gravel roads, anywhere but this place. When I drive through the gate to this place, I just get psyched out."

Trevino finished the day with a three-over-par 75 and gave the media in the press hut plenty of copy. He told them how he couldn't play the course and how he had hit more than four hundred balls on the practice range to get ready. But the shots required to play the Augusta National were just not in his bag. Trevino further stated that he had won too much money with his swing to try to fool around with it for one tournament.

The question then came up as to why he had even bothered to show up. Trevino replied, "It's a lot easier to put up with a course I can't play for four days than to have you sportswriters cut me up for not showing up." Trevino finished in forty-third place that year and then missed the 1974 tournament. He won the PGA that year, which then left the Masters as the only major tournament he had not won. Trevino returned in 1975 and finished tenth, and in the 1976 tournament he dropped back down to the twenty-eighth spot. He was not in the field for the 1977 Masters.

Trevino returned in 1978 and got off to his best start ever. He opened with a two-under-par 70 and followed that up with a three-under-par 69 in the second round that put him in a tie for first place. In the third round he played steadily over the first four holes, picking up a birdie and three pars.

At the fifth hole Trevino's drive was in the right side of the fairway, and he elected to go with a three-iron. It was too much club, and the ball flew over the green and over the safety-net bunker into the woods behind the green. His only shot out the woods was low and into the bunker. He failed to get out of the sand on his first effort. His next sand shot put him three and a half feet from the hole. He missed that short putt and tapped in for a triple-bogey seven and then said to his caddie, "I think my green jacket just flew the hell out the window."

Trevino finished in fourteenth place that year. He would make thirteen more Masters appearances, with a tenth place in 1985 being his best finish.

Whereas Trevino's chances went out the window at the fifth, Trevor Immelman's play of the hole in the final round in 2008 was a turning point that would lead to his slipping into a green jacket three hours later.

The South African had started the day with a two-stroke lead, but he was having a problem keeping his nerves in check. Immelman bogeyed the first hole and followed with three shaky pars before he found the antidote for his case of nerves at the fifth: an eight-iron approach to within four feet of the hole that he poured in for birdie. Commenting on that moment after the round, Immelman said, "That got my day going . . . settled me down."

Trevor would go on to win by two strokes.

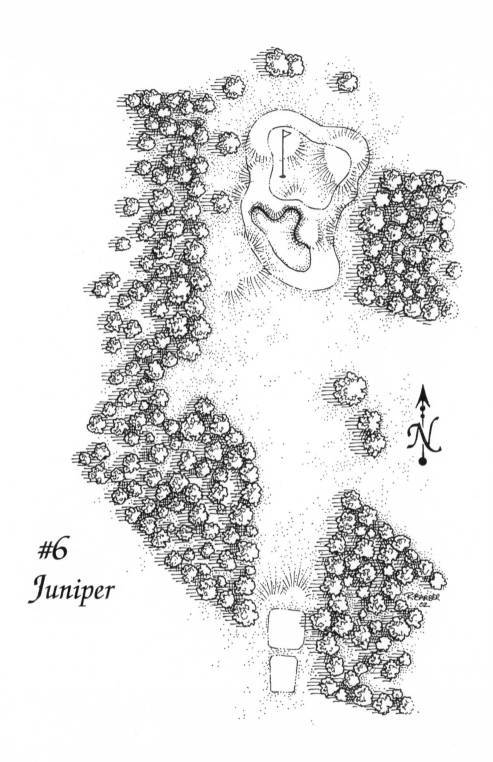

#6
Juniper

Hole No. 6

PAR THREE—180 YARDS	JUNIPER

The designation of the Masters as one of golf's four major championships did not occur at a summit meeting of the governing bodies of golf. When Bobby Jones won his Grand Slam in 1930, the four majors were the United States Open, the United States Amateur, the British Open, and the British Amateur. Shortly after Jones's retirement, the two amateur tournaments began to lose their stature, with the British version fading much faster than the United States Amateur.

The Masters and PGA Championship eventually took their places, but there is considerable debate as to when this actually occurred. Some believe that the Masters assumed the role in 1935 with Gene Sarazen's dramatic victory, while others take a much longer view and think it did not occur until Arnold Palmer and Jack Nicklaus were on the scene in the late 1950s and early 1960s. Noted golf writer and authority Herbert Warren Wind, who covered the Masters from 1947 until 1989, was of the opinion that the 1954 Masters ultimately crowned the event as a major tournament.

If one subscribes to Wind's belief, one of the loudest cheers heralding the Masters' coronation as a major occurred at the sixth hole in the final round that year. The cheers were generated by one of the most unheralded players ever to tee it up at the Masters. He looked more like a divinity student than a golfer, but he started a charge at the sixth hole that made that Sunday at Augusta one of the most memorable ever.

Those in the gallery around the sixth green that day were staring high up the hill to the tee 180 yards away. They were waiting for this golfer who had been the big story of the tournament to play his tee shot. But they would have to wait for several more moments because he was having difficulty finding just the right spot to tee up his ball. No one could really complain about his taking a little extra time. After all, he was what the press used to call a "Simon Pure," an amateur.

Given that all his major titles were won as an amateur, Bobby Jones always wanted there to be a strong representation of amateurs in the field at the Masters. When the qualifications criteria were being reviewed for the 1954 event, it was decided that members of the Walker Cup team would be sent an invitation. As almost an afterthought Cliff Roberts asked Jones if he wanted the alternates of that squad invited as well, and Jones said yes. With that decision, into the Masters field slipped a hardwood lumber dealer from Morganton, North Carolina, father of three, and weekend golfer William J. "Billy Joe" Patton.

Patton was already a legend in the hills of western North Carolina. He had been somewhat of a golfing child prodigy. Patton's father had been the first club champion at the Mimosa Country Club in Morganton. Patton stepped on that course for the first time at the age of ten. He shot a very credible 106. Some ten years later, he would set the course record of 62. By his early twenties, Patton had won many area, state, and regional tournaments. Patton served in the navy during World War II. After the war was over, he settled down to life as a family man and took a position as a lumber salesman. He kept his golf game tuned by hustling out to the Mimosa Country Club for twilight rounds during the week and playing in club matches on Saturday and Sunday. But he could find the time to play in only two or three big amateur events a year.

Patton contended that there were ten guys back at the Mimosa Country Club in Morganton who beat him regularly, and when one saw his swing, one would have thought that number should have been much larger. Patton left nothing in the bag when he swung.

It was the fastest swing anyone had ever seen at Augusta, and it was anything but picturesque.

The lumber salesman began to create a stir at the Augusta National on Wednesday not only by winning the long-driving contest but by the way he won it. Each contestant was allowed to hit three balls, the longest of those three being his mark for the event. Patton hit only one. It traveled 338 yards and outdistanced runner-up Cary Middlecoff's longest drive by 9 yards.

Legend has it that he then turned to the official running the contest and said, "That's the best I can do. I'm not going to hit any more." Years later, Patton set the record straight. The real reason he had hit only one ball was that he had shown up for the event with only his driver, thinking that balls were going to be provided. When he discovered they weren't, he had to borrow three balls from a fellow competitor. After his initial drive flew so well, he decided not to incur any more debt and returned the other two balls to the lender.

Ben Hogan had established a scoring record at the Masters the year before, but 1954 was not going to be a year for low scoring. When all the scores were posted after the first round, there were two co-leaders at a score of two-under-par 70. One of them was Patton.

Patton bathed happily in all the media attention, and he was certainly good copy for the opening round. He was thought to be just a flash in the pan, and it was expected that he would be deep down the leaderboard by the same time the next day. Even Patton was hedging a little, remarking that his game could quickly fall apart.

To everyone's surprise, his swing held up in the second round. Patton's playing partner was everyone's favorite, Byron Nelson, which was indeed a huge dose of good fortune for Patton. Patton awed Nelson at the fifth hole. Nelson required a driver and four-wood to reach the green, while Patton used a driver and a six-iron. Patton had a strong front side but slipped a little on the back nine and came home with a score of one-over-par 73. But that score was still strong enough to give him first place all by himself, one stroke ahead of Hogan. Patton again basked in the press coverage and had many people scratching their heads. Cary Middlecoff lamented, "If he wins, it will set golf back fifty years."

Patton's luck did change on Saturday. He drew Lloyd Mangrum as his playing partner. Mangrum, the no-nonsense, decorated World War II veteran, was all business and appeared to be in the Middlecoff camp in his regard for Billy Joe. It was a definite oil-and-water mix. Whether it was the pairing, or the pressure, or the natural cooling off of a streak player, Patton had his worst round of the week and ended the day with a three-over-par 75. He slipped down the leaderboard, while Hogan and Sam Snead moved to the front. The cream had finally risen to the top. The golf universe, which had been out of kilter for almost three days, now seemed to be back in its natural alignment.

In the press hut several writers filed their obituaries on Patton. Most had probably been written the day before, expecting the predicted undoing of the upstart amateur to happen in the second round instead of the third. One writer likened it to watching a fire in a fireworks factory; sooner or later, there had to be an explosion.

Shortly after playing in the 1948 Masters, Bobby Jones began to experience the onset of the illness that over the next twenty-three years would claim his mobility—syringomyelia—a rare chronic disease that attacks the spinal cord. He would soon be required to use a cane, then a cane and a leg brace, and then two leg braces and crutches, and ultimately he would be confined to a wheelchair. The illness quickly robbed him of the ability to play golf. One of the last pars he made at Augusta National was at the par-four eighteenth, and it required three three-wood shots and a chip-in.

As a result of his increasing lack of mobility, Bobby Jones used to love to monitor the action in the tournament from the porch of the Jones Cabin, which is situated on high ground near the tenth tee. He once told reporters in an impromptu session, "There is only one place to watch this tournament. On that porch ... You can hear the groans that mean a fellow has missed a putt. You can hear the shouts that mean he made it. You can hear every sound made on the eighteen holes, and on the quiet days, you can even hear the whispers."

Jones was manning his favorite spot on the porch that Sunday afternoon in 1954 when a huge roar went up at the sixth green. Jones said instantly, "Billy Joe's done something again." Of course, he was right.

Moments before, Patton had been stalking the tee box looking for just the right spot to tee up his ball. His round had gotten off to a bad start when he buried his approach shot in the bunker at the first hole and made bogey. He regained that stroke with a birdie at the second and parred 3, 4, and 5. He teed and then moved his ball two more times before finding the right spot. It has been said the third time is the charm, and that turned out to be the case. Patton adjusted his stance twice and let it rip. A few seconds later, there was a loud whack when the ball slammed into the flag stick about two feet above the ground and spun down the stick. There was not enough space between the stick and the edge of the cup for the ball to go completely into the hole. Luckily for Patton, it did not kick out but wedged itself between the flagstick and the top of the cup. All hell broke loose in the gallery.

A large portion of those in attendance that day began to head for the sixth hole, because most of them, like Jones, knew Billy Joe had done something spectacular. Patton still had some work to do when he got to the green. He had to make sure the ball stayed in the hole when he took the pin out. He consulted with the official at the hole, Joe Dey, executive director of the United States Golf Association. He then went to the hole and ever so carefully removed the flagstick. The ball dropped down to the bottom of the cup, making it official, and another huge roar went up in the gallery.

So many of the spectators were now flocking to the scene that a police officer was quickly assigned to Patton. A few holes later, additional reinforcements would be required. Patton was going to take his cheering throng on a wild ride over the remaining holes. The rest of that fateful Sunday will be chronicled in the remaining chapters.

The decibel level of the roar generated by Patton at the sixth hole would not be surpassed until fifty-one years later in the second round in 2004, and the shot that created it would be by a super-senior golfer, seventy-four-year-old Arnold Palmer.

Arnie had announced prior to the tournament that 2004 would be his last appearance in the Masters. Arnie's Army had showed up in full force to escort Arnie around Augusta National one last time, and rousing applause greeted him at every tee box and green.

This was Arnie's fiftieth appearance in the Masters, and he was hoping to tally at least one birdie. The throng marching with him and those situated around the sixth green sent out a deafening roar when Arnie's tee shot there checked up three feet from the pin.

Arnie's farewell birdie was now just a short roll away.

Those around the green that had been treated to a very special Masters moment with Arnie's tee shot were about to be treated to another. This would be one of the most poignant in the annals of Augusta National history.

As Arnie neared the green he caught the attention of another golfing legend who was stepping onto the nearby sixteenth green: Jack Nicklaus. The two titans tipped their caps to each other and exchanged a thumbs-up. The crowds at both holes sent out another thunderous roar.

Just minutes later, those in attendance at the sixth hole generated one of the loudest groans ever at the Masters when Arnie missed his putt and had to settle for a par.

Arnie winced when his short putt failed to drop, but in a manner of seconds his trademark smile returned. He would finish the day with an 84, but to the appreciative patrons it might as well have been a 64.

The sixth-hole tee is elevated about fifty feet higher than the green. It is a delight to the eye with the tall pines towering over the tee box and the bank of azaleas lining the path to the green. Because of the downhill trajectory of the shot, the hole plays considerably shorter than its listed yardage.

The sixth green is large, and its claim to fame is the large hump on its right side. The hump was even larger in earlier Masters tournaments, and a favorite remark of players was that Cliff Roberts had buried an elephant on that portion of the green. The green's surface slopes down from back to front and also from right to left, and there is a large bunker on the front left side.

The toughest pin location is back right on top of the hump, which is traditionally used in the final round. This location requires a very accurate tee shot to get the ball to this section of the green and have it hold. If one comes up short, he is faced with a very difficult chip or long putt.

Other than reduction of the size of the hump on the green, the changes to the sixth hole have been mainly cosmetic in nature. Originally, the tributary to Rae's Creek that passes in front of the thirteenth hole could be seen flowing across the fairway of the sixth, but it was well short of the green and did not come into play. In 1955 the creek was dammed, and a pond was formed in the fairway. It also proved inconsequential to the play of the hole, plus it became somewhat of an eyesore. It was difficult to keep the water looking clean, so it was covered up in 1959.

The sixth has been a key hole in a number of Masters tournaments. Battling a suspected case of food poisoning in the third round in 1940, Jimmy Demaret put his tee shot ten inches from the cup for an easy birdie and wrestled the lead away from Lloyd Mangrum. His two-under-par 70 gave him a one-stroke lead over Mangrum, which he expanded to a four-stroke win in the last round.

The sixth hole seems to be partial to players having stomach problems. In his 1942 playoff with Ben Hogan, Byron Nelson started his comeback from the stomach problems that had plagued him the night before and during the early part of that day's match. He was three strokes down when they arrived at the sixth tee. Nelson got on the road to recovery here when his tee shot settled down seven feet from the hole and he made the putt for birdie. Hogan missed the green with his tee shot and made bogey. Nelson would surge ahead by three strokes over the next several holes and then hold Hogan off down the stretch for a one-stroke win.

In 1967 Gay Brewer's play on the front nine and the sixth hole in particular was the key to his one-stroke victory. He played the front nine for the tournament at nine under par and the back nine at one over par. At the sixth he posted birdies in rounds one, two, and three. Brewer edged out Bobby Nichols by one stroke for the win.

There must have been a huge smile on the face of legendary college football coach Bear Bryant's face when these two players finished first and second in the Masters. Bryant had played a part in both Brewer's and Nichols's development as golfers. He had signed both of them to football scholarships: Brewer while he was the head coach at the University of Kentucky and Nichols while he was head coach at Texas A&M. Neither Brewer nor Nichols ever played a down of football for Bryant. He gave them football scholarships simply because there were no golf scholarships available and he wanted to help both of the schools' golf programs.

José María Olazábal was the third-round leader in 1999, but his chances for claiming his second green jacket appeared to be in jeopardy on the front nine in the final round. Olazábal bogeyed the third, fourth, and fifth holes. As he stepped on the tee at the sixth hole, he was probably having flashbacks about how brutal this hole had been to him in the 1991 Masters.

In that tournament Olazábal had opened with a four-under-par 68 and was one under par on his second round when he reached the sixth tee. He left his tee shot short of the green, and he had to chip up the hump on the right side. He had a muddy lie, and his first effort got almost to the top of the hump and then rolled all the way back to him. He chipped again, and the same thing happened. He chipped it again. This time he chipped it much too hard, and it went up over the hump and then off the back of the green. He chipped back on the green and two-putted for a quadruple-bogey seven. Olazábal's misfortunes at the sixth hole loomed big when the tournament was over. He finished in second place, just one stroke behind winner Ian Woosnam.

Despite his string of bogeys for the day and his tragic history at the sixth hole, Olazábal rose to the occasion in that final round in 1999. He dropped his tee shot just seven feet from the pin. His putt was crucial for his state of mind. To have such a fine tee shot without getting a birdie could have easily added more fuel to his slide, but he made a good stroke, and it caught the left side of the hole, dropping in for a two. After his birdie here, Olazábal played bogey-free golf the rest of the round and made three more birdies to win by two strokes.

England's Danny Willett started a charge at the sixth that would end with his donning the green jacket in 2016. Willett was one of the last competitors to arrive in Augusta. In fact, he didn't even think he would make the Masters at all. His wife, Nicole, was expecting their first child. The due date was the same as the final round.

Twelve days before the due date, Nicole's doctors decided that a C-section was necessary, and the Willetts became the proud parents of a boy that they named Zachariah. Danny flew to Augusta several days later for his second Masters appearance and got in just two days of practice.

Danny was at even par when he arrived at the sixth tee on Sunday. He had stumbled a bit over the final holes on Saturday and to this point in the fourth round had tallied all pars. A few holes behind him was Jordan Spieth, who appeared to be well on his way to his second straight Masters title.

Danny's tee shot at the sixth was a good one that left him with a twelve-foot birdie putt that he rolled perfectly into the cup. He would go to tally four more birdies over the next twelve holes while Spieth would experience one of the biggest collapses in Masters history. Danny's charge pulled him away from the rest of the field to a two-stroke victory.

In 1952 Ben Hogan, the previous year's winner, hosted a dinner for all the past winners of the Masters. It became a Masters tradition and is called the Champions Dinner. It is held at the club on Tuesday of Masters Week. The winner from the previous year serves as host, selects the menu, and picks up the tab. Ben Crenshaw had barbecue flown in from his native Texas in 1985.

The increasing number of international players winning the Masters has spawned quite the mix of interesting offerings on the Champions Dinner menu. In 1989 Sandy Lyle, who is from Scotland, served haggis, a traditional Scottish dish that is cooked inside a sheep's intestine.

In 2009 Trevor Immelman's selection was South African bobotie, a minced-meat dish with an egg topping. Ángel Cabrera had Argentine barbecue as his choice in 2010, featuring barbecued chorizo, short ribs, beef fillet, sweetbreads, and blood sausage. Australian Adam Scott served New York strip steak accompanied with an interesting selection from the waters around his country in 2014. They were Moreton Bay bugs, a type of Australian lobster

Phil Mickelson chose lobster ravioli as the main course when he hosted his first Champions Dinner in 2005. For his second in 2007, there were four choices: southern-fried chicken, barbecued babyback ribs, beef brisket, and smoked sausage.

At his third in 2011 Mickelson went international with Spanish seafood paella with ice cream–topped apple empanadas for desert. Phil choices were to honor two-time Masters Champion Seve Ballesteros, who was battling cancer and could not attend the dinner. Seve passed away four weeks later.

As Tiger Woods was about to claim his first green jacket in 1997, Fuzzy Zoeller, the 1979 champion, made some remarks that had racial overtones to a news crew about what Tiger should not serve at the Champions Dinner. When Zoeller's comments about fried chicken and collard greens reached the airwaves, they stirred up quite a storm of controversy that needlessly took focus away from Woods's record-breaking victory. It took several weeks for the storm that Zoeller's comments created to subside. About a month after the comments, Zoeller and Woods had a meeting in which Zoeller apologized for his remarks.

Zoeller was at the Champions Dinner hosted by Woods in 1998. The menu consisted of cheeseburgers, chicken sandwiches, and milk shakes. As fate would have it, Zoeller and Woods ended up paired together in the second round that year.

No second-round pairing has ever stirred up as much interest among the media and the patrons. Those looking for fireworks between the two were extremely disappointed. The biggest bang of the day came at the sixth hole when Woods, Zoeller, and the third member of the group, Colin Montgomery, all made birdie at the hole.

Woods did create some fireworks at the sixth hole in the final round in 2002. His tee shot to the daunting back-right pin placement was long and ran off the back of the green. Woods then hit a perfect chip from thirty-five feet that rolled into the heart of the cup for birdie, which for all practical purposes locked up his third Masters win.

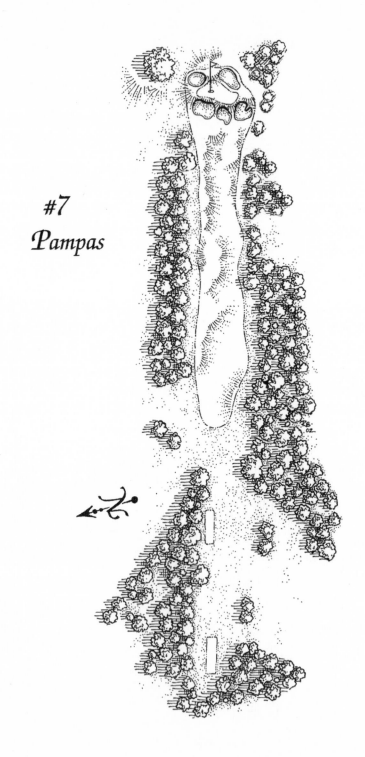

#7
Pampas

Hole No. 7

The seventh hole was considered the weakest on the course when Augusta National first opened. It was a plain-vanilla, drive-and-pitch par four that measured only 340 yards. The green was designed to receive one of those run-on approach shots that Bobby Jones liked so much. In the first round of the 1937 Masters, Byron Nelson ran his shot onto the green, but it wasn't his approach shot. It was his tee shot. Nelson made a two-putt birdie, and he went on to win the tournament.

Nelson's reaching the green with his drive that year highlighted the fact that something needed to be done about the seventh hole. Shortly after the tournament, Horton Smith, who had won the first Masters in 1934 and the third in 1936, offered a plan to change the hole that Jones and Cliff Roberts liked very much.

Golf course architect Perry Maxwell, a former associate of Alister MacKenzie who had already supervised changes to the tenth hole the year before, was given the assignment of carrying out Smith's plan. It called for the green to be moved 20 yards farther back and to the right, where it would sit at the top of an upslope and would be almost in a direct line with the tee box. Pine trees were already present on the right side of the fairway, and they were added down the left side as part of the makeover to create the narrowest fairway on the course. The new green became one of the smallest at Augusta National. It is very wide but not very deep, and it has a ridge running from back to front in its center that divides the putting surface into two sections. The green also has a pronounced tilt from the back to the front. Also, five sand traps were placed around the green, three in the front and two in the back, making it the most protected putting surface on the course. With the changes, which increased its length to 365 yards, the seventh would still be a drive-and-pitch hole, but it would require a very exacting pitch.

The cost of the changes to the seventh totaled $2,500 and was picked up by Augusta National member and washing-machine magnate Lewis B. Maytag. The early membership was very small and totaled only about eighty, but it was a very powerful group. Joining Maytag in the magnate category were Robert W. Woodruff, head of Coca-Cola, and W. Alton "Pete" Jones, head of the Cities Service Company, an oil and gas conglomerate.

Woodruff had taken over the reins of the Coca-Cola Company from his father in 1923 and was a close friend of Bobby Jones. He held memberships at the nation's golf meccas: Augusta National, Burning Tree, and Cypress Point. He was, however, a poor golfer who played the game for its business and political returns. He did like to wager on the course and was an aggressive negotiator for strokes. It was said he would demand so many strokes that even Bobby Jones couldn't beat him.

Pete Jones was a close friend of Cliff Roberts, and his was a rags-to-riches story. He was born in rural Missouri and started his career as a meter reader for the local gas company while he began studying bookkeeping through a correspondence school. His hard work and a series of acquisitions and mergers eventually landed him in New York, and by 1929 he was president of the Cities Service Company. He successfully guided the company through the Great Depression and made it a leader in the industry.

Jones was instrumental in America's industrial effort during World War II. He helped end an explosives shortage with the construction of a top-secret plant in Arkansas, and he led the effort to get two pipelines built from Texas to the East Coast that were completed in time to support the D-Day invasion.

Jones was one of the most enthusiastic members of the club. He signed on early and also acquired several memberships for his friends, and, like Maytag, he was always ready to support the club with any financial assistance it needed. It was in Jones's New York City office that the plans for the first Masters tournament were finalized.

In 1962 Jones and ninety-three others were killed when an American Airlines jet crashed moments after taking off from New York. He had been on the way to spend a weekend with former president Eisenhower.

Although the membership roster is not made public, it is believed that the club currently has approximately three hundred members.

Bobby Jones went to great lengths to make sure that those who supported the Masters with their attendance had a very enjoyable experience. He even wrote a small booklet titled *Spectator Suggestions for the Masters Tournament* to guide them around the course. In this booklet Jones detailed where he thought the prime spots were for the spectators to view the action on the course. The area behind the seventh green is one of the spots he highly recommended.

Those in the gallery might also want to keep an eye on who's watching the action with them. Over the years the likes of Bing Crosby, the Duke of Windsor, Donald Trump, and Jack Nicholson have been observed taking in the action on the course. Baseball great Ted Williams once took a little time off from work to go to the Masters. The Boston Red Sox were working their way back home from spring training in Florida and were playing an exhibition game in Augusta during Masters Week. Williams played a few innings and then ducked out of the ballpark and headed over to Augusta National for the rest of the afternoon.

In the early years of the tournament, the opening-day galleries were bolstered by the employees of the City of Augusta who were given half a day off so they could attend the first round.

The ultimate public servant's experience at the Masters would have to be Jack Westland's. Westland was a U.S. representative from the state of Washington. In the final round of 1953 he received a nice round of applause from the gallery at the seventh green. They weren't applauding his work on Capitol Hill; they were applauding his holing a birdie putt.

Westland's appearance in the tournament was the culmination of what had been a very fantastic previous nine months for him. In September 1952 the forty-seven-year-old Westland had earned an invitation to the Masters when he became the oldest player ever to win the United States Amateur. Three months later Westland was elected to Congress as a Republican, thanks to plenty of campaign help from an Augusta National member and the top man on the Republican ticket that year, Dwight Eisenhower. Eisenhower campaigned for Westland on a whistle-stop tour of Westland's district. To show his appreciation, Westland gave Eisenhower the putter he had used to win the Amateur.

The first eagle at the seventh was by Dick Mayer in the final round in 1955. He holed an eighty-yard wedge shot that helped him to his highest finish at the Masters, tenth place.

There have been a number of eagles at the seventh since Mayer's. One of the most notable was by Tiger Woods in the final round in 2010. Tiger had started the day four shots behind leader Lee Westwood, but he had slid far down the leaderboard by going three over through six holes.

Tiger's tee shot at seven almost missed the fairway on the right. He played his approach well to the left and well above the front-right pin. The green's slope slowly brought his ball back toward the pin. It rolled slowly but surely toward the hole and dropped for an eagle.

The eagle at 7 and birdies at 8 and 9 vaulted Tiger back into contention. He cooled off on the back nine and ended up finishing in a tie for fourth, two strokes behind the winner, Phil Mickelson.

The record for highest score at the seventh hole is held by Richard von Tacky Jr. He carded an eight in the second round in 1981. That score broke the old record of seven, which was shared by several players, one of them being Charles Coody, the 1971 Masters winner.

In the first round in 1972 Coody's tee shot strayed into the pines on the right side. He pulled his approach shot into the front bunker on the left side of the green. Coody was one of the most methodical players on the pro circuit. He always went to bed twelve hours before his tee time, and he kept copious notes on each round he played. He always seemed to be in control of his emotions and would be the last player you would expect to come unhinged in a sand trap, but that is exactly what happened.

Coody's third shot from the bunker hardly moved at all, and it left a sort of half grin on his face, which appeared to say, "Well, everyone leaves one in the bunker every now and then." The look on his face changed to stunned astonishment a few moments later when his next shot stayed in the bunker as well. The astonishment turned to utter disbelief when his next shot also failed to make it out. Finally, his fourth blast from the sand was played like a Masters champion, and it stopped a few feet from the hole. Coody then one-putted for seven. When he walked off the green, he must have been thinking he was in some sort of twilight zone, because fifteen minutes earlier, he had made a hole in one at the par-three sixth.

The seventh hole has also provided its share of superb moments during the tournament.

When the third round started in 1940 Jimmy Demaret was locked in a battle with fellow Texan Lloyd Mangrum. Demaret was also battling stomach problems from tainted shrimp he had eaten the previous evening.

Demaret had started the day tied with Mangrum for the lead and was holding his own. He had parred the first five holes and then had picked up a birdie at the sixth hole.

At the seventh tee Demaret pushed his drive into the pines on the right side. He boldly attempted to go for the green instead of just punching his ball back into the fairway. Demaret struck the shot, and a split second later his ball hit a pine tree and ricocheted hard to the right out into the seventeenth fairway.

Laying two and still eighty yards from the hole, Demaret lofted a wedge high into the air. The shot cleared the bunker on the right front, bounced once, and then rolled to just six inches from the cup for a gimme par.

Demaret never stumbled again after that shot. He finished the day with a two-under-par score of 70 that placed him in the lead by one shot over Mangrum. Mangrum shot a 74 the final day, while Demaret ran off fourteen consecutive pars, birdied the fifteenth hole, and then parred 16, 17, and 18 for a one-under-par 71 and a four-shot victory.

The seventh green was a birdie haven for the four leading players in the third round of the 1970 Masters. Billy Casper, Gene Littler, Tommy Aaron, and Bert Yancey all made birdies in a wild round that saw multiple lead changes. Yancey's curling birdie putt briefly gave him the top spot.

Yancey was playing in his fourth Masters. In his previous three starts in the tournament, he had finished third twice and thirteenth once. Yancey was almost consumed by his desire to win the Masters. His means for attempting to fulfill this desire had placed him in hot water with the tour's commissioner, and he was facing the possibility of being temporarily suspended from the tour.

Yancey was convinced that having the best putting stroke and a high degree of knowledge of Augusta's undulating greens was how he was going to claim a green jacket. The Greater Greensboro Open was the tournament that preceded the Masters that year on the schedule. Yancey had made a commitment to play in that tournament but had a change of heart. He wanted to spend the week at Augusta concentrating on his putting. Yancey went to the sponsor of the Greensboro tournament and asked to be released from his commitment, but the sponsor declined.

In a very unprofessional move Yancey thought of another way to solve his problem. After the first round at Greensboro, he deliberately turned in an unsigned scorecard, knowing that meant automatic disqualification. As soon as he was disqualified, he took off for Augusta. Needless to say, the sponsor and the tour were not happy about Yancey's actions, and he was advised to expect disciplinary action.

Waiting for Yancey in Augusta was a model that he had made of all the greens at Augusta. The models were made out of clay and affixed to a large sheet of plywood. Yancey worked on his putting stroke by day and studied the model of the greens by night at the house he had rented in Augusta.

Yancey's plans seemed to be falling into place at the end of the second round. He was tied for the lead with Gene Littler. Plus, the threat of suspension had been settled, and he was advised at the conclusion of his round that the penalty for his actions in Greensboro would be a fine and not suspension. After receiving that word, Yancey told reporters, "I have an obsession with the Masters. . . . It was wrong [deliberately getting disqualified]. It was one of the worst things I have ever done."

Yancey's putting held up throughout the tournament, but a poor tee shot in the third round at the par-three twelfth resulted in a triple-bogey six that proved too difficult to overcome. He finished in fourth spot, two strokes out of a playoff with Casper and Littler.

After the tournament he stored his model of the greens under the bed at his rental house. The next year when he returned to Augusta to begin practice, he pulled out the model from under the bed and received a very disturbing shock. The year under the bed had taken its toll on the clay model of the greens, and it had been reduced to little mounds of dust. Yancey would finish in fifty-fourth place that year, which would be his all-time-worst finish in the Masters. He would play in three more Masters, but his desire for a green jacket would go unfulfilled.

In the 1989 Ryder Cup, Fred Couples had hit a shot into the water on the last hole that cost the United States the victory. Shortly after that devastating loss, Raymond Floyd, who had been captain of that Ryder Cup team, took Couples under his wing. The rap on Couples had been that he was a great talent but lacked the motivation and focus required to take his game to the top level.

Under Floyd's guidance Couples reached the heights he had always been capable of achieving. Couples won the Masters in 1992, and one of the players he had to battle tooth and nail was none other than his mentor, Raymond Floyd.

The two were paired in the third round, and at the seventh hole the twosome treated the gallery to two outstanding approach shots. Floyd flew his approach shot directly over the flag by about fifteen feet, and his ball then spun back to within four feet of the pin. Not to be outdone, Couples brought a nine-iron in from the left rough that hit the flag and rattled around the hole before spinning out to the right about eighteen inches away from the cup. Floyd made his four-footer for birdie, and Couples tapped in for his.

It would be quite a battle over the remaining twenty-nine holes, but the protégé would finish on top, and the mentor would finish in second, two strokes behind.

Johnny Miller wrapped up an amazing start to his third round in 1975 at the seventh hole. Miller started with par at the first hole and then caught fire. He almost holed out from a greenside bunker at the second hole for an eagle and had a twelve-inch tap-in for birdie. At the third hole he sank a fourteen-footer for birdie number two. His two-iron on the par-three fourth stopped ten feet from the hole, and he sank that putt for birdie number three. On the fifth hole Miller hit his approach to within fourteen feet, and his putter was still red hot as that putt fell for birdie number four. On the par-three sixth he hardly needed a putter. His tee shot stopped a foot from the cup, and he made another birdie.

It appeared Miller's streak was over at the seventh hole. His tee shot was in the fairway, but he had caught a bad lie, and his approach shot just missed the green. Miller had thirty-five feet left to the hole and elected to go with his hot putter instead of chipping the ball. It was the right decision; he drained the putt for his sixth birdie in a row, which was a record. His streak ended on the eighth hole, but it had shot him up the leaderboard and set up what would be an unforgettable three-way battle with Jack Nicklaus and Tom Weiskopf in the final round.

Miller's record of six straight birdies was equaled by Mark Cal-cavecchia in 1992 and David Toms in 1998. In 1999 Steve Pate bird-ied the seventh hole to start a run of seven consecutive birdies to establish a new mark in that category. On his way to his third green jacket in 2005, Tiger Woods matched Pate's mark. Tiger's string of seven also started at the seventh hole.

In the first round of the 1996 Masters, Greg Norman seemed to be off to anything but a record-tying pace. He had strung together six pars, but at the seventh hole he snaked in a thirty-five-foot birdie that turned what looked like a ho-hum round into one that was unforgettable. Over the remaining eleven holes Norman would pick up eight more birdies and tie the course record of 63 established by Nick Price in 1986.

Over the years the seventh hole had become more and more vul-nerable to the increased driving distance of the players. Even those players electing to go with a one-iron off the tee were hitting wedge and sand-wedge approach shots. Those who could drill a three-wood down the narrow fairway only had to hit half wedge shots to the green. In the third round of the 2001 Masters, Tiger Woods, on his way to his second Masters win, had a second shot to the green of only fifty-five yards and easily picked up a birdie, which would be one of three he would make at the seventh during the tournament. The second-place finisher that year, David Duval, did Woods one better: he birdied the hole in all four rounds.

To give the hole some much-needed toughening, 45 yards were added to its length as part of the 2002 changes. Also, additional pines were added down the left side to extend the chute of trees even farther. These changes had a big impact on the scoring at the hole. In 2002 it gave up only twenty-two birdies compared to fifty-six in 2001.

Before the 2006 Masters the hole was stretched out 40 more yards, bringing its length to 450 yards, and more trees were added to both sides of the fairway. Plus, the green was redesigned to cre-ate a pin placement on the right rear. The green was also lowered on the right rear. This was done to thwart players from flying their approach shots long when the pin is front right and letting spin and the green's slope bring their ball back to the hole.

In the 2012 Masters the increased distance wasn't a problem for Bubba Watson, but the trees were.

Bubba was trailing Louis Oosthuizen, his playing partner and the man on top of the leaderboard, by two strokes. It looked like Louis was in position to expand that lead, as he had just hit a fine approach from 150 yards that checked up 5 feet below the hole.

Bubba had outdriven Louis, but he was in the trees on the left. The ball was in a spot that even the ultracreative Bubba had no shot to the green.

Bubba was looking at the real possibility of losing two shots to Louis. He pitched back into the fairway and had 90 yards left to the flag. Bubba's next shot traveled 89 yards, landing softly and coming to rest 12 inches below the hole.

Louis, who had made a 15-foot putt from the fringe above the hole at the sixth green to save par, misread the 5-footer. He played it to break left, but it did the opposite. He tapped in for par, and Bubba followed suit, saving par and escaping without losing any ground to Oosthuizen.

Bubba would pull even with Oosthuizen late on the back nine. And then in a playoff he would pull off one of the greatest shots in the history of Masters at the tenth hole to win his first green jacket.

#8
Yellow
Jasmine

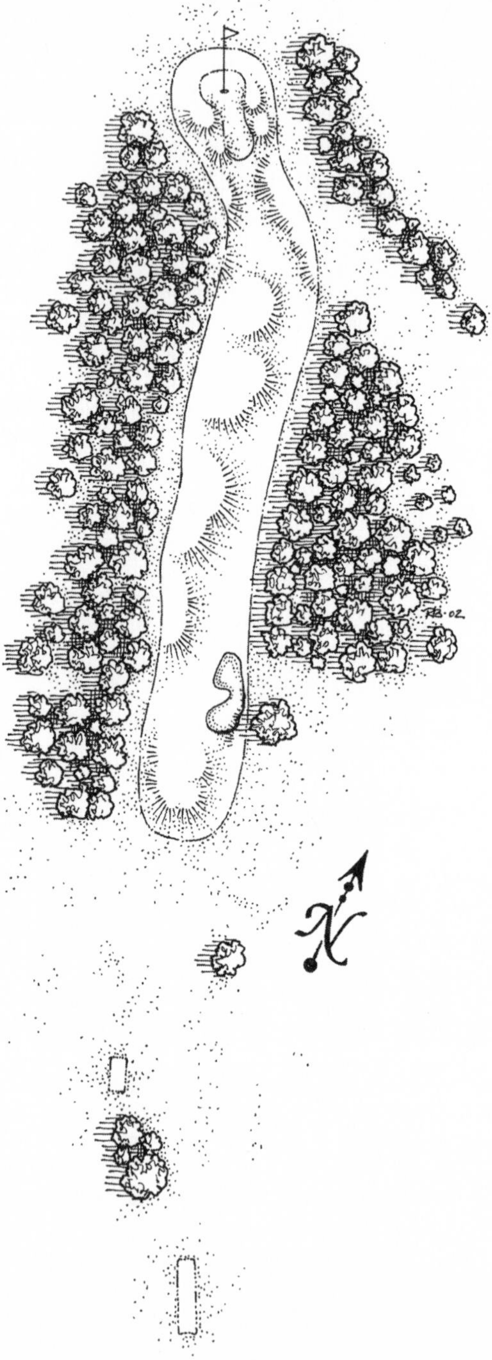

Hole No. 8

| PAR FIVE—570 YARDS | YELLOW JASMINE |

The eighth hole is the longest and toughest of Augusta National's par fives. It plays even longer than its listed yardage because it is uphill practically all the way from the tee to the green, and it requires two really big blows for an eagle opportunity.

To reach the eighth green in two, the player needs to carry the fairway bunker on the right side. From this area he will have the best angle to attempt to get home in two shots. The green, which is tucked over to the left just beyond the end of the tree line that parallels the left side of the fairway, is not in view from this range, so the shot is played blind.

Reaching the eighth hole in two shots became even more difficult in 2002 because the hole was lengthened by 20 yards and the size of the fairway bunker was doubled. Previously, a drive of 275 yards would clear the bunker; now a carry of 315 yards is required. Also, the tee was moved over to the right by 10 yards to make the route over the bunker even more difficult.

Those players who lay up with their second shots normally play up the right side of the fairway, which will give them the most green to work with on their third shots.

The green is approximately 100 feet in length from back to front. It is very narrow for its first half and then begins to widen. At about 60 feet into the green, a ridge runs across it from right to left, with the right-side portion of the ridge more pronounced. There are no bunkers around the green. Instead, it is protected by mounds on both sides. The mounds on the left side are significantly larger than the mounds on the right side and cause the most problems for the players. If a shot bounds over these mounds or lands on their left side, it can roll into the trees and pine straw to the left of the green. From this area the player will have an extremely tough pitch back over the mounds to a green that it is running away from him.

This green looks much like it did in 1934, but not how it looked from 1957 through 1978. Cliff Roberts was concerned that the mounds around the green blocked the views of the gallery and had them removed. With the mounds gone, the green was certainly highly visible, but many were of the opinion that the hole had lost much of its character. Although it took more than twenty years, Roberts reached that conclusion as well, and shortly before his death in 1977 he decided that the mounds should be brought back. In 1979 Byron Nelson helped supervise the restoration of the mounds.

This hole has always given up plenty of birdies but has been very stingy in the eagle category. Even before the 2002 changes, the hole had not given up an eagle since the final round of the 1999 Masters, and it kept that streak going in 2002.

David Duval came very close to making an eagle in the final round in 2001. His second shot from the right rough beyond the fairway bunker had the distance but appeared it was going to miss the green to the left. Duval caught a break, however; his shot struck one of the large mounds on the left side of the green and kicked dead right. Duval's ball ran almost directly over the top of the ridge on the green and came to a stop just a few feet from the left fringe.

Duval was left with a sixty-foot eagle putt that he paced perfectly, but it was just a hair off line and stopped just a couple of inches from the left side of the cup. The tap-in gave him his fourth consecutive birdie and placed him in a tie with Tiger Woods for the lead at thirteen under par. Duval's birdie string would be stopped at the ninth hole, but he would keep the pressure on Woods, the eventual winner, on the back nine and would come up two strokes short.

The eagleless streak ended in 2003 when two were made.

Prior to the 2002 Masters, Tiger Woods had birdied the eighth sixteen times in thirty attempts. In the 2000 Masters he birdied the hole in all four rounds. Woods also made six consecutive birdies at the hole, beginning in the second round of the 1997 Masters and ending with the third round of the 1998 tournament.

Before the 2002 tournament Woods had birdied the hole at least once in each of his seven previous Masters appearances. The changes made in 2002 may not have "Tiger-proofed" the eighth hole, but they did appear to slow him down some. In 2002 Woods was held to par at the hole in each of the four rounds and had to work really hard to avoid a bogey in the final round. The fairway bunker caught his drive, and his second shot could be advanced only 100 yards up the fairway. The shot just reached the area where a player can see the green, and Woods had 140 yards left to the flag. His third shot came up just short of clearing the ridge on the green. This left him with a very tough 20-foot putt over the ridge to the hole. Woods left this effort 4 feet short and had a slick downhill putt to save his par. After considerable study he dropped the putt and kept humming along toward his third green jacket.

The 2007 U.S. Open champion, Ángel Cabrera, was anything but humming along when he played the eighth in the final round in 2009. Ángel had started the day tied with Kenny Perry and Chad Campbell for the lead. When he arrived at the eighth hole, both he and Campbell were one behind Perry.

To this point Ángel's round had been shaky, and it was about to get even shakier. Paired with Perry, he outdrove Kenny by 20 yards and had 262 yards left to the hole.

Ángel, who dropped out of school in Argentina at the age of ten to begin his life in golf as a caddie, pulled out a long iron for his second shot and proceeded to strike the most dreaded shot in golf and one that is a rarity in Masters competition: a shank! Cabrera's ball shot out to the right and left him with about 100 yards to the pin. Rattled, he left his approach some 50 feet from the hole. His lag putt left him with a knee-knocker for par.

Perry had a slightly longer putt for birdie to extend his lead to two strokes. He missed. Ángel dropped his testy par putt, surviving the shank and staying just one behind.

Cabrera and Perry would battle the rest of this Sunday afternoon, with Cabrera ultimately defeating Perry in a playoff.

Jordan Spieth had started the day tied for the lead and paired with Bubba Watson. By the time they reached the eighth tee, Spieth had taken a two-stroke lead. He flared his three-wood second shot right, leaving a 60-yard pitch to the green.

Bubba had outdriven Jordan by 30 yards, but his second shot carried deep into green and ran off the back some 15 feet. Jordan's pitch checked up too early, leaving him a 50-foot birdie putt that he left 5 feet short. His par effort rimmed the left side of the cup, and he tapped in for bogey.

Bubba came close with his eagle chip and tapped in for birdie, wiping out Spieth's lead. Spieth would give up another two-shot swing at the ninth, clearing Bubba's path to a second green jacket.

With a little luck in the second round in 1956, Ken Venturi snapped a four-year eagleless stretch at 8.

Venturi's tee shot at the eighth hole had trouble written all over it. It was heading deep into the woods on the right side. The shot rattled around in the pines but then caromed back in the direction of the green and came to rest just a few feet from the edge of the fairway. Venturi found he had a good lie and chose to go for the green, and he rifled a three-wood 280 yards. The shot had the distance, but it was off line to the right, and it finished approximately 35 yards from the flag. When Venturi's tee shot flew into the woods, he must have been thinking that he would be lucky to make a bogey six on the hole, but thanks to receiving the fortuitous carom out of trouble, he stood a chance for a birdie. A birdie wasn't in the cards that day; however, an eagle was. Venturi played a chip with a six-iron on his third shot, and his ball took a long, curling journey before bumping into the flagstick and dropping into the hole.

Prior to Venturi's three, it had been since the second round in 1952 that the eighth had last given up an eagle.

In the 1970 Masters there were 2 eagles, 79 birdies, 158 pars, 19 bogeys, 1 double bogey, and 1 other recorded at the eighth hole.

The double bogey was made in the final round by the eventual winner, Billy Casper, and it was very costly because it played a big part in putting him in an eighteen-hole playoff with Gene Littler the next day. Casper had a one-stroke lead when he teed off at the eighth, but by the time he reached his tee shot, which had landed in the fairway bunker, his lead was gone. Littler, playing in the group directly in front of Casper, had rolled in a 20-foot birdie putt to move into a tie for the lead.

From the fairway bunker, all Casper was able to do was get his ball back in the fairway. He was 250-plus yards from the hole hitting his third shot. Casper went for the green but hooked the shot deep into the pines on the left side. His ball stopped on a service road 50 yards short and to the left of the green. Casper tried to get through an opening in the pines with his wedge, but his ball hit a limb and dropped down about 30 feet short of the green. Casper then chipped on and two-putted for a double-bogey seven.

The player whose efforts at the eighth hole in 1970 had made the dreaded "other" category was Jack Nicklaus. When Nicklaus teed off at the hole in the second round, he was even par for the tournament and just three strokes off the pace being set by the leader at that time, Bert Yancey.

Nicklaus's drive put him in position to go for the green. His second shot, however, was not one of his better efforts. He hooked it into the same area of the woods short of the green on the left side that Casper would find in the final round. Despite having a huge part of the gallery assisting him, Nicklaus could not find his ball. He had to take a stroke and distance penalty and go back to the spot from which he had played the shot, drop a ball, and play it again. Nicklaus's next shot landed short of the green. He chipped on, but he was still obviously upset over the lost ball and proceeded to three-putt for a big fat eight. It was the first time he had ever made a triple bogey at Augusta. The big eight dropped him well back into the pack. Nicklaus played well over the remaining forty-six holes and had worked his way back up to eighth place by the end of the tournament.

In the final round in 1986, Nicklaus was in the woods at the eighth hole again. He had started the day four strokes out of the lead, but when Nicklaus reached the eighth tee, he had not made up any ground and was languishing at even par for the round.

Given the fact that he would soon be running out of holes, Nicklaus needed to reach the eighth in two shots for a shot at eagle or at least to pick up an almost sure birdie.

The safe play for the next shot would have been to punch his ball back into the fairway. There was an inviting opening six feet wide, however, that Nicklaus believed he could get a three-wood through and with a little cut action get the ball to the green. Nicklaus made all the preswing adjustments he thought he would need to pull off the shot. He opened his stance, he aligned his clubface for the proper action, and he positioned the ball back in his stance to keep it low.

Nicklaus's calculations and actions had a flaw somewhere. When he hit the shot it did not take the desired path for the six-foot opening. It shot off well to the right of it. Lady Luck was shinning on Nicklaus, however, because the ball zipped through a twelve-inch opening between two pines and carried almost to the green. Nicklaus chipped onto the green and two-putted for a par five. If his ball had struck a tree, Nicklaus could have been looking at another eight on the hole. And the 1986 tournament would surely not have gone down as one of the most memorable Masters ever because the man who was to be the star of the great show, which would begin to unfold in a matter of a just a few minutes, would have been eliminated from the cast.

Two groups behind Nicklaus that day in 1986 was the pairing of Tom Kite and two-time Masters champion Seve Ballesteros. Greg Norman had the lead. Kite trailed him by four strokes, and Ballesteros was one behind.

Kite had always been handicapped at Augusta National by his lack of length off the tee and from the fairway when trying to reach the par fives in two shots. In his fifty-three previous rounds at the Masters, he had made just three eagles on par fives. His chances for an eagle at the eighth hole on this day would have been considered pretty remote. In fact, there had not been an eagle at the eighth in the entire tournament.

Kite laid up on his second shot and had eighty yards left to the flag. His third shot was very high and right at the target. It landed short of the pin, took two bounces, and then rolled into the hole for Kite's first eagle of his career at the eighth hole.

Ballesteros appeared to be unaffected by Kite's splendid shot. He was fixed on his own situation. His second shot was only forty yards short of the green. He opted to go with a different type shot: a pitch and run. The ball was hit low and carried just over the fringe of the green and began tracking for the hole. It hit the flagstick and dropped into the hole for another eagle to put him in the lead by one stroke over Norman.

On his way to his first win in 1977, Tom Watson birdied the eighth hole in all four rounds. Watson was wobbling a bit in the third round that year. He started the day tied for the lead and parred the first six holes, but he bogeyed the seventh hole to drop back into second place. Watson immediately got back on track at the eighth hole when he sank a fourteen-footer for birdie to regain a share of the lead, and he would conclude the round in that position.

In Sunday's round Watson went on a birdie binge that would help secure his first green jacket. He made birdies at the fifth, sixth, and seventh and then dropped another fourteen-footer at the eighth for his fourth birdie in a row on the front side and his fourth birdie of the week at the hole.

Watson extended his streak of birdies at the eighth the following year to six, picking up birdies there in the first and second rounds before finally registering a par in the third round.

The eighth hole turned out to be just as important in Watson's second and final Masters win in 1981, as he again birdied the hole in all four rounds.

Fuzzy Zoeller has the best record at the eighth hole by any winner. In his 1979 win, which was his first Masters appearance, he eagled the hole in the first round and birdied it in the remaining three rounds for a tally of five under for the tournament.

Bruce Devlin holds the record for the best score at the eighth hole. He recorded the second double eagle in Masters history at the hole in the first round of the 1967 tournament.

On that day Devlin was dealing with painful blisters on both of his heels and was one over par for his round when he reached the eighth tee. Devlin's drive placed him in good position. He had approximately 240 yards left to the green and believed he could get there with a four-wood if he hooked the shot just a bit.

Later in press interviews, Devlin would describe the stroke "as the perfect golf shot." He would also say it was the only decent shot he hit all day. The ball landed on the front of the green and began to track for the cup, which was located on the back right. It was running on fumes when it seemingly crawled to the front of the cup and tumbled in.

Since it was a blind shot Devlin did not see the ball go into the hole. He heard the three hundred or so spectators at the green having a fit, and it took about five seconds for word to reach him that the ball had gone into the hole.

The double eagle Gene Sarazen made at the fifteenth hole in the final round of the 1935 Masters propelled him to victory. Unfortunately for Devlin, his splendid stroke did not. After the double eagle, Devlin made five bogeys and ended the round with a two-over-par 74. From that start, Devlin worked his way up the leaderboard and finished the tournament in tenth place.

When told about Devlin's double eagle, Sarazen stated that his double eagle was easier because he could at least see the target he was shooting for. One member of the Devlin family almost got a chance to see the ball go in the hole, and that was his father. The senior Devlin was up ahead near the green on the left side of the fairway, and as his son's shot streaked by, he darted out into the fairway, hoping to follow the rest of the flight of the ball. He was immediately stopped by a Pinkerton Security guard who ordered him back behind the ropes.

The spectators following the Ben Hogan–Byron Nelson eighteen-hole playoff in 1942 didn't have to worry about staying behind the ropes, because there weren't any at that time. If spectators were so inclined, they could walk along with the players in the fairway.

The gallery walking along in the fairway with Nelson and Hogan that year was thick with their fellow playing professionals because most of the Masters field had stayed over for the Monday playoff.

When they had reached the eighth hole, Nelson was storming back after spotting Hogan an early three-shot lead. Nelson had shaved two strokes off that lead at the sixth hole when he birdied and Hogan bogeyed. Nelson outdrove Hogan from the eighth tee. Hogan laid up, but Nelson elected to go for the green in two. He then showed his contemporaries walking along with him how to hit a three-wood. He smoked the shot, and it disappeared over the ridge and toward the green. Nelson knew it was a good shot by the crowd's reaction up at the green. When he had walked far enough to bring the green into view, he had to be pleased. His ball was resting five feet beyond the hole. Hogan pitched on and two-putted for par. Nelson slipped his five-footer into the hole for an eagle to take the lead, which he would hold for the remainder of the playoff.

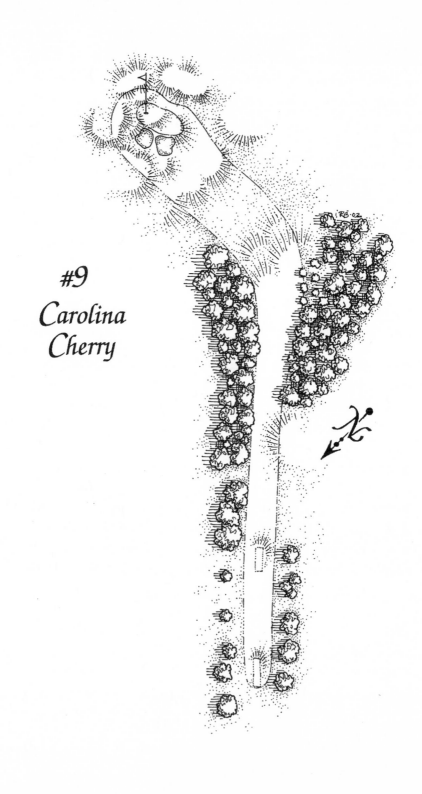

#9
*Carolina
Cherry*

Hole No. 9

| PAR FOUR—460 YARDS | CAROLINA CHERRY |

The ninth hole is a dogleg-left par four. From the tee to the bend of the dogleg, there is a fifty-foot drop in elevation. At that point the fairway rises approximately thirty feet over the remaining distance to the green.

Pine trees line the fairway down the left and right sides until the bend of the dogleg. The best route for the drive is slightly to the right of the center of the fairway. This path opens up the green for the second shot and reduces the threat of the two bunkers that guard its left side.

The second shot used to be one of the prime challenges of the hole because it typically was hit from a downhill lie to an uphill green. Over the years the players' increased driving distance put most drives at the foot of the hill with a level lie for the approach shot.

Even from a level lie, the approach shot is daunting. It must be played deep into the green because this putting surface is severely sloped from the back to the front and very quick. Any shot that is not well past the center is in great peril of being repelled by the slope and sent streaming backward off the front of the green and often well back down the fairway.

The ninth hole was originally 420 yards in length. In 1973 this distance was increased to 435 yards. The distance was increased an additional 25 yards as part of the 2002 changes. Also, more pine trees were added to the tree line on the right side of the fairway to tighten up the landing area.

The ninth green is located at one of the highest points on Augusta National. It is in this area that Bobby Jones, on his initial visit to the property, had first stood and marveled at the beautiful vista that lay before him. It has been said that after taking in this view, he knew immediately that it was the location he had been looking for to build his dream course.

This area is one of the most exposed to the high winds that are often present during Masters Week. Ironically, if it had not been for hurricane-force winds, it is quite possible the view would have been enjoyed by hotel guests, from as high as fifteen stories up, instead of golfers and golf fans.

In the fall of 1925, several years before Jones was shown the property, Commodore J. Perry Stolz paid a visit to Augusta. Stolz owned a fifteen-story hotel on Miami Beach named the Fleetwood, and he had ambitious plans to create a chain of hotels modeled after his Miami operation. Augusta was still a thriving winter resort at that time, and Stolz liked the city very much and picked it for the location of his second hotel. He selected the former Fruitlands Nurseries property as the site.

Stolz returned to Augusta in early 1926 and broke ground on the site. His plans called for the hotel to be built behind the Berckmans's Manor House—now the Augusta National clubhouse and one of the most revered buildings in golf—and for this magnificent structure to be torn down.

After the groundbreaking the project seemed to stall, and in the fall of that year it was ultimately done in by a big wind. One of the most damaging hurricanes ever to hit Florida slammed into Stolz's Miami Beach hotel. The damage was so severe that Stolz was forced to file bankruptcy, and the old Fruitlands Nurseries property went back on the market.

During the first Masters in 1934, the ninth hole was the eighteenth hole, and it was the scene of a nail-biting finish. Horton Smith had grabbed a three-way share of the lead after the first round, and at the end of the second round he held the lead outright by one stroke. Smith maintained that advantage after round three with a total score of four-under-par 212.

Craig Wood had been lurking just behind Smith throughout the tournament. Wood had one of the earliest starting times for the final round. He shot a two-under-par 70 and finished the tournament with a total score of three-under-par 285. Smith was on the fourth hole when he received word of the score that Wood had posted. To that point in his round Smith was one over par for the day and in a tie with Wood at three under par.

Smith moved out in front by a stroke with a birdie at the sixth hole (now the fifteenth). He extended his lead to two strokes with a birdie at the tenth hole (now the first). Smith stumbled midway through his back nine with bogeys at the fourteenth hole (now the fifth) and the fifteenth hole (now the sixth) to fall back into a tie with Wood. On the par-five seventeenth hole (now the eighth), Smith stuck his third shot twelve feet from the hole and dropped the birdie putt to regain the lead by one stroke.

At the eighteenth hole (now the ninth), Smith was in good position with his drive. The wind had been blowing strongly throughout the day and had firmed up the green considerably. When Smith's approach landed, it bounced hard and ran to the back of the green.

Smith was then faced with a thirty-five-foot downhill left-to-right breaking putt. He played too much break on the putt and came up short. He was left with a four-footer above the hole that was lightning fast with a wicked break. Smith took his time and studied the putt from every angle. He then tapped the putt ever so lightly. It appeared that Smith might have tapped the ball too lightly. The ball hung on the lip just long enough for Smith's heart to reach his throat and then toppled into the cup to make him the first winner of the Masters.

In the final round in 1954 Billy Joe Patton wrapped up his front nine as if he were heading down the glory road. Patton hit his approach to within a few feet of the hole, and he confidently nailed his short birdie putt to finish the front side with a four-under-par 32. The birdie burned the ears of leader Ben Hogan with another loud roar from Patton's ever-increasing gallery. The ninth hole had been Patton's hole all week, making birdie there in each of the three previous rounds.

Patton would make another birdie at the ninth hole several days later, in a friendly round with President Eisenhower, who had been very impressed with Patton's Masters performance. Eisenhower had sent word from the White House that he would like to play a round with Patton a few days after the tournament concluded, when he arrived at Augusta National for his annual spring vacation. Patton accepted the invitation, but since he had been on vacation from his job as a lumber salesman during the tournament, he decided he had better make the two-hundred-mile drive back to Morganton, North Carolina, to check on things at the office. After making sure everything was running smoothly there, he drove back to Augusta for his round with the most powerful man in the world.

The ninth hole would have to be one of Ben Crenshaw's favorite holes because of the success he enjoyed in his two Masters victories in 1984 and in 1995.

In the 1984 tournament he holed out for a birdie from a green-side bunker in the third round. In the fourth round he brought his six-iron approach right over the flag. The ball carried twelve feet past the hole and then trickled back down to within seven feet. It was a lightning-fast putt, but Crenshaw smoothly stroked it into the hole to take the outright lead, which he would maintain for the remainder of the tournament.

Crenshaw's approach shot with a sand wedge in the final round in 1995 was one of the biggest shots of the tournament. It checked up a foot from the hole for a tap-in birdie, which gave him a two-stroke lead at that point. Crenshaw would ultimately win the tournament by one stroke.

Gary Player took an unusual approach to reaching the ninth green in the third round of the 1961 Masters. Player and Arnold Palmer were fighting it out for the lead in what would turn out to be a very interesting two-day battle that Player would win.

Player's tee shot had strayed into the pines on the left side of the fairway. He was 160 yards out, but trees blocked a direct shot to the green. Player had two options. He could take his medicine for an errant drive and just punch the ball back into the fairway, with the likelihood that he would almost surely make a bogey. Or he could go for the green by a very unusual route, which would be by hitting a big slice out of the pines up the first fairway and hope it would curve enough to get him to the green.

Player chose the latter option. He signaled to the green to have the spectators on the left side move back. When they were safely out of harm's way, Player hit what he hoped would be the big slice he needed with a four-wood. His ball shot out of the woods up the first fairway and was seemingly heading straight for the clubhouse, but then it began to take its planned big curve to the right and headed for the green. The shot had just enough distance to clear the bunkers and struck the edge of the green, but it ran hot and rolled just off the backside.

Player chipped down close to the flag and one-putted for a very unusual par. He would make a number of key shots in his battle with Palmer, but this was one of the biggest.

One of the most ill-fated approaches to the ninth green was made by Greg Norman in the final round of the 1996 Masters. The six-stroke lead he had teed off with some two hours before was beginning its disappearing act. He had just lost a stroke at the eighth hole to his pursuer Nick Faldo, and he then hit an approach shot to the ninth green that sent a message that possibly the flood gates were about to open.

Norman's drive at the ninth hole had left him only one hundred yards to the pin, which was cut on the front portion of the green. Norman made the cardinal sin of not hitting the ball well beyond the flag. It landed about five feet below the hole and then kicked into reverse. It rolled off the front of the green and some fifteen yards back down the fairway.

Faldo had played his approach well above the hole, and his thirty-five-footer for birdie caught the edge of the cup but lipped out, and he tapped in for par. Norman could not get up and down to save his par. From that point forward, it seemed he could do no right and Faldo could do no wrong. When the day ended, Faldo was slipping on his third green jacket.

The false front claimed another victim in 2014.

Jordan Spieth had given up a two-stroke swing to Bubba Watson, his playing partner, at the eighth hole, and the two were tied for the lead. His approach to 9 landed a yard short of carrying the false front and rolled back down into the fairway. Bubba stuck his second shot eight feet from the pin.

Spieth's chip almost dropped but ran four feet by the hole. Bubba curled in his birdie, while Jordan overread his par putt and made bogey and Bubba took a two-stroke lead. He would go on to win by three. Jordan would finish in a tie for second.

Of course, those who go long with their approach shot must still handle the treacherousness of the slope of the green carefully. In the 1939 Masters one particular participant's approach shot was too strong, and it rolled just off the back of the green. His playing partner was the defending Masters champion, Henry Picard. Picard told the player that he would not be able to keep his next shot on the green, and he was right. Picard's playing partner chipped his ball very softly, and it streaked down the slope and off the front of the green.

Picard's partner and victim of the slope that day was Bobby Jones, and by the next Masters Jones had the ninth green redone and the amount of its slope reduced. Most players, however, would contend that this reduction could have been carried a lot further.

In the final round of his one-stroke win in 1977, Tom Watson was a little too strong with his approach shot, and it ran off the back of the green by a couple of feet. His putt back down the slope mirrored Jones's effort from thirty-eight years earlier, and his ball sped by the hole and well off the front of the green. Watson chipped back to within four feet and dropped that knee-knocker for a bogey.

The green's slope got Watson again in the final round in 1983. He had just cut Seve Ballesteros's lead from four strokes to two at the eighth by knocking in a sixty-foot eagle putt. At the ninth hole he played his shot well above the pin. His downhill putt for birdie had too much speed and went five feet by the hole. Ballesteros dropped a birdie putt from eighteen feet. Watson then missed his par putt to give the two strokes back to Ballesteros, who coasted home to win by four strokes over runner-up Ben Crenshaw. Watson would finish in the third spot, five strokes back. Short putts on the ninth green are most likely where the term *knee-knocker* originated. In his 1956 bid to become the first amateur to win the Masters, Ken Venturi missed a two-footer for par in the third round. In the fourth round Venturi started an extremely bad run at the ninth green when he missed a three-footer for par. He would go on to bogey six of the last nine holes and miss tying for first place by one stroke.

The record for the shortest putt ever missed at the ninth green would have to belong to Lanny Wadkins. Wadkins shot his best eighteen holes ever at Augusta in the opening round in 1991, a 65. In the second round he was one over par for the day through the first eight holes. At the ninth green Wadkins had a four-foot uphill putt for his par. He pulled the putt slightly, and the ball just missed on the left side, slid by the cup, and stopped just six inches beyond it. Wadkins was fuming over the miss and in the heat of the moment decided to hit his tap-in bogey putt backhanded. It turned out his backhand needed a little work. The ball missed the cup and rolled four feet by the hole. He was now looking at the same putt for double bogey that he had for par.

Wadkins was now twice as hot as he had been when he hit the backhand; however, he did go back to a conventional putting stroke and drilled his ball into the cup for a big six. Wadkins was steaming when he walked off the green, but he was somehow able to harness his anger. On the backside he shot a very fine three-under-par 33 and would end the tournament in third place two strokes back, which was his best Masters finish ever.

A pressure putt does occasionally go in at the ninth hole. In the final round in 1986 Jack Nicklaus, obviously bolstered by his most fortunate escape from the woods off the eighth fairway, hit a fine approach shot to the ninth green that left him with a twelve-foot birdie opportunity. Nicklaus was about to stroke the putt when the roar at the eighth green for Tom Kite's eagle pitch-in broke loose, and he had to back away. After things had calmed down, Nicklaus started his putting routine over. He was just about to pull the trigger when a second roar went up from the eighth green, and he backed away again from the putt. This roar was for Seve Ballesteros's eagle chip-in.

The back-to-back gallery explosions at the eighth hole were causing quite a buzz in the gallery at the ninth green. To quiet things down, Nicklaus looked over at the section of the gallery nearest to him and said, "Okay, now let's see if we can make that same kind of noise here." The gallery responded with a short burst of applause and then quickly quieted down.

The exchange with the crowd served to relax Nicklaus. When he addressed the putt he felt good about his chances. He believed he had the line and the speed he would need to apply to the putt properly calculated. A player knows some putts are going in the moment they are stroked, and this was one of them. It hit the hole dead center, and the gallery at the ninth green made itself heard over the course.

The birdie still left Nicklaus five strokes off the lead. The crowd continued to cheer him as he departed the green. They were paying tribute to a great former champion who was having a fine tournament. You can bet no spectators in the ninth green gallery would have predicted they would be applauding Nicklaus as the current champion a few hours later.

Twelve years later in the final round in 1998, the "Old Bear" was on the prowl once again. Nicklaus started the day at one under par, seven strokes out of the lead. Nicklaus was getting plenty of praise from the media and great applause from the gallery for being able to put on such a show at age fifty-eight, but hardly anyone gave him a serious chance, except one person, Nicklaus himself.

At the second hole Nicklaus's eagle putt from twenty feet burned the right edge of the cup, and he tapped it in for birdie. At the third hole his approach shot fell short and left him with a delicate seventy-foot lightning-fast downhill chip. To everyone's surprise, including his own, he holed it for another birdie. Nicklaus slipped at the fourth hole when he made a bogey, but came back at the sixth with a tee shot that stopped five feet from the hole and resulted in another birdie. Another big roar from the gallery rocked the pines. At the seventh hole Nicklaus stayed hot, dropping down his approach eight feet from the hole and then holing the putt for another birdie. Another loud roar went up, and the course was buzzing with the news that the Old Bear was on a rampage.

Nicklaus cooled down at the eighth hole and had to settle for a par. At the ninth hole his second shot sent up another big roar when it stopped nine feet from the hole. Nicklaus had lit the fuse for his great run in 1986 at the ninth green and appeared to be poised once again to do the unimaginable on a Masters Sunday. His putt was perfectly paced, but his line was just a hair off, and it turned away from the hole in the last foot. Nicklaus's momentum was broken, but it still had been a great run. His 33 on the front side at Augusta in the final round is a great score whether a player is twenty-eight or fifty-eight. Nicklaus would shoot one under par on the backside and finish the tournament in sixth place.

While Nicklaus had been creating all the noise, Fred Couples and Mark O'Meara, the last pairing of the day, had been having a seesaw battle. Couples had started the day two ahead, but O'Meara had pulled even by the third hole. Couples regained a two-stroke advantage with birdies at the seventh and eighth holes.

Couples unleashed a big drive at the ninth tee that left him 105 yards to the green. O'Meara's tee shot strayed too far left and tangled with pines that border the fairway. When O'Meara arrived at his ball, he found he was blocked from going for the green by several trees, and the only play he had was to punch his ball down the fairway. Given the circumstances, O'Meara hit a good recovery shot and advanced his ball to within 75 yards of the green.

At this point it appeared that Couples was going to expand his lead by at least one stroke. His approach shot quickly wiped out that possibility. The ball did not carry deep enough into the green, landing just a few feet short of being an excellent shot. It spun back, and the slope quickly took the ball off the front of the green and several paces back into the fairway.

O'Meara's sand-wedge third shot flew directly over the flag stick and climbed to a spot about twenty feet above the hole and then rolled backward and stopped six feet above the hole.

Couples hit his chip shot much too hard, and it sped by the hole some twelve feet. His par putt slid off to the left, and he tapped in for a very costly bogey. O'Meara made his six-footer for a great up-and-down par. The stroke O'Meara saved and the one Couples let get away would loom very large at the end of the day.

Phil Mickelson made quite the par at nine in the fourth round of the 2009 Masters to tie the tournament record for the lowest score on the front nine at 30. Johnny Miller first set the mark in 1975. It was later matched by Greg Norman (fourth round, 1988) and K. J. Choi (second round, 2004).

Trailing the leader by seven at the start of his round, Phil birdied the eighth, his sixth birdie of his opening nine, to move within one of the lead.

A birdie at the ninth would give him a share of the lead; it would also have established a record of 29 as the lowest score ever recorded on the front nine. But Phil struck a poor drive that landed deep in the pines on the fairway's right side.

The record was safe. Bogey would have been a good score from where he was, but Phil managed to squeeze out a gutsy par. He somehow threaded a low shot through the pines that found the bunker on the green's left side. Phil then a hit fine blast from the bunker that stopped four feet beyond the hole, and he curled in that sidehill putt for a par, to match the front nine record score of 30.

Phil would stumble on the back and finish the day with a score of 67 for a fifth place finish.

Thanks to rain in 2005, the ninth hole had the honor of hosting one of the most special moments ever in Masters history. Saying farewell to the event's leading champion: six-time winner Jack Nicklaus.

With the second round delayed by rain until Saturday, split tees were used, with half the field going off number one and the other half going off ten. Nicklaus, who was taking part in the Masters as a competitor for the forty-fifth and final time, was among the players going off on number ten, making his finishing hole the ninth.

The sixty-five-year-old Nicklaus was hoping to make the cut, something he hadn't done since the 2000 Masters, but an opening-round 77 indicated that the second round would be Jack's final eighteen in the Masters.

He handled the round with quintessential Nicklaus class, acknowledging the generous ovations he received at tee boxes and greens with a wave of the hand and a warm smile.

Jack reached the ninth tee four over par. His last drive was a towering, solid one that left him with an approach from the fairway of 158 yards. During his walk to his drive, the reality of the moment became immense. He was fighting back tears. Once at his ball that old Nicklaus magic kicked in, and he hit a six-iron that came to rest just three feet from the pin. The patrons packed in around the green responded with a tremendous roar that rattled the pines.

As he walked up to the green, Nicklaus could no longer hold back the tears, and neither could many in the gallery. A birdie at his final hole in the Masters would have been quite a storybook ending, but it wasn't to be. Jack's putt slid by the hole, and the crowd groaned in disappointment.

But the groans gave way to rousing applause as Jack left the green. His storied Masters career didn't get its Hollywood ending, but it couldn't detract from the Golden Bear's legacy at Augusta—one that may never be equaled.

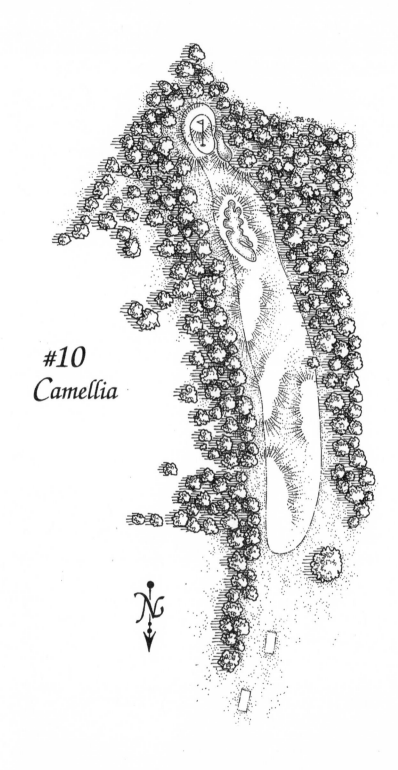

#10
Camellia

Hole No. 10

PAR FOUR—495 YARDS	CAMELLIA

Playing as the first hole in 1934, the tenth tee was where the first ball was struck in the Masters by Ralph Stonehouse on March 22, 1934, at 10:00 a.m. Although it played as number one only one year, it has often been said that the tee at number 10 is where the tournament really begins in the final round on Sunday.

The Bobby Jones Cabin sits just down from the tenth tee on the left side of the fairway. As discussed in chapter 6, it was one of Jones's favorite spots at Augusta National. Sportswriters loved the Jones Cabin porch as well, because on numerous occasions they could catch Jones there and engage him in conversation about almost any topic under the sun, but golf in particular.

At one of these impromptu sessions during the 1951 Masters, Jones offered these opinions on measuring a player's game: "Frankly, I find that you can't measure a fellow's game by the way he hits them on the practice tee. A lot of golfers have a marvelous game in practice, but you have to play with them, watch all their shots in various situations, observe their attitudes and how they react to pressure to know them as golfers. That's the main thing, I think, how they react to pressure."

On his own approach to the game, he said this: "J. H. Taylor [one of the top players in Britain in the late 1890s and the early 1900s] gave what I consider the finest description of the perfect approach to golf—courageous timidity. I guess that was about the way I approached the game. I never hit the ball hard the first few holes. After that, I let the circumstance control my courage."

The 1968 Masters was the last year Jones's failing health would allow him to attend. While in his cabin at the conclusion of the tournament, he experienced possibly the darkest moment ever in his long association with the game of golf.

Roberto De Vicenzo had turned the tournament upside down in the final round with a brilliant 65. The seven-under round included the eagle that was discussed in chapter 1. But shortly after the conclusion of his amazing round, De Vicenzo exclaimed in utter anguish, "What a stupid I am!" At the par-four seventeenth hole, he had made a birdie. But Tommy Aaron, his playing partner, who was responsible for keeping De Vicenzo's score, wrote down a four instead of a three on De Vicenzo's scorecard. When he was given the scorecard to check, De Vicenzo gave it only a cursory glance and did not detect the error. He then signed the card and turned it in at the scorers' table.

A bogey at the eighteenth hole left De Vicenzo in a tie with Bob Goalby. Everyone then began to think about the eighteen-hole playoff that would take place the following day to determine the winner. It all changed, however, when the officials at the scorers' table did the math on De Vicenzo's scorecard. Despite the fact that thousands of people who were following the action in person at the seventeenth hole and the millions who had watched De Vicenzo play the hole on television could attest to the fact that De Vicenzo had made a three, the rules of golf are brutally strict in this area. The rules require a player who turns in a score on a hole lower than he actually made to be disqualified. And when a player turns in a score on a hole that was higher than he actually made, the score has to stand.

When the scoring officials found the error, they went to the Jones Cabin, where Jones had been following the tournament's action on television. They wanted his opinion before they made a final ruling. After Jones was apprised of the situation, he desperately wanted to find a way within the rules to correct De Vicenzo's mistake in order to have the Masters decided on the course the next day and not at the scorers' table. But after a review of the rule, including the opinions of some of the most knowledgeable rules authorities in the game who had come to the cabin to assist in the matter, it became apparent there was no remedy to the situation that would not violate the rules of golf. Jones then ruled that De Vicenzo's scorecard would stand and that Bob Goalby would be declared the winner. Those in the room when Jones made the decision commented later that they had never seen a more tragic look on a man's face than the one on Jones's as they exited the cabin to make the announcement that Goalby was the winner.

Just a few paces from the tenth tee, there is a white house with a gold American eagle mounted on its gable. This structure was actually the White House a number of weeks each year during President Dwight Eisenhower's regular winter and spring vacations at Augusta National.

Cliff Roberts, Bobby Jones, and the Augusta National membership played a huge part in Eisenhower's run for the presidency. Roberts made frequent trips to Paris to confer with Eisenhower, while he was serving as the NATO commander, about a possible run for the presidency in 1952. Eisenhower waited almost to the last minute to decide to enter the race. Many thought Eisenhower had waited too long to make his decision and that Senator Robert Taft already had the Republican nomination locked up.

Roberts was one of the key members of Ike's campaign and did what he did best—handling the financing. Roberts mobilized the Augusta National membership that was spread practically all over the country, and they formed what were called "Ike Clubs" in their areas to raise money and work for the campaign.

It was a touch-and-go battle for Eisenhower. But with Roberts raising money and Bobby Jones working for him in the South and at the Republican Convention, he defeated Taft for the nomination. Eisenhower then handily defeated Adlai Stevenson in the general election. On election night Roberts was a kind of caddie for Eisenhower. Eisenhower was tired and needed a place to rest while the returns were coming in. Roberts found a vacant room at the hotel that was serving as the election-night headquarters and stood guard at the door while Eisenhower got some sleep. When word came that Stevenson was ready to concede, Roberts woke Eisenhower to give him the news.

Eisenhower had been kept off the golf course for political reasons during the campaign, and he went to Augusta National immediately after his victory for a working vacation. In the morning he worked on setting up his new administration, and in the afternoon he played golf.

Having the president of United States as a member quickly taxed the existing facilities at Augusta National. Ann Whitman, Eisenhower's personal secretary, recalled that first visit after the election: "It was a chaotic place for everyone, and just finding a phone to use was a major accomplishment." It was while trying to locate a telephone that Whitman had an up-close-and-personal encounter with boxing great Gene Tunney. She made a wrong turn and ended up in the men's locker room, where Tunney was toweling off after exiting the shower. After getting a quick and inadvertent eyeful, she decided the call could wait and quickly departed the area.

Roberts immediately went to work on this problem. He solicited funds from fifty Augusta National members to build the Eisenhower Cabin and make other improvements to the club, so it could now accommodate its most important member. It was originally called "Mamie's Cabin," in honor of Eisenhower's wife. The "cabin" part is a bit of a misnomer, however, for it had eighteen rooms and seven bathrooms.

Eisenhower made twenty-nine trips to Augusta, and it has been said that you could set your watch by him every morning. Promptly at eight, he would walk across the tenth tee to an office that had been built for him above the pro shop, where he would work until lunch and then golf in the afternoon.

When Eisenhower made those trips across the tenth tee each morning, he was treated to one of the most spellbinding views in golf. It is one of the most picturesque holes in the game. From the tee the fairway flows down toward the green and takes a slight turn to the left at about 250 yards out. It continues to flow downward until it has dropped almost 100 feet in elevation. It then rises slightly to an elevated green that is nestled in a natural amphitheater of tall Georgia pines.

The tenth hole was not always so spellbinding. It was the first hole at Augusta to undergo a major change, and it was this change that turned it from a wallflower into a raving beauty. The original location of the green was approximately 50 yards up the fairway and to the right of where it is now located. In the area of the old green is a huge bunker that is known as the MacKenzie bunker. Many first-time Augusta National visitors and viewers on television must wonder what purpose it serves, because it is too far from the green to affect approach shots. It used to provide protection for the original green, but now its duties are purely cosmetic. The bunker performs these duties quite splendidly, because this large white island of sand in a sea of green fairway adds much to the splendor of the hole.

These first changes to the tenth were made in 1937 and carried out by golf course architect Perry Maxwell, who had been a protégé of Alister MacKenzie. Maxwell picked the spot for the new green. This location was on high ground, which would avoid the drainage problems that had plagued the previous location. It also made the hole more formidable by increasing the distance significantly and gave it its beauty by framing it in a backdrop of tall pines.

The changes made it one of the most challenging par fours in golf. The tenth has often ranked as the toughest hole at Augusta National in the tournament's cumulative ranking. Its 4.691 stroke average in the 1956 Masters is the highest amount over par a hole has averaged in the tournament's history.

The location of the tee shot is the key factor on this hole. On the left side of the fairway, there is a steep incline. If a player can reach it with his drive, the ball will kick forward an additional thirty to forty yards. If he misses the incline and goes right in the fairway, he can be looking at a two- to three-club difference for his approach. Like the other dogleg-left holes that precede it, the woods on the left side can play havoc with a drive if a player gets too greedy.

Going too far to the right off the tee can also be problematic because it is easy to run a driver through the fairway. This leaves the player with a difficult angle to the green that slopes severely from right to left.

This green best receives a shot that is played with a little fade. However, it is easy to fade the shot too much and drop the shot into the greenside bunker on the right side. Players will always try to have their approach shot stop below the hole on this green.

Tiger Woods made one of the biggest shots of his career from the tee of the tenth hole in the first round of the 1997 Masters. Woods had played the front nine in a very dismal four over par. As he was walking from the ninth green to the tenth tee, he had a revelation as to what was wrong with his swing. He had been taking the club too far back on his backswing and needed to shorten it. Woods initiated the shortened swing with his tee shot at the tenth, which he hit perfectly. His approach shot to the green was equally impressive, and he made his first birdie of the tournament. Woods would go on to win the tournament with a scoring record of eighteen under par. Amazingly, after making the change to his swing, Woods played the remaining sixty-three holes of the tournament at twenty-two under par.

In the final round of the 1989 Masters, Seve Ballesteros pulled his drive along the left side of the tenth fairway. His ball did not make it into the woods but stopped short of the trees in an area that Ballesteros believed had been adversely affected by the gallery walking down that side of the fairway. He wanted to be given a free drop out of the trampled area. An official was called over to the scene, and he was inclined to go along with Ballesteros's request, until Ken Green, Ballesteros's playing partner, came over to see what was going on and then began to protest vehemently against the relief being granted. After Green's protest, it was decided that another official would be brought in to render a second opinion.

Green's ball on the second hole earlier that day had been in what he believed was a far worse circumstance than Ballesteros's. When Green had sought relief he was told by an official that he would have to play it as it laid.

Because Ballesteros was one of the front-runners in the field, a good bit of this brouhaha was being shown on television. Tom Weiskopf, one of the commentators, lauded Green's actions and stated that Green had an obligation to the rest of the players in the field to protect them from a bad ruling.

The second official who was sent to examine Ballesteros's lie was Michael Bonallack, secretary of the Royal and Ancient Golf Club at St. Andrews. Bonallack took one look at the ball and told Ballesteros to play away; no relief would be given. Ballesteros missed the green with his shot and ended up with a bogey five. He finished the tournament at three under par, two strokes out of first place.

Earlier in the week, Green would have probably welcomed the assistance of a marital rules official to help him in a dispute with his wife (now ex-wife). Shortly before the Masters, the couple had experienced a case of marital disharmony that spilled over into tournament week. His wife did not come to the Masters, choosing to stay at home in Florida. The problem was that she had seven Masters tickets in her possession. Green had invited twelve people to spend the week with him in Augusta, and four were members of his wife's family. Green requested that his wife send the tickets to him, but she refused.

Green went to Masters officials and explained the situation to them and tried to obtain replacement tickets. They turned him down. Green then had to resort to sneaking in the ticketless members of his party, going so far as to place some of them in the trunk of his car.

Greg Norman, the man practically everyone would have liked to have seen in a green jacket, had come so close so many times. The one

hole more than any other that has kept him from the champions dinner is the tenth. In his first Masters in 1981, Norman was in excellent
shape when he reached the tenth tee in the final round. He was just
two strokes out of the lead and could have really put some pressure
on eventual winner Tom Watson. But Norman then learned in his
first Masters how true that old adage can be about the tournament
not starting until the back nine on Sunday. Norman pulled his drive
into the woods on the left side. He ended up with a double-bogey
six on the hole and finished the day three strokes behind Watson.

The tenth would also be a huge hole for Norman and the ultimate
winner, Jack Nicklaus, in the final round in 1986. Nicklaus started
what would be an unforgettable back-nine charge with a birdie from
twenty-five feet at the hole, while Norman experienced a disaster.

Norman had started the round in the lead, and when he reached
the tenth tee, he and Seve Ballesteros were tied for the top spot.
Once again Norman pulled his drive, and it appeared to be heading
deep into the woods. But it caromed to the right off a tall pine and
bounced back into the edge of the left side of the fairway. Norman
then hooked his second shot into the gallery short of the green on
the left side. His backswing was restricted by a pine tree, and he
could only jab at his ball. Norman hit the shot too hard, and it ran
across the green into the bunker. His bunker shot was well short
of the cup, and he two-putted for double bogey. The three-stroke
swing between Nicklaus and Norman here at the tenth would be
huge at the conclusion of the day, because Nicklaus would end up
nosing out Norman for the win by just one stroke.

A bogey at the tenth in the final round in 1987 was very costly
to Norman. He finished in a three-way tie for first place with Seve
Ballesteros and Larry Mize. Mize would win the playoff on the
second extra hole with an incredible shot, which will be detailed
in the next chapter.

In 2011 Rory McIlroy hit a tee shot left in the final round at 10
that would result in his joining Norman (1996) and Ken Venturi
(1957) as the sufferers of the most epic collapses in Masters history.

The twenty-one-year-old McIlroy had at least a share of the lead for the first three rounds and a four-stroke advantage entering Sunday's final round. When he arrived at 10 he was clinging to a one-stroke lead. A host of challengers—among them Tiger Woods, Ángel Cabrera, and Charl Schwartzel—were closing in, and Rory was feeling the pressure of a Masters Sunday.

As previously described, Norman's and Ballesteros' problems at 10 started with a pulled shot from the tee. Rory McIlroy's tee shot at 10 was well beyond that category. It was a big hook that came off McIlroy's driver like a bullet. It struck a pine just off the fairway and ricocheted to an area where no Masters competitor had ever been.

The ricochet had carried the shot farther away from the green and farther left. When his ball came to rest, it was between two of the bungalows provided for Augusta National members, 50 yards from the fairway and just 125 yards from where he had struck the shot.

Rory's only option from that spot was to play the ball out almost sideways. This left him with 275 yards to the green. His third shot with a three-wood was also hooked. It ended up behind a tree to the left of the green. Rory tried to go over it with his fourth shot, but it clipped one of the tree's branches and fell short of the green. His next shot was a chip that just made the putting surface. From there he two-putted for a triple-bogey seven.

He left the tenth green now two behind, and he continued to unravel. He bogeyed the eleventh, double bogeyed the twelfth, and bogeyed the fifteenth. He finished the nine with a total of 43 and a score for the round of 80. After stepping onto the tenth tee with a one-shot lead, he finished the day ten strokes behind the winner, Charl Schwartzel, in a tie for fifteenth place.

Prior to the 1984 Masters, Ben Crenshaw had been in a long slump that had made him doubt whether he still had a future on tour. During this period he was seeking advice on his game from practically everyone. Finally, he returned to his longtime instructor and mentor, Harvey Penick. Penick helped him get his game back on track. Crenshaw was in the hunt when the final round started.

Long considered to have a putting stroke that other golfers would kill for, Crenshaw caught fire on the finishing holes of the front nine. He made a birdie from eight feet at the eighth hole and a birdie from seven feet on the ninth hole. These two crucial putts pulled Crenshaw one stroke ahead of his teenage rival and former teammate on the University of Texas golf team Tom Kite.

Tom Watson was also in the hunt that day, and he was playing in the group immediately in front of Crenshaw. At the tenth hole Watson made a bogey, and he was walking to the eleventh tee when he saw Crenshaw's approach shot. It was less than stellar and landed on the front-right portion of the green. With the pin located clear across the green on the left rear, Watson took some solace in the fact that it looked like he would drop only one stroke to Crenshaw, based on where his ball was.

When Crenshaw arrived at Augusta that week, he received some additional advice from former Masters champion and fellow Texan Jackie Burke. Burke told Crenshaw to concentrate on keeping his ball in the fairway (over his career Crenshaw had picked up the nickname of "Jungle Ben" because of the amount of time his errant tee shots kept him in the woods) and then put his approach shot on the green. If he did that, he would have just as good a chance as anybody. Burke might have understated the last part of his advice, because with Crenshaw's putting stroke, he probably had a better chance than most.

Crenshaw had another person in his corner giving him critical advice. This was Carl Jackson, his caddie. Jackson, an Augusta National caddie, had been on Crenshaw's bag since the 1976 Masters. Crenshaw had decided to stay with Jackson instead of going with his regular tour caddie after the caddie policy was changed following the 1982 tournament. Jackson's ability to read the difficult Augusta greens was second to none.

At the tenth green that day Crenshaw and Jackson conferred on his line, which was made much more difficult to read because the green was now almost totally covered in late afternoon shade.

Jackson read the putt and gave Crenshaw a line that would have a huge right-to-left break.

Crenshaw looked relaxed as he addressed the ball. His stroke was silky smooth. Watson was walking down the eleventh fairway when he heard the gallery's roar go up. Having seen the location of Crenshaw's approach, he could not believe his ears. Tom Kite couldn't believe it either, and he had seen it. He had reached his tee shot on the tenth, and he and his playing partner, Mark Lye, were watching as Crenshaw's ball made that long journey across the green and then disappeared.

Crenshaw's putt was tantamount to a knockdown punch to Kite. Lye looked over at him and could see Kite was stunned. In an interview after the round, Kite reflected on the putt and how he knew what Crenshaw could do when his putter got hot. He said, "When Ben gets in one of those moods, he can line up in the wrong direction, and it will still go in."

The putt at the tenth definitely got Crenshaw going in the right direction and broke the backs of two of his closest pursuers. Kite would three-putt the tenth to begin a big slide down the leaderboard. Watson, perhaps benefiting from only hearing what had happened and not seeing it, played gamely down the stretch but still finished two strokes behind Crenshaw.

While Watson heard Crenshaw's birdie and Kite saw it from afar, Ben Hogan received such an unsettling blow at close range at the tenth in his 1954 playoff with Sam Snead that Hogan had to take a break for some nicotine. Snead had put his approach shot over the green by about six feet. Hogan was the picture of accuracy in the playoff. As he would do on each of the eighteen holes that day, Hogan reached the green in regulation and was about twenty-five feet from the pin. Snead had a very treacherous sixty-five-foot downhill chip that he ran right into the hole for birdie. After Snead's ball fell in the hole, Hogan pulled out a cigarette and lit it. He smoked it almost down to his fingers before he was ready to putt. The nicotine did not produce a birdie, but it may have prevented a three-putt.

Hogan's first putt came up short by about two feet, and he tapped in for a four. The chip-in turned out to be a big factor in Snead's winning the playoff by one stroke.

In the final round in 1982 Craig Stadler had walked down the eleventh fairway with a six-stroke lead, thinking about how he was going to look in his green jacket. But when he walked off the eighteenth green, he was probably thinking about how he would look in a straitjacket. The six-stroke lead had disappeared, thanks to a rash of bogeys. Stadler's last bogey, which occurred at eighteen, was particularly painful to watch. He was thirty feet from the hole and needed to get down in two putts for a par and a one-stroke victory. Stadler's first putt was worse than ugly, and it stopped six feet short of the hole. His next putt did not even come close, and he fell into a tie for first and a playoff.

The tournament had changed its policy from an eighteen-hole playoff to sudden death in 1976. Originally, plans called for the sudden-death playoffs to begin at the first hole, but it was switched to a back-nine start, commencing with this tournament.

Stadler's opponent in the playoff, Dan Pohl, who was playing in his first Masters, was probably just as surprised to be going back to the tenth tee as Stadler. Pohl had started the day six strokes behind. He knew he would have to get off to a fast start to have a chance, and he did. He birdied the first and second holes and went on to shoot a 33 on the front. But he gained no ground on Stadler, who turned the front in the same number of strokes. At that point Pohl began playing conservatively so he wouldn't lose second place. When Stadler collapsed over the last seven holes, there was probably not anybody more surprised than Pohl by the turn of events.

As Stadler was making that short trek back to the tenth tee, he encountered his wife. He gave her a look of exasperation, and then she said to him, "Craig, hang in there; you can't do a thing about those putts you've missed. Just go out there and play your best. One of you has to win. It might as well be you." Stadler would say later, "Her words really pumped me up."

Stadler hit his drive like he was six strokes ahead again. Pohl also hit a fine drive. On their second shots, Stadler hit the green but was thirty-five feet from the hole. Pohl, who had been hooking his irons all day, pushed a seven-iron out to the right and missed the green. His chip still left him six feet from the hole. Stadler curled his first putt around the hole and tapped in for par. Pohl missed his putt for par, and shortly afterward Stadler was putting on the green jacket that had been on his mind all day.

The next playoff to end at the tenth hole was between Len Mattiace and Mike Weir in 2003. Mattiace was on the brink of becoming the all-time Cinderella story at the Masters. But the conclusion of his story would turn out to be a far cry from a fairy tale, as it was almost too painful to watch.

A journeyman player, Mattiace had moved to Augusta National's center stage with a marvelous closing round of 65. A par at the eighteenth would have given him the win, but he made his only bogey of the day, which would leave him tied with Weir. Weir fashioned a closing-round 68, thanks to a rock-solid putting performance, which featured the canning of a testy six-footer for par at the eighteenth to force the playoff.

Their playoff was the first at the Masters in thirteen years, and when both players hit rock-solid drives off the tee, it had the makings of a classic shoot-out. But then things went terribly wrong for Mattiace. He hooked his approach shot into the pines just short of the green on the left side, while Weir played a fine approach onto the green.

Mattiace had a pine directly in front of him on his third shot. So he couldn't chip straight at the hole. He had to play out to the right. His chip was too strong and ran to the backside of the green, which left him with a very slick putt coming back to the hole. He caught a break when Weir put his birdie putt seven feet by the hole. But there was quick reversal of fortune when he was too strong with his putt, and it almost went off the front of the green. His effort for bogey still left him a painful five feet from the hole. Weir then two-putted for a five to become the first left-hander to win the Masters and the first player ever to win a major in a playoff with a bogey.

Put your feet together end to end and take a look. In his playoff with Nick Faldo in 1989, that's how close Scott Hoch came to winning the Masters at the tenth green.

Faldo had tried to fade his approach shot into the green, but he hit more of a slice than a fade, and the ball landed in the greenside bunker. Hoch's second shot made the front of the green but was thirty-five feet from the flag that was cut on the back-right side. Faldo's sand shot was nothing to write home about and left him fifteen feet from the hole. Hoch's putt was a touch too strong and slightly off line, and it left him two feet above the hole. Faldo's putt for par wasn't even close, and when it stopped rolling, he had not lost his turn. He had left himself with a first-class knee-knocker that he drilled into the cup for a bogey with the look of defeat engraved in his face.

Hoch, a second-generation Wake Forest University golfer (his dad had played on the Wake Forest team with Arnold Palmer), was twenty-four inches from golf immortality. All he had to do was make a two-footer, but being above the hole had increased the difficulty factor considerably. He studied the putt for a good while. Ben Crenshaw, monitoring the action on television back at the clubhouse, believed Hoch was overstudying the putt and pleaded to the screen, "Go ahead and hit it!" Hoch did finally hit it, and the ball never had a chance. It barely grazed the left lip as it sped by. When it stopped rolling, it was twice as far from the hole than when it began. Hoch later stated, "I had some indecision [about the line], and then I pulled it, too." Hoch made his bogey putt, but Faldo had been given new life, and fifteen minutes later he would make the most of it at the eleventh hole.

Perhaps the greenside bunker at the tenth should be named "Faldo's Bunker," for in 1990 Nick Faldo survived two trips to that trap on a pressure-packed Masters Sunday. Faldo and Ray Floyd were tied for the lead at the end of regulation, so for the second straight year extra holes would be required. Floyd, charged up from getting up and down from a greenside bunker at eighteen to force the playoff, outdrove Faldo. Faldo's approach shot landed in the greenside bunker. Floyd hit a fine approach, and it stopped fifteen feet below the hole. For Faldo, it was the second time in three hours he had been in that spot. He had gotten his back nine off to a sour start with a bogey at the tenth when his approach shot drifted to the right and landed in that trap. Faldo hit a weak sand shot that left him fifteen feet from the hole, and he two-putted for a five.

Faldo's shot from the sand in the playoff was struck with more authority and confidence than his earlier effort. It flew straight at the pin and checked up shortly after landing just three feet below the hole. Floyd's birdie attempt from fifteen feet was headed straight for the heart of the hole, but it had only enough gas to travel fourteen feet, six inches. He tapped in for his par and then Faldo rolled in his three-footer for his, and Floyd had lost the opportunity to be the oldest Masters champion ever at age forty-seven. Faldo would take the playoff at the next hole.

Kenny Perry, forty-eight, was vying to become the oldest winner of a major in 2009 when a dreadful approach at the tenth shattered his chances in the playoff against Ángel Cabrera.

Perry, Cabrera, and Chad Campbell had finished in a three-way tie. Campbell bogeyed the first playoff hole, now the eighteenth, and was eliminated.

Cabrera hit two bad shots on that first playoff hole. But thanks to good fortune and grit, he had survived and matched Perry's par.

The playoff moved to the tenth. Perry's second shot was his worst swing of the tournament and left him sixty feet from the left side of the green.

Cabrera put the heat on with his approach, which stopped fifteen feet below the hole. Perry couldn't get up and down for his par, and Cabrera cozied his birdie putt up by the hole and tapped in for the win.

Decades of frustration finally came to an end for Australian golf fans in 2013, when Adam Scott defeated Ángel Cabrera in a playoff with a birdie at the tenth. Since 1950 Aussies had finished second or tied for second nine times, with Greg Norman accounting for three of that number. In 2011 Scott, along with fellow Aussie Jason Day, had finished tied for second, two strokes behind Charl Schwartzel.

At the seventy-second hole Scott had dropped a long birdie putt to take the lead, prompting a wild celebration, as it looked like he was going to be the winner. However, Cabrera, in the next and final pairing, hit a stellar approach and made his birdie putt to tie Scott.

Eighteen was the first playoff hole, and they halved it with pars. Cabrera caused Aussie fans' hearts to stop when he narrowly missed with his birdie putt.

The playoff moved to ten. Both players hit approach shots that left them with makeable birdie putts. Cabrera once again narrowly missed his effort. Scott got help with the read from his caddie, Steve Williams, and then rolled it into the cup for the win.

In the final round in 2012, nobody could argue that it had been Louis Oosthuizen's day. His double eagle at two three and a half hours before appeared to be ready to take the spot as the third-greatest shot in Masters history behind Gene Sarazen's double eagle at 15 in 1935 and Larry Mize's chip-in to defeat Greg Norman at the eleventh hole in a playoff in 1987.

After the second hole, further indicators that it was Louis's day kept showing up. At the par-three sixth he was not on the green after two shots but drained a speedy fifteen-foot downhill putt from the fringe to save par. He had a great up-and-down from the bunker at 17 to save par. Louis had also survived a makeable birdie attempt by Bubba Watson at the eighteenth green that would have given Bubba the win. The miss left them tied and in a playoff.

They played the eighteenth as the first playoff hole, and Louie just missed his birdie putt. Watson, from only eight feet, missed as well.

They moved to the tenth for the next playoff hole. Bubba's drive was long and right, straying deep into the pines 150 yards from the green.

Louis's tee shot also went to the right and into the pines. It was well short of Bubba's tee shot, but another indicator that it must be Louie's day occurred. His ball kicked out of the pines and came within a foot of making it back to the fairway.

Louis had a clear shot to the green from 231 yards. With Bubba deep in the pines, he could really put the pressure on him, if he could put his ball on the green. But Louis's good fortune ran out on his next swing. His four-iron came up short of the green by 30 feet.

The door that looked closed for Bubba was now half open. His next swing would open the door wide open. One of Watson's claims to fame is that he's never had a golf lesson; he is the quintessential "natural" with the ability to shape shots like no one else.

Despite his ball being deep in the pines, Bubba had an opening back to the fairway, and that was all he needed. Using a gap wedge, he hit a big hook that took a sharp right turn over the fairway and carried all the way to the green, coming to rest 20 feet from the hole.

Louis's chip from in front of the green was long. His putt for par turned away an inch in front of the hole, leaving Bubba two putts to win. Bubba cozied his first putt to a few inches from the hole and tapped in for his first green jacket.

#11
*White
Dogwood*

Hole No. 11

PAR 4—505 YARDS	WHITE DOGWOOD

The eleventh is the start of "Amen Corner." This name was given to the eleventh and twelfth holes and the tee shot at 13 by the legendary golf writer Herbert Warren Wind in a feature story he wrote for *Sports Illustrated* in 1958. Wind took the name from a recording he had listened to during his college days titled "Shouting at Amen Corner."

Surviving this stretch of holes, particularly in the last round, is often the key to victory. Dave Marr, who finished second to Arnold Palmer in 1964, summed up many Masters participants' feelings when he said, "If you get through these holes in even par, you believe a lot more in God."

The eleventh did not come off the drawing board as a very formidable hole. From the first Masters in 1934 through the 1950 tournament, it was just a bland drive-and-pitch par four. It was 415 yards in length but played considerably shorter because the fairway ran downhill from the tee to the green. The tee was to the right of where the tenth green is now located. Its tournament history was pretty bland as well; the most notable occurrence at the hole had been both Byron Nelson and Ben Hogan birdieing the hole by running in long putts in their eighteen-hole playoff battle in 1942. In the final round in 1949 Sam Snead was on his way to his first Masters win when he stumbled a bit at the eleventh and took a bogey. In a press conference after his win, he was asked about his bogey at the eleventh. Snead blamed his poor play at the hole on his being distracted by two dogs fighting in the woods off the fairway.

Obviously, a hole that did not offer enough challenge to maintain the undivided attention of the tournament leader in the last round was long overdue for some modification. After the 1950 Masters, following a plan devised by Cliff Roberts and endorsed by Bobby Jones, the hole underwent a major overhaul. The tee box was moved to the left of the tenth green. A chute was cut through the trees, and a new fairway was created that ran practically straight for 200-plus yards, and then it swept to the left down to a new green. The new green now called for a very demanding approach shot because an extension of Rae's Creek had been dammed and turned into a small pond. The green was set where its left side was afforded maximum protection by the new water hazard. The left-side pin location became one of the most treacherous in golf, and its use is traditionally reserved for the final round. The other pin locations available on the green are no picnic either. Locations in the rear usually result in a player letting up on the shot for fear of being long and getting into trouble behind the green, which features the often swift-running water of Rae's Creek. A front pin location always raises the possibility of an underplayed shot bounding left into the water.

When Ben Hogan arrived for the Masters in 1951, he thoughtfully surveyed the changes at 11. In regards to the approach shot, Ben concluded that the pond was too formidable a hazard and the penalty for a mistake too great. He declared it would now be a serious mistake to be aggressive with his approach shot, and one of his most famous "Hoganisms" was articulated for the first time: "If you ever see me on the eleventh green in two, you'll know I missed my second shot." His strategy for the hole was now to take the pond completely out of play on the approach shot by aiming the shot at the right-hand fringe of the green. From there he would try to get up and down with a chip and a putt for par.

This strategy has been chronicled countless times in print, and it has been espoused by Ken Venturi when he was a CBS golf analyst and by other members of the broadcast team during almost every telecast of the event for many years. Venturi was speaking from experience. In the final round in 1960 he had gone in the pond and made his only bogey of the day, finishing one stroke behind the winner, Arnold Palmer.

In that 1951 Masters Hogan wasn't given too much of a chance. He had played in only one tournament in the preceding three months. He had, however, been practicing rigorously, had arrived at Augusta two weeks early, and had gotten in eleven full practice rounds. When the third round started, Hogan was one stroke behind the co-leaders, Sam Snead and Skee Riegel. At the end of the day he was slipping into his first green jacket.

His victory was undoubtedly the most popular since the tournament had begun. He had come close twice before, losing the playoff with Byron Nelson in 1942 and finishing one stroke behind Herman Keiser in 1946 by three-putting the last green. Add to that the fact Hogan had come back from the serious injuries he had sustained when a Greyhound bus rammed into his car in 1949. It is hard to believe anyone in the gallery could have not been pulling for him.

The eleventh proved to be a pivotal hole on the final day. Hogan had played his new strategy to perfection in the first three rounds, recording a par every day and continuing the streak on Sunday. He placed his approach in the right fringe and then used a six-iron to chip within a few feet and made par. Riegel, who would finish second two strokes behind, made a bogey at the eleventh. The hole did the most damage to Snead. His first approach shot ran across the green into the pond. His next shot came up short and landed in the pond. His sixth shot finally stopped on the green, and he two-putted for a quadruple-bogey eight. For all practical purposes, he was done for the day. He would finish fifth.

The next year Snead still had problems with the eleventh, playing it two over for the week, but he won the tournament. Hogan finished seven strokes behind Snead, but he parred the eleventh in every round. In 1953 Hogan extended his streak of pars to nine at the eleventh before making his first bogey in the second round.

He made pars in rounds three and four and picked up his second green jacket, setting a new record for total score at 274.

In 1954 Hogan possibly could have picked up a third green jacket and been the first player to win back-to-back titles, if he had not strayed from his strategy for the eleventh in the final round. Billy Joe Patton, who had captured practically 80 percent of the gallery on the course with his hole in one at the sixth hole, was playing several groups ahead of him. Hogan had started the day five strokes ahead of Patton, but the upstart amateur had turned the front nine in 32 to erase Hogan's advantage. Before Hogan played his approach shot to 11, which he had played even par for the week, a tremendous roar went up from Patton's gallery at 13. Hogan must have believed that Patton had made birdie or even an eagle, because he abandoned his strategy on how to play the approach to the eleventh green. Hogan fired straight at the flagstick. His aim was just a little off. His ball came down twenty feet to the left of the pin, which, on this day with the hole tucked on the left side, meant it was in the pond by a couple of feet. Hogan took a double-bogey six on the hole.

It turned out Hogan had been deceived by the roar from thirteenth. Patton was actually in deep trouble. He had attempted to reach the par-five thirteenth in two, but his shot had landed in the creek in front of the green. Patton went down to the creek bed to survey his ball's position. He decided that it was playable and that he would play the shot from the water barefooted. He then climbed back up the bank and began to take off his shoes. When the gallery saw Patton unlacing his shoes, they let out a huge roar of approval for Patton's bravado. This was the sound that Hogan thought was probably a birdie or eagle roar.

When Patton went back down into the creek and addressed his ball, he thought better of the situation and decided to take a penalty stroke and drop the ball in the fairway behind the creek. Patton played his next shot poorly and ended up with a double-bogey seven. This disaster and another like it two holes later at the fifteen stopped Patton's quest for glory. If Hogan had played his "patented" approach shot, he would have made possibly a par or at worst a bogey and would have won the tournament by either one or two strokes. The double-bogey six put him in an eighteen-hole playoff with Sam Snead the next day, which he lost.

There were two other later noteworthy occasions in Hogan's Masters career where he ditched his own strategy at the eleventh. The first was in the third round in 1966 when the Masters patrons were treated to a dream pairing of Hogan and Arnold Palmer. Palmer by this time had collected all of his four green jackets, and his playing partner that day had been instrumental in his claiming the first one back in 1958.That year, Palmer had played a practice round with Hogan prior to the start of the tournament and had played badly. In the locker room after the round was over, Palmer overheard Hogan asking another former Masters champion, Jackie Burke, a question. "Tell me something, Jackie. How in the hell did Palmer get an invitation to the Masters?" Hearing the remark really stung Palmer, and he decided he would show Hogan why he had been invited. And he did, as he claimed his first green jacket that year.

In 1966 a huge throng followed the twosome around the course, and there even seemed to be a few defections from "Arnie's Army," judging by the cheers that went up for Hogan at the eleventh that day. He put his strategy aside on his approach and put the shot on the green and then rolled in a twenty-footer for a birdie. The putt was decisive in his duel with Palmer, as he bested him by one stroke, shooting a 73 to Palmer's 74.

Hogan made Saturday at the Masters special the following year (1967) as well. In his last Masters appearance the fifty-four-year-old legend gave all in attendance and the home television audience a golf moment to remember. After shooting an even-par 36 on the front nine, he blistered the back nine with a record-tying performance of six-under-par 30. Hogan started the inward half with a birdie at 10. He then placed his drive at 11 in the middle of the fairway. Once again he discarded his strategy and fired a six-iron straight at the flag. The shot came to rest twelve inches from the cup for an easy birdie. Ben would post four more birdies on the way in to tie Jimmy Demaret and Gene Littler for the back-nine record.

Art Wall used Hogan's strategy in the final round in 1959 when probably every fiber in his being was telling him to go for the pin. He had made the cut by only two strokes and was seven strokes behind when the last round started. He had a good front side of two-under-par 34 but started the back nine with a bogey at 10. Wall had half jokingly said before teeing off that if he shot a 66, it might give somebody a scare, but he was a long way from scaring anybody when he teed off at 11. Despite his position on the leaderboard, he chose to be patient and conservative with his approach and play it Hogan's way. He placed his three-iron shot to the right of the green, some three feet off the putting surface. Wall almost holed his next shot with his putter and then tapped in for par. At Augusta it is often the golfer who can be patient and who makes the right decisions who comes out on top. Wall got an up-and-down par at 12 and then caught fire. He birdied five of the last six holes to post that 66, and it did more than scare someone; it won the tournament by one stroke.

In 1978 Gary Player started the final round seven strokes behind the leader, Hubert Green. As Wall had done in 1959, Player posted a two-under-par 34 on the front side, but unlike Wall, he birdied the tenth. He drove the ball well at 11 and played a "Hogan" approach shot. His ball landed just to the right of the green. His chip shot rimmed the hole, and he tapped in for his par. Player then went on a tear, picking up birdies at 12, 13, 15, 16, and 18. In the process he tied the back-nine record of 30 and also tied the course record with an eight-under-par 64.

Forty minutes after Gary had played the eleventh that day, third-round leader Hubert Green arrived at the hole. He played an "un-Hogan" approach and hooked his shot into the pond. He was fortunate to get out with a bogey, but he would be unfortunate to make two more bogeys on the back nine. Green would finish in a three-way tie for second, one stroke behind Player, who claimed his third and final green jacket.

In the final round of his win in 2008, fellow South African Trevor Immelman escaped a situation that was ripe for a bogey at 11 by making par without ever playing a shot from the green.

When he teed off on the hole, Trevor was holding a two-shot lead. He bailed out to the right of the green with his 220-yard second shot. His ball rested in the same area that the second most famous shot in Masters history was played from in 1987. That shot will be detailed in a few pages.

Trevor had a pitch of 75 feet to hole with the green sloping away from him toward the water. He was a little too cautious with his pitch, and it hung up in the fringe 14 feet from the cup. Electing to use his putter, he was facing a lightning-fast path to the hole. Trevor took his time and gave the putt plenty of study. His stroke sent the ball on line and at just the right pace. It trickled into the hole for par.

Trevor would go on win by three strokes over runner-up Tiger Woods.

Bruce Devlin was in a tie for the lead as he teed off at the eleventh in the second round in 1968. He missed the fairway by just a foot with his drive. He then hooked his three-iron approach shot into the pond. He took his drop at the water's edge and then misfired his pitch shot. Instead on lofting it softly into the air, Devlin caught it thin and hit a low liner into the bank of the pond in front the green. The ball tried to roll back into the water but was halted by a patch of grass near the edge. From an awkward stance, he tried to hack the ball out of the thick grass and moved it only a few inches. As a result of the force he had expended with his swing, Devlin began to lose his balance on his follow-through. To keep from falling back into the water, he opted for an emergency landing on the bank. He landed on his posterior, and with a wry smile on his face he carefully raised his backside from an imbedded lie and slowly rose to his feet and collected himself. His next effort came out cleanly onto the green, and Devlin kept his balance. He then two-putted for an eight. He did record two birdies coming in and finished with a 73, but the damage inflicted by the eleventh would prove to be too much to overcome. He would finish the tournament in fourth place, three strokes behind the winner, Bob Goalby.

Cary Middlecoff struck one of the ugliest shots ever at the eleventh in the final round in 1955. Despite having a four-shot lead, Middlecoff admitted he was very nervous before the start of his round, as anyone would be who had Ben Hogan lurking behind him in second place. He turned in a solid two-under-par 34 on the front nine and had improved his lead over Hogan to seven strokes, but then disaster stuck at the tenth. Middlecoff bunkered his approach shot and then took two shots to extricate himself from the sand and two-putted for a double-bogey six. A haunting memory then crept into Middlecoff's mind. In 1950 he had been paired with Jim Ferrier in the final round, and he had watched Ferrier lose a five-stroke lead on the back nine to Jimmy Demaret.

Middlecoff hit a decent drive off the tee at the eleventh and had a three-iron left to the green. This stroke went terribly wrong. He jerked his head up a fraction of a second before hitting the ball. The ball took off like a bullet, but it had no altitude. It was only three feet off the ground, but it was on a line for the right side of the green. Middlecoff could tell it was going to land well short of the green and could easily kick left into the pond. After his blowup at the tenth, his heart had to be in his throat as he watched the ball's flight. If it went in the water, Middlecoff could easily make six, and back-to-back double bogeys would be the makings of a very sorrowful Masters back-nine obituary. But Providence was on Middlecoff's side that Sunday. When the ball landed, it bounded directly forward. When it began its roll, it stayed on a path safely away from the pond and rolled onto the green. Middlecoff then two-putted for his par. He sealed his win with a birdie at the twelfth and cruised home to a seven-stroke win over Hogan.

The eleventh had plagued Tiger Woods more than any other hole at Augusta National, but even it finally succumbed as Woods marched to his unprecedented fourth consecutive major triumph, when he captured the 2001 Masters. In the third round he was lurking just a few strokes off the lead and launched a 300-yard-plus drive and then hit a nine-iron for the approach shot. He played it cautiously and landed his ball on the green but some 30 feet right of the hole. Woods then stroked a sweet putt that had the line and the pace, and it dropped into the cup for birdie.

In the final round on Sunday, by the time Woods had reached the eleventh hole he was in the lead but still being challenged by Phil Mickelson and David Duval. He again bombed a drive out 300 yards, and once again he had a nine-iron approach shot to the green. This time, he threw caution to the wind and launched a nine-iron for the flag, which was set on that dangerous left side. The shot landed about 15 feet short of the hole and then rolled straight for it. It missed going in by a hair, almost grazing the cup as it trickled by on the left side and stopping just 18 inches or so beyond it. Woods then nonchalantly tapped in for birdie, picking up one stroke on Duval, who had parred the hole, and two strokes on his playing partner, Mickelson, who bogeyed it. Woods would end the day two strokes ahead of Duval and three ahead of Mickelson.

The eleventh was significantly lengthened as part of the changes prior to the 2002 Masters. The tee was moved back 35 yards, increasing its length from 455 to 490 yards. The tee was also repositioned slightly more to the right to make it more difficult for a player to play a draw from the tee. The fairway was recontoured in the landing area to eliminate drives bounding hard toward the green.

The effect of the changes was skewed by wet conditions in the first three rounds that year, and the hole's ranking in difficulty dropped from third to ninth. However, in the final round that year, the course had dried out, and with its traditional Sunday pin placement of back left, the eleventh was a bear. It played as the toughest hole on the course for that round, giving up only one other birdie beside Tiger's.

In 2003 the eleventh played as the toughest hole on the course. In 2004 thirty-six pine trees, measuring twenty-five to thirty-five feet high, were planted along the right side of the fairway to deny the players the option of bailing to the right with their tee shots. In spite of these new fortifications, the hole slipped a bit in difficulty that year, dropping back to third. However, it recaptured the top spot in 2005.

The eleventh was tweaked some more before the 2006 Masters. The tee was again shifted to the right and moved back an additional 15 yards, bringing its length to 505 yards, and more pine trees were added down the right side of the fairway.

These changes to 11 made one of the most intimidating approach shots in golf even more daunting. This makes the fantastic approach shot Bubba Watson struck in 2012 all the more extraordinary because he was not even in the fairway. He was in the woods.

Although Bubba Watson's shot from deep in the trees and off pine straw at 10 in the playoff in 2012 was a phenomenal one, he does not consider it his best shot of the tournament. What he consider his best shot of the week came in the first round. It was his approach to 11, and it, too, was from the pine straw. If he had not pulled it off, there is a good chance he would have not made it to a playoff for that year's green jacket.

Bubba's drive at 11 missed the fairway on the right side and came to rest under a tree in a lie of pine straw that looked like a bird's nest. One hundred and eighty yards from the hole, Bubba assessed the situation for several moments. He decided that he would go with a nine-iron, keep it low, rope-hook it over the pond, and stop it on the green.

When he told his caddie, Ted Scott, his plan, he advised Bubba not to try it. To which Bubba replied. "No, no, I got this."

Bubba hit a low screamer with more hook on it than his shot at 10 in the playoff. It made the green and rolled to a stop forty feet from the pin. He escaped with a two-putt par, and he would go on to shoot an opening-round 69.

In 2004 the Masters altered its sudden-death playoff format of having the competitors start on the tenth tee and continue on the back nine until there was a winner. This format had been in effect since 1979. The new format called for the players to return to the eighteenth tee for the first hole of the playoff. If there was not a winner after the first playoff hole, play would be rotated between the tenth and the eighteenth hole until there was a victor.

Prior to this change four of the first six sudden-death playoffs were decided at the eleventh. The first of these four was in 1979 between Ed Sneed, Tom Watson, and Fuzzy Zoeller. Sneed was not a marquee player by any stretch of the imagination, but he had appeared to be on his way to Masters glory. He was the third-round leader, and he had made it through Amen Corner without a scratch on him on Sunday, but he bogeyed the sixteenth, seventeenth, and eighteenth to fall back into a playoff with Watson and Zoeller.

All three players failed to convert on reasonably good birdie chances at the tenth hole. They all hit drives that placed them in good position in the fairway at 11, but Zoeller outdistanced his rivals considerably. Sneed was away and hit a five-iron right at the pin, which was tucked on that perilous left side. The shot was dead on line but just a touch long and flew over the flag and bounced into the back bunker. Watson went with a five iron as well. He hit an excellent shot that came to rest just twelve feet short of the hole.

Now it was Zoeller's turn, and he was in conference with his caddie, Jerry Beard, over what club to hit. Zoeller had spent a considerable amount of time in conference with Beard, a veteran Augusta National caddie, all week. This was Zoeller's first appearance at the Masters. He had gotten in only one practice round before the tournament began, and he needed all the help he could get. He had received a really big break when Beard was assigned as his caddie. The two meshed together like beer and pizza. Beard was masterful all week in giving Zoeller good reads on the greens and in clubbing Zoeller from the fairway.

This critical juncture was one of the few times all week Zoeller had differed with Beard's advice. Beard wanted Fuzzy to hit a nine-iron. Zoeller stated that one of his best shots was a knocked-down eight-iron. Zoeller was about to hit what could be the most important shot of his life, and he needed to feel confident about the club he had in his hands. As any good caddie would do under the circumstances, Beard dropped his nine-iron proposal and endorsed the eight-iron. Zoeller then hit one of the prettiest knocked-down eight-irons ever; it carried over the edge of the pond and stopped eight feet below the hole.

Sneed, in the back bunker, was the first of the trio to play his third shot. At the twelfth earlier in the day, he had saved par with a seventy-foot sand shot that had stopped just a few inches from the cup. After all Sneed had gone through in the two hours since that recovery and now finding himself in this predicament, one had to wonder if he had anything left. In regular tournament play, this would have been an extremely tough bunker shot, but in a playoff for the Masters title, it could easily compete for the title of the Mother of all Bunker Shots. Sneed was facing the water, and he had a downhill lie. Also, he had lost a three-shot lead over the last three holes of regulation play. It was one of those shots that would make a spectator want to turn away and not watch. To his great credit, Sneed almost holed the shot. He hit a soft blast that landed a few feet on the green. The ball then began to track toward the cup. When it was a foot away from the cup, it looked as if it was going to drop, but it peeled away to the left, just an inch or so from the hole.

Watson was next; he stroked his twelve-footer on line, but it did not have the pace. It ran out of steam just short of the hole and fell slightly away toward the pond. It came to rest directly beside the hole but a few inches to the left.

Now it was Zoeller's turn. He stood behind his ball, and Beard stood directly behind him. Beard confidently spoke into Zoeller's right ear, giving him the prescribed line. He then patted him on his left shoulder and stepped away. Zoeller coolly addressed the putt and then made a smooth stroke that put the ball solidly on Beard's line, and it dropped into the cup. Zoeller hurled his putter high into the air and danced to his left about ten yards. Then he stopped dead in his tracks; he was forgetting the other half of the pizza-and-beer team. He wheeled around and raced toward Beard with outreached arms. They embraced and pounded each other on the back in a level of pure exhilaration that only a few people ever get to experience. The two had truly been a masterful combination.

The next playoff conclusion at the eleventh came in 1987, and without a doubt it is the most famous. Augusta native Larry Mize had started the final round two strokes off the lead in the fourth-to-last group. His chances had seemed to be over when his second shot at 15 was long and ran into the pond behind the green and he made a bogey. This should have finished him off, but the other leaders, Ben Crenshaw, Roger Maltbie, Seve Ballesteros, and Greg Norman, failed to make a move.

Mize was still two under when he teed off at 18, and it looked as if a birdie there stood a chance of getting him a share of the lead. All the other leaders were still playing behind him, and they were at either three or two under. Mize connected for a solid drive and had a 140-yard approach shot to the flag. He then hit a splendid nine-iron shot that came to rest just 6 feet from the hole. He made his putt for his third birdie of the tournament at 18 and then had to wait for the others to finish. When the dust had settled, Mize was in a three-way playoff with Greg Norman and Seve Ballesteros.

The threesome teed off at the tenth, and Mize outdrove his two competitors. His approach shot came to rest 10 feet from the hole. Ballesteros and Norman had longer and tougher birdie efforts, and both failed to convert. Mize's birdie putt was on line but was lacking about 6 inches in distance. He tapped in for par. Norman made his par as well, but Ballesteros missed his short par putt and was eliminated from the playoff. Norman and Mize both hit good drives from the eleventh tee.

Prior to the tournament, the knock on Mize, who was then twenty-eight, had been that he had all the tools, but he might not have what it took to stand up to the pressure. He had one tour victory in five years. The year before he had blown a four-stroke lead in the final round of the Tournament Players Championship and had lost to Norman in a playoff at the Kemper Open. His clutch birdie at the eighteenth, his confident play on the first playoff hole, and his drive at the eleventh would appear to have been putting those knocks to rest. Mize's next swing, however, quickly brought them back to life. He pushed his approach way to the right, missing the green by 30 yards. Mize reacted with sheer disgust. His caddie, Scotty Steele, had been telling him all week "Don't worry about it" after every poor shot or bad break. He repeated those words after this shot, but, as Mize recalled later, Steele added a few more words to it, something to the effect that it would all work out somehow.

Norman's approach shot didn't improve the situation, as it landed safely on the right side of the green. When Mize reached his ball, he discovered that this dark cloud did have a little trace of a silver lining. Earlier in the day when he had played the eleventh, he had sunk a gut-checking 16-foot putt to save his par. His ball lay now, although some 100 feet farther away, on that same line to the hole. He would at least have a reasonably good idea how much the ball was going to break, once it was on the green and started its roll toward the hole. His main focus was to get it close, so he could save his par with his next shot and require Norman to hole his lengthy putt to beat him.

Mize played the ball back in his stance. His backswing went back to about knee high, and then he smoothly made the transition into the downswing, and the ball was launched on what would be a historic 130-foot, six-second journey. Norman was watching Mize's shot intently. He wanted to get a read on the speed of the green, so he could gauge how firmly he would have to stroke his own putt. Although he had lost the final major of the year before, the 1986 PGA, in a playoff when Bob Tway had holed out from a greenside bunker, that event was actually far from Norman's mind. He thought he was in excellent shape and believed it would be a difficult proposition for Mize to get down in two from his position.

Mize's ball landed about 6 feet short of the green and then skipped onto it. The ball settled down nicely on a line about a foot to the right of the hole, but it was rolling at a pace that was going to put it 5 to 8 feet by the cup. The ball quickly began to take the break, and when it got to within in a few feet of the hole, it was dead on line. The ball slammed into the pin and disappeared into the hole.

The fifteen thousand spectators who had been following the action went wild. To Norman, it was another devastating blow at the Masters; unfortunately, there would be more to follow.

Two years later, in 1989, Nick Faldo was squatting down, peering through the Georgia twilight at the eleventh green. He was trying to get a line on a 25-foot putt that would give him a playoff victory over Scott Hoch. He asked his caddie, Andy Podger, a fellow Englishman, who was looking over his shoulder, what he saw. Andy replied, "Don't ask me, Gov; I can't see a bloody thing." Faldo picked his own line and made what he would call the best putting stroke of his life, rolling it in the cup for the win.

A year later Faldo returned to the eleventh in another playoff, but with a new caddie. He would not need to seek any advice on a putt this time. His opponent, forty-seven-year-old Raymond Floyd, had made a gallant effort to become the oldest player ever to win the Masters, but he made a bad swing with a seven-iron, and his approach shot had gone into the pond. Faldo was on the green in two and watched Floyd take his drop at the water's edge and then make his last-gasp effort to par the hole with a pitch shot. Floyd missed, and Faldo two-putted to join Jack Nicklaus as the only other player, up until that time, to win two consecutive Masters.

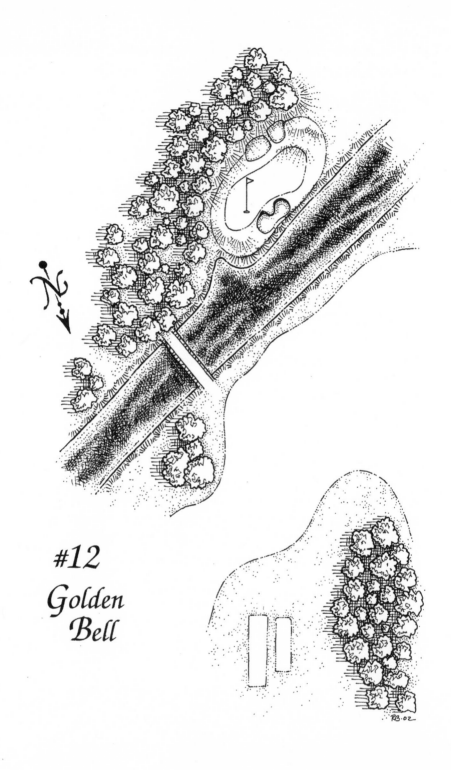

#12
Golden
Bell

Hole No. 12

PAR THREE—155 YARDS | GOLDEN BELL

If there was one swing Tiger Woods would want to have over again from his remarkable 2000 golf season, it would have to be his tee shot at the twelfth hole during the first round of the Masters. This shot may have cost Woods the most treasured prize in golf, the "Grand Slam."

No one had ever arrived at Augusta as a bigger favorite to win the tournament than Woods. Out of the last eleven tournaments he had entered, he had won nine and finished second in the other two.

He was two over par on his opening round when he arrived at the twelfth tee, but with his supreme length off the tee and two par fives just ahead, he could easily get back to even par or possibly into red numbers for his opening round.

The tees were set just 140 yards from the flag, but there was wind present. Woods decided to go with a knockdown eight-iron. He struck the shot solidly, but the wind grabbed it and slammed the ball down short, into the bank, just below the front bunker. It then spun back into the hole's famous guardian, Rae's Creek.

Woods hit his next shot from the drop area to within 15 feet of the hole. He was too strong with his bogey putt, and it went 3 feet past the hole. He then missed that putt coming back to take a triple-bogey six. Although he was able to stay near the lead over the rest of the tournament, Woods was never able to recover from the wound the twelfth had inflicted on him, and he finished the tournament in fifth place.

Woods would go on to win golf's remaining three major titles in 2000, running away with the U.S. Open, the British Open, and taking a pressure-packed win at the PGA Championship. He would later win the 2001 Masters to become the first player in the modern era of golf to hold all four major titles at the same time. Many would argue that Woods had achieved the Grand Slam. Others would contend it was not a Grand Slam since the four wins were not in the same calendar year. The latter group appears to hold the edge in the debate, however, because Woods's amazing accomplishment is now referred to as the "Tiger Slam."

The fifty-yard walk from the eleventh green to the twelfth tee has been described as one of the great walks in golf. This is more than fitting, because after receiving a round of applause from the huge gallery behind the tee box, the player is faced with one of the most challenging shots in golf.

The twelfth is only 155 yards long, but it has frequently played as the Masters' toughest hole. It is often referred to as the meanest par three in golf.

Cliff Roberts once stated that the twelfth was the easiest hole at Augusta to build because it was a nature-made hole. The only money spent was to smooth off the ledge where the green was placed and build the tee. The engineers who headed up the work had a very different opinion. It was quite an undertaking, because a large amount of dirt had to be excavated from the opposite side of the creek to complete the building of the green. During its construction it was discovered that the location had once been an Indian burial ground. Many have blamed the difficulty of the hole and the strange occurrences that have happened there on Indian spirits who are upset that their final resting place has been disturbed.

The hole has had no significant changes made to it since the day Augusta National opened. Although it was enlarged slightly in 1951, it still features the smallest green on the course. In 1960, in response to floodings, the entire hole from tee to green was elevated 2 feet. In 1981, to give the green protection from the sweltering Georgia summer and frosty winter mornings, a heating and cooling system was installed beneath it.

The green is provided with more than adequate protection in the front. The game's most infamous water hazard, Rae's Creek, flows directly in front of it. The closely mowed and super-slick creek bank and a bunker that is located in front of the center of the green provide additional frontal protection.

From above the green looks like a shoe print (, with the left side being the front of the foot; the center, a narrow instep; and the right side, the heel. It is 101 feet wide and 42 feet deep at its widest point, which is on the far left side. There is a 5-foot rise from the front of the green to the back.

During the first three rounds, the consensus strategy is to aim for the center of the green, make a three, and go quietly. The center-of-the-green strategy becomes doctrine on Sunday, since the traditional final-round pin placement is just six paces from the right edge of the green. A shot fired at that pin location must have the carry measured perfectly, or it will hit the bank and roll back into the creek.

Players, guarding against going into the water, are often too strong with their tee shots and end up going over the green, where plenty of trouble awaits as well. Two side-by-side bunkers protect the right rear. A shot played from these bunkers ranks among one of the most terrifying in golf. The player must execute a very delicate shot to a narrow putting surface that is running away from him and has Rae's Creek eagerly waiting in the background. The left rear is no bargain either; a player who ends up there will find himself playing off a shrub-laden bank.

There is usually one more element that adds to the twelfth's difficulty, and that is the wind that is often present during the week of the Masters. Since the hole is located at the lowest part of the course, the winds swirl around the green and the tee box. These are not typical wind swirls. They behave in a manner that could be best described as "mystical."

A player's preshot observations can be quite confusing as he attempts to gauge the wind's direction. The teeing area is protected to the right and to the rear by a thick stand of Georgia pines, so that even in a stiff wind, the player will be standing in a pocket of relative calm. A player will often check the treetops to his right and see the wind blowing them from left to right. When he looks at the flag on 12, it is fluttering from right to left, and when he looks to his left at the flag on the eleventh green, it is being blown left to right.

It can be equally vexing for the player to factor in the wind's intensity at the twelfth because it can shift from one extreme to another in a heartbeat. Perhaps the best example of this was Bob Rosburg's experience in the second round in 1956. The wind was blowing stiffly into his face, so he elected to go with a four-iron shot. Just as he went into his swing, the wind abruptly stopped. It was as if it had been turned off by a remote control. With no wind to resist its flight, a four-iron was way too much club, and the shot sailed over the green, over the back bank, over a fence (since removed), and out-of-bounds. Almost as soon as the ball had disappeared from sight, the wind started blowing briskly again as instantaneously as it had stopped. Rosburg elected to fire again from the tee with the same four-iron. This time the ball landed softly on the green—ten feet from the pin.

When there is wind present, there is probably no tougher par-three tee box in golf for a player to get committed to his club selection than the twelfth. It is not unusual for a player to pick a club and address the ball, only to feel a change in the wind's force or direction and decide to go with another club, address the ball again, feel the wind change again, go back to his original selection, and address the ball once more—and then back away to study the treetops and the flags on the greens once again.

It is during conditions like these that a player will seek the advice of his caddie, which can produce mixed results, as the following examples will demonstrate.

Sam Snead looked as if he would be the sure winner when he arrived at the twelfth in the final round in 1952. He had played steadily for eleven holes and held a four-shot lead. But the twelfth had been on the warpath since the first round, when it claimed the scalp of the man whose double eagle at the fifteenth had put the Masters and Augusta National on the map seventeen years earlier: Gene Sarazen. After going one under on his front nine, Sarazen put three balls in the water at 12, took an eight, and then withdrew from the tournament.

At the tee Snead and his caddie, O'Brien, who had been on his bag when Snead had won his first Masters in 1949, got into a debate over what club Snead should use. O'Brien wanted Snead to hit a seven-iron. Snead wanted to go with a six-iron. O'Brien won the debate, and Snead hit the seven-iron, and his shot plunged into Rae's Creek.

Snead took a drop. He was obviously upset by his drowned tee shot and hit a poor pitch shot that barely cleared the creek and then began to roll back toward the water. Luckily for Snead, the practice of closely mowing the bank had not yet begun, and his ball's roll was stopped at the water's edge by a clump of grass. From an awkward stance and staring a triple-bogey six right in the face, Snead pitched the ball. It landed about three feet from the pin and then bounced into the hole for the best bogey "Slammin' Sammy" ever made. Obviously charged up by his great recovery, Snead birdied the next hole and went on to coast home with a four-stroke victory.

Twenty-one years later, in 1973, Snead's nephew J. C. Snead arrived at the twelfth in the final round, locked in a three-way battle for the lead. Uncle Sam had repeatedly told him to make sure he took enough club at this hole, but in the heat of the moment J. C. had a memory lapse. He initially reached into his bag and pulled out a six-iron, but when he did, he saw his caddie's facial expression, which was that of someone who had just swallowed a mouthful of Listerine. J. C. placed the six-iron back in the bag and pulled out the seven. His caddie's expression turned to a big smile, but that smile would be short-lived. J. C.'s tee shot barely cleared the creek. Unfortunately for him, the practice of closely mowing the bank had begun, and his ball quickly rolled back into the water.

J. C. made a double-bogey five and ended up in second place, one stroke behind Tommy Aaron.

Of course, there has certainly been very positive caddie input at 12 as well. For example, in 1959, William Hyndman III, an amateur, made the second ace in the history of the twelfth, thanks to his caddie, who went by the name of First Baseman. Hyndman had asked First Baseman for a club recommendation, and he answered forcefully: six-iron. Hyndman initially balked at the suggestion, thinking it was too much club. First Baseman adamantly defended his choice and further added that even with the six, Hyndman would have to get all of it. Hyndman went with his caddie's choice, and his shot landed a few feet behind the pin and then spun back into the hole.

The disrespect and consternation the twelfth was going to inflict on the biggest names in golf was displayed from the day Augusta National was officially opened. When Bobby Jones was playing his first official round on the course he brought into existence, and with newsreel cameras chronicling his play, his tee shot here ended up at the bottom of Rae's Creek. In 1934 the little hole gave its creator a working over in the inaugural Masters. In the first round his tee shot barely cleared the creek, but he recovered with a good pitch and made par. In the second round he made a two-putt par, but in the third round he dropped his tee shot in the water and made five. Jones found the water again in the final round but managed to make bogey, thanks to a fine pitch shot.

Arnold Palmer needed a favorable ruling from the Rules Committee in the final round in 1958 to prevent the twelfth from denying him his first Masters victory. Palmer was in the lead by one shot over his playing partner, Ken Venturi, when the two reached the twelfth tee. Palmer admitted to being pumped at that moment and attributes an adrenaline rush to the fact that his seven-iron shot flew over the green and landed in the area between the green and the back bunkers. Venturi's tee shot also carried the green, but it hit the rear bank and spun back onto the green.

An overnight rainstorm had left the area behind the green very soggy. When Palmer arrived at his ball, he discovered it had plugged in the soft ground. Palmer then advised the rules official on duty at the twelfth, Arthur Lacey, that he was going to take a free drop, as provided by a local Augusta National rule for wet conditions that he understood to be in effect for that day's play. Lacey was no rules lightweight; he was a member of the Royal and Ancient at St. Andrews and had been a player on two British Ryder Cup teams. He advised Palmer that he was not entitled to relief. He would have to play it as it lay.

Approximately ten minutes later, Palmer and Venturi walked off the green and headed for the thirteenth tee with differing opinions as to what had just transpired at the twelfth green. Palmer was not sure if he was in the lead over Venturi by one stroke or behind by one. Venturi, on the other hand, was convinced he knew exactly where he stood. He was in the lead. For the rest of their lives, what happened here would be a point of contention between them.

When the dispute had broken out between Lacey and Palmer, Venturi had joined in, arguing that Palmer was entitled to relief. But when it appeared the debate was going to be a long one and fearing he would lose his concentration, Venturi opted out of the discussion and had putted out, almost holing his twenty-footer for birdie and then tapping in for par.

Venturi detailed his version of what happened next in his book *Getting Up and Down: My 60 Years in Golf*, which was published in 2004.

After barely missing my birdie attempt, I rejoined Palmer and Lacey to catch the rest of their discussion. Nothing was resolved. I sat on my bag with Mutt, my caddie. This matter was obviously going to take longer than I thought. While I sided with Palmer's interpretation, I realized I might capitalize from his misfortune.

Finally, an angry Palmer played the shot. Not surprisingly he flubbed the chip and the ball did not even reach the putting surface. He then hit the next one five feet past the hole but then missed the putt, making a five. The two-shot swing put me in the lead for the first time since early in the third round. . . .

Only Palmer wasn't ready to give up on the 12th hole just yet. "I didn't like your ruling," he said, glaring at Lacey. "I'm going to play a provisional ball." (He was really playing what is called a "second ball.") "You can't do that," I told him. "You have to declare a second before you hit your first one. Suppose you had chipped in with the other ball? Would you still be playing a second?"

But Palmer had his mind made up. I turned to Mutt.

"Mutt we got 'em now," I said knowing Palmer was in violation of the rules. "It doesn't make any difference what he does with his ball."

Palmer didn't say another word. He took the drop. The ball rolled toward the hole two times in a row, allowing him to place it. This time, with a better sense of the speed of the green, he almost chipped it in, tapping in for par.

Palmer has always insisted that before he hit his embedded ball, he declared to Lacey that he would play a second ball. He rendered his account of the events at the twelfth that day in his book *Playing by the Rules*, which was published in 2003:

When I saw that my ball was embedded behind the 12th green, I called a rules official over and explained my situation, fully expecting him to give me the relief I was entitled to under the local rule. . . . That's exactly the way we had played all week.

So imagine my surprise when the rules official, a fellow named Arthur Lacey, said, No, you don't do that at Augusta.

"I beg your pardon?" I said. "We're playing wet-weather rules."

"No sir," he said. "You can't do that. You have to play it as it lies."

That sent my heart rate and blood pressure up a notch or two. I knew I was right, but I wasn't in much of a position to argue. Finally, I said, "I'm going to play two balls and appeal to the tournament committee." I knew I had that option under Rule 3-3a. . . .

"No sir," Mr. Lacey said with a slight edge to his voice. "You can't do that either."

That's when I knew my official was out of bounds. There was a one-in-a-million chance that I was wrong about the embedded ball rule. Even though it had been in effect all week, I could have been wrong. It could have been rescinded on Sunday without my knowledge. But I knew I was right about playing a second ball. That is always an option under the rules.

"Well," I said, "that's exactly what I'm doing."

I played the embedded ball still buried in the pitch mark, and took a double-bogey. Then I returned to the spot where the original ball had been, and I dropped a second ball. From there I chipped up to about three feet and made that putt for par.

Palmer played the par-five thirteenth as if he were several strokes behind. From a difficult lie, he scorched his three-wood second shot to within about twenty-five feet of the hole and then rammed in the putt for an eagle.

A few minutes later on the fourteenth hole, Palmer received the official word that he had won his appeal and would be given a three on the twelfth instead of a five. Those two shots would prove to be very huge. Palmer would bogey the sixteenth and the eighteenth, but would still be able to claim his first Masters win by one stroke.

The ruling in Palmer's favor had to throw Venturi out of sync, as he three-putted the fourteenth, three-putted the par-five fifteenth after reaching the green in two, and three-putted the sixteenth. He would finish the day in fourth place, two shots behind Palmer.

The spirits at the twelfth hole must have been upset that Palmer had gotten away on a technicality in 1958 and gave him a one-two punch the following year. Palmer had parred the hole in each of the three previous rounds and was in the lead by two strokes when he arrived at the twelfth tee on Sunday. He walked briskly to the front of the tee box to gauge the wind, which he found was blowing stiffly into his face. He considered hitting a five-iron but decided to go with a six because he had been striking the ball so well. The shot took off perfectly, but when it was at its highest point, the wind grabbed it, and it plunged into Rae's Creek just a few feet from the bank. Palmer took a drop and pitched over the creek. The shot was too strong, and it ran over the green. The spirits at 12 struck again. The ball trickled into an indentation behind the green. The only club Palmer could get on the ball was his putter. He managed to pop it out onto the green and then two-putted for a triple-bogey six. Palmer would end the day in third place, two shots behind the winner, Art Wall.

The next year, 1960, seemed to be a case of déjà vu for Palmer and the twelfth during the first round. His tee shot was long, and it flew over the green and plugged in soggy ground. This time there was no rules debate at all, and Palmer was granted a free drop. He made an excellent chip and one-putted for a par. Palmer went on to post a five-under-par 67 for the day, which gave him the opening-round lead.

Playing several groups behind Palmer that day was Ken Venturi, who had just set a record for the front nine with a five-under-par 31. His tee shot at 12 landed on the green but ran off the back and came to rest in the pitch mark of a previous ball. Venturi sought relief, but the official on duty at the green ruled that since his ball was not plugged in its own pitch mark, he would not be entitled to relief.

The proverbial wheels came off for Venturi at that point. He chopped the ball out of the pitch mark and then pitched onto the green and two-putted for a double-bogey five. He went on to post a back-nine score of six over par, which was an eleven-stroke differential from his front side and gave him an opening score of 73.

Venturi fired subpar rounds on Friday, Saturday, and Sunday, but would finish one stroke behind the ultimate winner, who was Palmer.

In the second round in 1972, one of the last years he was considered a serious contender, Palmer suffered another disaster at the twelfth. Players often leave the twelfth green in a rage, but Palmer was in one on the tee box because a ruling had not gone in his favor.

Despite having missed a two-foot birdie putt on 12, Palmer was coming off his best opening round in seven years and had been in third place when the day started. He was playing well until the ninth hole. His approach shot there missed the green, and the ball came to rest in an indentation left by a folding chair. Palmer thought he should be entitled to a free drop, particularly since he believed the indentation had been made by an official's chair. The situation could not be resolved immediately, so he played the original ball as it lay and played a provisional ball as well. He made a bogey five with the original ball and a par four with the provisional ball. The matter was then referred to the full Rules Committee.

When Palmer was leaving the eleventh green, he received word that the Rules Committee had ruled against him. His score with his original ball would stand. He was fuming when he reached the twelfth tee. "Arnie's Army" watched in horror as their beloved general took a triple-bogey six without going into the water or taking a penalty stroke. His tee shot landed in the front bunker. His sand shot skidded over the green into a stand of heavy grass on the left side. He then caught his chip shot thin, and it blazed across the green back into the front bunker. From there he hit an excellent sand shot to within two feet of the hole and then missed the putt to take a six, and for all practical purposes, took himself out of the running for the rest of the tournament.

Palmer probably takes some solace in the fact that 12 has been equally hard on his archrival, Jack Nicklaus. Nicklaus has said about the twelfth tee: "Sometimes I get there, and my hands just shake." This could explain what happened to him in the third round in 1964. He was attempting to challenge Palmer, the ultimate winner, for the lead when he hit quite possibly the most embarrassing shot of his career. He shanked his eight-iron tee shot.

The ball flew off to the right at an almost ninety-degree angle. It narrowly missed a TV tower before coming to rest almost one hundred yards from the tee box. To add insult to injury, the shot was witnessed by Bobby Jones, who was sitting in a golf cart near the tee with Cliff Roberts. Nicklaus hit a fine recovery shot to about eight feet from the hole, but his par putt slid by the cup, and he tapped in for bogey.

The twelfth was successful in knocking Nicklaus off his stride in the third round in 1981 and keeping him from claiming his sixth green jacket for another five years. Nicklaus had started the day with a four-stroke lead, but by the time he reached the twelfth, his lead was down to two over Tom Watson. He put his six-iron tee shot into the creek and took a double-bogey five. Watson would ultimately win the tournament by two strokes over Nicklaus.

Nicklaus's play from the eighth to the eighteenth hole in the final round of the 1986 Masters has been described as the greatest stretch of competitive golf ever played. His score of 30 on the backside could have been an incredible 29 if it had not been for the twelfth. When Nicklaus walked onto the tee there, he had run off a string of birdies at 9, 10, and 11, which had vaulted him into a three-way battle for the lead. Pumped to the max, he tried to quell his adrenaline rush and carefully gauge the wind conditions. It felt to him as if it had picked up a little. The pin was in its traditional Sunday position of far right. Nicklaus wanted to go with a six-iron but was afraid that would put him in one of the back bunkers, so he went with a firm seven. As he started his swing, the wind gusted. Fearing going right and landing in the water, he pulled the shot and ended up in the back fringe on the left-hand side of the green.

Nicklaus hit what he thought was a fine chip on a target line that would have it run down to the hole, but the ball took a strange hop when it landed on the green. Instead of running down toward the cup, it clung to a little ridge above the hole, and when it stopped Nicklaus was faced with a seven-foot downhill putt.

As if the gust of wind and the strange hop had not been enough, when Nicklaus lined up his putt, he saw a spike mark with blades of grass that stood up like the ends of a fork directly in his line, about a foot in front of his ball. When Nicklaus stroked his putt for par, his ball rolled over the spike mark, toppled slightly off line, grazed the hole, and slid by. Nicklaus slumped down as if all the wind had been let out of him. He quickly regained his composure, tapped in for bogey, and marched to the thirteenth tee. What would happen over the remaining six holes would become legendary—three birdies and an eagle—and Nicklaus would get that sixth green jacket, despite the efforts of the twelfth hole to derail him.

Nicklaus was recovering from hip-replacement surgery in 1999 and had to miss playing in the Masters for the first time in forty years. On Tuesday during a practice round before the tournament, he was touring the course in a golf cart with tournament chairman Hootie Johnson. When they reached the twelfth tee, he couldn't resist the urge to take a whack at his old nemesis.

Carlos Franco was about to tee off. Nicklaus asked him if he could borrow a club and a ball. He requested the six-iron. The hole started playing its old tricks, and a little indecision crept into Nicklaus's mind. He then gave Franco back the six-iron and asked for a five-iron. It turned out to be the right choice. Nicklaus's shot carried the creek, landed just on the top of the bank, and bounced onto the green, and the crowd gave out a roar that would have made one think it was Sunday afternoon instead of Tuesday.

Gary Player is another great player the twelfth has loved to torment. His tee shot once found the cup on the fly, but instead of a hole in one, he wound up with a par. The ball bounced off the lip of the cup and ended up fifteen feet away. In another year he putted the ball off the green into the creek, on consecutive days. In 1962 he had the lead but bogeyed 12 on Sunday and dropped into a three-way tie. In the playoff the next day, he came to the twelfth with a three-shot lead and bogeyed it again, which started a downhill slide that would result in his losing to Arnold Palmer by three shots.

In the first round in 1966 his tee shot landed on the bank above one of the back bunkers in a horrendous lie. Player believed he had no shot and was considering taking an unplayable lie but decided instead just to slap it down into the bunker and play his third shot from the sand. Player used too much force on the shot, and the ball raced through the bunker, over the fringe, onto the green, and into the hole for a birdie two. Go figure.

Vijay Singh had to be happy that his tee shot at 12 ended up in one of the back bunkers in the final round in 2000. Singh was clinging to a one-shot lead. His tee shot was way too long and landed in the shrubs beyond the bunkers. It appeared that Singh would be facing a similar situation to Player's in 1966, but his ball took a fortuitous bounce and bounded back toward the green. It came to rest in the left bunker. He got up and down from the sand for par to keep his lead. He would go on to expand his lead over the remaining six holes and win by three shots.

To cross Rae's Creek to the green, the players use the Hogan Bridge. This bridge was built in 1958 and named for Ben Hogan in honor of his record-setting performance in the 1953 Masters. In the 1999 Masters Greg Norman never dreamed he would have to make two trips across the bridge in the third round.

Norman hit an eight-iron that was a little long and carried the green on the left side and bounded into some shrubs up on a bank. Norman, his playing partner, Lee Janzen, their caddies, and an official searched diligently, but they could not find the ball. When the five minutes allotted for such searches had expired, Norman and his caddie, Tony Navarro, trudged back across the bridge to the tee to play another ball.

Norman elected to go with an eight-iron again. This time, the ball held the green and was twenty-two feet from the hole. On the way back to the green, Navarro said to Norman, "Let's just make a hard four and get out of here." Norman said he never doubted he would make the putt, and that's exactly what he did. Keeping the damage to just a bogey helped Norman stay in contention. He would finish the tournament in third place.

CBS announcer Bobby Clampett, who covered the twelfth hole during the telecast, went back and found Norman's ball after play had concluded. It was ten feet away from where the search party had been concentrating their efforts.

Norman's four would have to rate as the second-best bogey ever made at the twelfth, behind Sam Snead's chip in 1952. Snead would also have to be given credit for being the best-prepared golfer at the twelfth in 1957. In the first round his tee shot wound up just a few feet short of clearing the creek. After Snead had located his ball in the water, he returned to his golf bag and pulled out hip waders, donned them, and stepped into the water to play his shot. Snead was barely able to splash his ball out onto the bank. He then chipped onto the green and one-putted for a bogey.

Phil Mickelson had the makings of one of the great charges ever in a major championship in the final round of 2009, but he stumbled hard at the twelfth. Phil had started the final round seven strokes behind. His amazing score of six under on the front nine had him just one stroke out of the lead when he arrived at 12.

Phil was paired with his old nemesis, Tiger Woods. Tiger had the honor at the twelfth tee and used an eight-iron for the 157-yard shot. He didn't go at the pin that was located in his normal final-round position on the right side. Tiger's shot was at the heart of the green, and it landed pin high before spinning back down to near the front of the green.

After consultation with his caddie, Jim "Bones" Mackay, Phil elected to go with a nine-iron. The swing looked nothing like the one that had look so perfect on the front nine. It appeared that he was not totally committed to the shot. There were murmurs from the patrons as his ball reached the halfway point of its flight that translated as "That one may not make it." It did clear the creek but hit the bank and trickled back into the water.

After taking a drop Phil's third shot was long but on the putting surface, and he two-putted for a double bogey. He would end the day in a tie for fifth place.

There have been three big-number meltdowns by contenders at 12 in the final round. They were by Payne Stewart, Jeff Maggert, and Jordan Spieth, with the latter being the most infamous of the three.

Stewart had begun the final round in 1985 four strokes off the lead. He started with six straight pars. He made a birdie at the seventh hole to go one under for the tournament. Bernhard Langer, the ultimate tournament winner, was at three under at that point. Stewart parred his way through to the tenth and then birdied the eleventh to go to two under. Langer remained at three under at that point.

At the twelfth tee Payne was a little pumped up on his tee shot and flew it over the green into the back-right bunker. His sand shot did not want to stop on the green, either. It skipped across the green and into Rae's Creek. Stewart dropped a ball on the tee side of the creek. He hit a nice pitch shot that landed just next to the hole, but it had so much backspin that it spun backward and didn't stop until it was in Rae's Creek.

Stewart dropped another ball. On his next shot he wanted to make sure he didn't duplicate the previous one, so he hit this next ball a little harder. But it was too hard. It landed again in the same back trap in which this nightmare began. Stewart somehow managed to collect himself and very tentatively chopped the ball out of the trap and onto the green. He then two-putted for a 9. He would finish the day in a tie for twenty-fifth place.

In the final round in 2003 the twelfth squashed the green-jacket hopes of Jeff Maggert, the third-round leader. Maggert had battled his way back from a disaster at the third hole, where his fairway bunker shot had ricocheted back into him for a two-stroke penalty and resulted in what would have been for many players a round-killing triple-bogey seven. But Maggert hung tough over the next eight holes. He made a birdie at five, pulled off a couple of tough par saves, and made another birdie on number 10. When he reached the twelfth tee he was just two shots off the lead.

The wind caused him some concern on the tee, and he elected to go with a seven-iron, which proved to be a shade too much club. The shot flew over the green and landed in the front of one of the back bunkers and then ran to the bunker's back lip. The ball then started to roll back down to the center of the bunker. But its journey was halted by a furrow that had been made by a caddie of an earlier player, who had been a little sloppy when he had raked the trap.

Maggert's ball settled into the furrow, which was high up on the bunker's backside, for his second extremely bad break of the day. Maggert had to hit his bunker shot from a kneeling position, and the shot came out too hot and ran across the green and into Rae's Creek. Because there was no place to take a legal drop near the green, Maggert had to take the long walk back across the Hogan Bridge to the drop area on the other side.

By his own admission, Maggert's concentration was nowhere to be found on his next shot, and it too splashed into Rae's Creek. Maggert dropped another ball, and his next shot found the green but was twenty feet from the pin. He somehow managed to regain his composure and drained that putt for a quintuple-bogey eight. Remarkably, Maggert was by some means able to put his misfortunes behind him over the next five holes, as he made three birdies and two pars to finish in fifth place, five strokes out of first.

In the final round in 2016 Jordan Spieth, the defending champion, finished his front nine with his fourth consecutive birdie and now held a commanding five-shot lead. He made the fifty-yard walk from the ninth green to the tenth tee, cheered every step by a throng of patrons. They thought they were acclaiming the twenty-two-year-old's march into history as a back-to-back, wire-to-wire Masters champion. They were wrong.

A little more than a half hour later, Spieth made the short walk from the eleventh green to the twelfth tee to a huge ovation from those situated in the bleachers by the tee and lining the eleventh fairway. Spieth was bruised at this point, having bogeyed the tenth and the eleventh. Two birdies by Danny Willett three groups ahead had cut his lead to just one.

With a nine-iron in his hand, Spieth stuck his tee in the ground, and a hush fell over the patrons. None of them could have known they were about to witness the twelfth's most brutal beat-down ever of the leader in the final round.

At this point what most were expecting was a safe, high-rising shot that dropped softly onto the center of the green. Jordan's swing was not Spieth-esque, however, and the shot drifted to the right. It cleared Rae's Creek but landed on the bank and trickled back down into the water.

From the drop area with help from his caddie, Spieth found a yardage he liked to take his drop, eighty yards out. His swing from that locale was not one of a defending Masters champion but that of a weekend hacker. He dug a trench before striking the ball. It never had a chance of clearing the creek.

Spieth took another drop. His next shot sailed over the green and into the back bunker. His bunker shot settled three feet from the hole, and he was in on his next stroke for a triple-bogey seven. It was just the second triple bogey of his professional career.

After arriving at the twelfth tee with a one-stroke lead, Jordan departed the twelfth green one stroke behind Willett, the eventual winner. Jordan would go on to finish in a tie for second place, three strokes back.

Numerous players are haunted by the fact that one miscue at the twelfth cost them a shot at the Masters title, but one has to feel extra pain for Jodie Mudd and Bobby Mitchell, as it was 12's cumulative effect that wrecked their chances.

Larry Mize would never have had the opportunity to pull off his miracle chip at 11 in 1987 if Mudd could have gotten a handle on the twelfth. Mudd finished in a three-way tie for second at two under par, one stroke out of a three-way playoff with Norman, Ballesteros, and Mize. He was four over at 12 for the four rounds with a lone par, two bogeys, and a double-bogey.

In 1972 Mitchell finished in second place with a one-over-par 289, three shots behind Jack Nicklaus. His scores at the twelfth during the four rounds were 5–5–5–4, seven over par.

Bernhard Langer, however, most likely began to think about a green jacket when he played the twelfth. Langer bested Stewart's score by seven strokes, when he dropped a twelve-foot birdie putt to get to four under. His winning score would be six under.

Only two players have put their tee shots in the water at 12 in the final round and won the tournament. They are Seve Ballesteros in 1980 and Sandy Lyle in 1988.

Ballesteros, at age twenty-three, appeared to be cruising to victory. He had an eight-stroke lead until he decided to fire at the pin at 12. His shot hit the bank on the front right side and rolled back into the water. He made a double-bogey five and then bogeyed 13 while several of his pursuers were making birdies. Ballesteros's lead slipped to just three strokes before he was able to get back on track and take a four-stroke victory.

Lyle had a two-stroke lead when he teed it up at 12. Although he admitted that he had been worrying about the twelfth during his front-nine play, he threw caution to the wind and fired straight at the pin. His ball, like Ballesteros's, struck the bank on the front right side and rolled back into the water. Lyle made a double-bogey five to drop into a tie for first. Lyle would save the day with a remarkable birdie at the eighteenth hole to win by one stroke.

Sometimes, something good does happen at the twelfth hole. Ben Crenshaw faded a six-iron to within twelve feet in the final round in 1984 and then rolled in the putt for a birdie that helped him claim his first green jacket.

In 1997, in the first round, Tiger Woods might have still been getting used to that swing adjustment he made at the tenth tee. He was a little left and long with his tee shot. He was off the green by about ten feet and had a difficult downhill chip. Woods deftly played the perfect chip, and the ball rolled into the hole. This shot added additional fuel to his remarkable turnaround that would see him go from a 40 on the front nine to a 30 on the backside and start him on the course to his runaway victory.

Patrick Reed used the twelfth in 2018 to help stave off Sunday charges by Rickie Fowler and Jordan Spieth. Leading by three at the start of the round, Reed had taken a hit at the eleventh when he missed the fairway with his tee shot and ended up with a bogey. His tee shot at 12 was just a little long, a few inches into the green's back fringe. He faced a tough downhill, sidehill twenty-five-footer that he stroked perfectly for a birdie. Although there would be some anxious moments at the thirteenth, Reed saved par there and then birdied the fourteenth. He held on from that point to win by one over Fowler and two over Spieth.

And, of course, in the miracle category, there is Fred Couples's remarkable tee shot in the final round in 1992. The usually super-relaxed Couples would admit later that he had never been so nervous before a shot in his life.

Couples had a three-stroke lead, but he knew the twelfth was famous for devouring leads. He knew what he was supposed to do: aim for the center of the green and not at that wicked right-side pin placement. But in golf, as in life, knowing what to do and actually doing it are two separate issues. Couples fired at the flag. In an interview later that day, he would say, "I didn't want to aim at the pin, but there was this thing in my brain that shoved the ball over there."

The shot came up just short and landed halfway up the bank, eight feet from the front of the green. Like hundreds of similar shots played on the hole during the previous Masters, the ball began its roll backward down the closely shaved slope toward a watery grave. But unlike all the other balls that had made this journey, this ball stopped just short of the water. There was nothing to stop it, but it stopped anyway. Veteran members of the media and seasoned Masters gallery members could not recall a shot ever landing in that area that did not end up in the creek.

When Couples reached his ball, he stood over it for a risky moment, full of wonder and astonishment. Then he chipped up to within a foot of the cup for a gimme par.

Nonbelievers contend that the ball must have settled in the pitch mark from the ball of a previous player. But true believers know that they could have stopped the tournament and named Couples the winner because there could have been no clearer evidence from above that he was the chosen one that Sunday. He went on to win the tournament by two strokes.

Two other players besides William Hyndman III have had the good fortune to record holes in one at 12. They are Claude Harmon in 1947 and Curtis Strange in 1988.

No history of this hole would be complete without an account of the most infamous score ever recorded at it: Tom Weiskopf's 13 in the opening round of the 1980 tournament.

When Weiskopf reached 12, he had a lackluster round of three over par going, but with 13 and 15 just ahead, he still had a chance to turn in a respectable score. Having not put a ball in Rae's Creek at the twelfth in the last twelve Masters, he had no reason to be overly concerned. The conditions were excellent, since no wind was present, and the pin was in its best scoring location on the left side.

Weiskopf hit an eight-iron, and it flew to the front fringe, where it hit, took a skip-hop forward toward the pin, and then spun rapidly backward, through the fringe and down the bank and into the water.

Weiskopf took his drop about sixty yards from the hole and hit a half wedge. The result was almost an exact copy of the first shot, as it, too, landed in the fringe, hopped forward, and spun back down the bank and into the water.

His situation went from bad to worse with his next drop, as his ball rolled into a barren spot. From that tight lie, he lined his shot dead into the creek.

Weiskopf dropped again, and this time he got a good lie, but he hit this shot dead into the water again. He dropped another ball, and there was another splash.

He dropped his sixth ball—with penalty strokes, he was now hitting his eleventh shot—and this ball finally carried the creek and ran to the back fringe of the green. He got down in two from that spot to become coholder of the record for the highest score ever recorded in the Masters: 13. Tommy Nakajima, of Japan, esablished that mark in 1978. His trials and tribulations in making his 13 will be covered in the next chapter. Despite a well-earned reputation of having an explosive temper, Weiskopf kept his composure and played the remaining six holes at even par. His score for the round was 85.

Needless to say, he knew he was not going to make the cut, but to his credit he showed up for the second round. In that second round Weiskopf's tee shot at 12 carried the creek but hit the bank and bounced back into the water. This time he chose to stay as far away from the water as possible and hit from the tee. His next effort landed in the creek. He teed up another ball, and this one sailed to the middle of the green, and he two-putted for a seven. He shot a 79 for the round and finished with a two-day total of twenty over par, with fourteen of those over-par strokes occurring at 12.

#13
Azalea

Hole No. 13

PAR FIVE—510 YARDS	AZALEA

It is a rare Masters when the thirteenth hole, the last leg of Amen Corner, is not the stage for some dramatic turn of events during the tournament. This hole has changed very little since it was first constructed. It was the first hole that Bobby Jones and Alister MacKenzie found on their initial tour of the property. MacKenzie thought it was the most natural golf hole he had ever come across; all that it needed was to add a tee and a green.

The hole doglegs to the left, and it has the shape of a boomerang. Its original distance was listed at 480 yards, and it stayed in that range, give or take 5 yards, until 2002, because the club's property line was directly behind it. As part of the 2002 changes, Augusta National purchased a small section of land behind the tee from the neighboring Augusta Country Club. This allowed the hole's distance to be increased by another 30 yards and for the tee box to be widened. These changes did not affect the character of the hole. It still remains a par five that is very reachable in two shots.

The thirteenth hole brings out the primal "go for it" instinct in the most cautious players and the players who should be thinking cautiously because of their position on the leaderboard. It is a hole on which a player can easily make a three or a six.

The closer one plays his tee shot to the lower left side of the fairway, the better his position will be to attack the green. While this route offers the most reward, it also provides the most risk. About 50 yards before the dogleg, there is a creek that will be in play on both the player's drive and his approach shot. It is a tributary to Rae's Creek, and it curls its path all the way down the left side of the fairway until just before the green. It then turns right and runs in front of the green, curls back to the left, and continues up the right side. To the left of the creek is a heavily wooded area, which parallels the fairway all the way to the green.

Near the dogleg the fairway begins to rise and gradually banks to the left toward the green. It is very rolling and undulating, which produces lies of virtually all descriptions, except in the area on the lower left side near the creek. This small strip of fairway provides a level lie, and it is the desired destination for a player's tee shot.

The farther to the right a tee shot wanders, the more distance that is added to the second shot and the more difficult the lie will become. The right side of the fairway is bordered by a stand of pine trees that can cause a great deal of havoc if a tee shot strays into them.

The green at the thirteenth is very large, as it is thirty-eight yards wide and about that same distance deep. It runs upward from front to back and slopes from left to right with a ridge running across its rear section. There is one bunker on the left side and three bunkers behind the green. The rear bunkers often come into play because this green can be one of the firmest on the course. When players attempt to reach the green in two, their shots often come in hot and hit the firm surface and run into these back bunkers.

The thirteenth has always ranked as one of Augusta National's easiest holes, and it gives up more than its share of eagles and birdies. But it has always had the penchant to ambush a front-runner from the creek and woods on the left side, or from a difficult lie in the fairway, or from the creek and bunkers at the green.

Paul Runyan was the first contender to be ambushed at the hole as he was picked off by trouble on the left side. In the final round of the first Masters in 1934, Runyan drove his tee shot into the woods on that side and ended up with a double-bogey seven. He finished the day two strokes behind the winner, Horton Smith. It turned out, in addition to helping Smith's cause by going in the woods at this hole, Runyan also helped Smith just as much by lending him a wood. Prior to the tournament, Runyan had lent Smith a driver.

Smith used it in all four rounds, and he claimed he had never driven the ball better.

In the final round in 1950 Jim Ferrier hooked his drive into the woods on the left side and started a slide that would result in his losing a five-stroke lead. He would finish in second place, two strokes behind Jimmy Demaret. Demaret's play at the thirteenth hole that year won him the tournament. He made birdie in the first round, eagle in the second and third rounds, and another birdie in the fourth round, which gave him a total of six under par on the hole for the week. His winning score for the tournament was 283, five under par.

The thirteenth was feast and famine for Fred Couples in 1998. In the third round Couples's drive hugged the left side and reached the ideal approach position on the lower left side of the fairway. He then hit a perfect five-iron to within three feet of the hole for an easy eagle. In the final round he pulled his drive so far left that it ended up on a service road deep in the woods. Couples somehow hit a lofted iron through the canopy of the trees and back into the fairway. He then pushed his next shot to the right and landed in the creek. Couples ended up with a double-bogey seven on the hole and would finish the day in second place, one stroke out of a playoff.

The shots that followed Ernie Els's errant tee shot to the left in the final round of the 2002 Masters were almost too painful to watch. Els stood the best chance of any of the other contenders in putting any pressure on Tiger Woods on the back nine. Els had made a tough par-saving putt at 12, and Woods had just bogeyed the eleventh to move Els within three strokes of the lead.

Els pulled his tee shot just over the creek into a grassy area on the edge of the tree line. Instead of simply punching his ball back into the fairway, Els elected to play a shot that would get him as far up the fairway as possible. This route was on a line directly over the creek. His shot struck one of the low-hanging branches and was knocked down into the creek.

Els was able to take his drop in an area that gave him a shot at the green from 190 yards. This shot landed high on the far bank of the creek, but fell back into the water. Els took another drop and pitched onto the green, and the ball finished about 20 feet above the hole. He then two-putted for an eight that ended any chance he might have had.

Attempting to avoid the creek and the woods on the left can often cause a player to block his shot to the right. This makes his second shot some 50 to 75 yards longer, and it will have to be played from a lie that is rarely favorable. In this situation the player is usually forced to lay up with his third shot. He will use a short iron to advance the ball down the fairway and hope to set up a birdie with an accurate pitch shot.

Between the ideal drive to the lower left side of the fairway and the one that strays too far to the right is that area where a player must make the decision whether to go for the green in two or play it safe and lay up. He will have to consider a number of factors: his standing on the leaderboard, how well he has been swinging, the lie of his ball, and wind conditions.

The most famous "go for it" decision was made here by Billy Joe Patton in the last round of that very memorable 1954 Masters. The charge he had started with his hole in one at the sixth hole had him in position to win it all. The huge gallery following Patton was sure that they were watching history in the making. An amateur was going to win the Masters. Before leaving Morganton, North Carolina, Patton had purchased a white sport jacket to wear at the awards ceremony in case he won low amateur. It was now looking as if there was a strong possibility a green jacket was going to be provided for him.

During the night Patton's followers had been reinforced by a throng of North Carolinians who had driven down to root on their native son in the final round. They must have been descendants of Jeb Stuart's favorite unit, the First North Carolina Calvary, because piercing rebel yells were sweeping over the fairways as Patton made his charge. When Patton teed off at the thirteenth, he was in a virtual dead heat with Sam Snead and Ben Hogan for the top spot. Snead was playing a couple of holes ahead of him, and Hogan was playing a couple of holes behind him. Patton's drive on 13 was not stellar, but it wasn't that bad, either. He was in no-man's-land. Before Patton reached his tee shot, his North Carolina faithful were already yelling, "Go! Go!" There was most likely never any thought in Patton's mind about laying up. Before the tournament he had said it would be his strategy to fire at all seventy-two pins, which he had done to this point. Throughout the tournament, before each bold shot Patton took, he liked to tell the gallery that he had not gotten this far by playing it safe.

Because of the location of his ball in no-man's-land and his position high atop the leaderboard, many observers thought even Patton would back off and lay up instead of taking such a huge risk with so much golf left to play. By laying up, at best he would still have a chance at a birdie, and at worst he would make par.

Of course, a layup shot wasn't in Patton's bag, at least not that day, and when he pulled a wood out of his bag, the crowd went wild. Their enthusiastic cheers, however, would turn to moans in just a few moments. Patton wasted no time in moving into the shot. His swing was as lighting fast as ever and maybe even a hair faster. The shot didn't come off the clubface with the zip everyone knew it would need to get to the green, and his ball fell into the creek. When Patton was walking toward the creek, there were some indications from the gallery that his ball was playable. He soon was bounding down the creek bank to take a look. After examining his ball's lie, he scurried back up the bank and began to take his shoes off, and a huge roar went up from the gallery. This was the roar that Hogan mistook as meaning that Patton had made another birdie or eagle. In his bare feet Patton then went back down in the creek to play the shot. Once he got over the ball, the risk-management department in his brain—although a shot late—kicked in. He realized that the shot was just too risky, even for Billy Joe Patton. He decided to take a penalty stroke and dropped the ball behind the creek.

Patton did not take the time to put his golf shoes back on and played his chip shot over the creek barefooted. He hit the shot poorly, and it barely cleared the bank on the other side of the creek. It took him three more shots to get down for a disastrous double-bogey seven.

The huge gallery was in a state of shock. Earlier, the throng had been moving down the fairway charged with unbridled enthusiasm, but now they were moving in a funeral march—in near silence. Patton seemed less bothered by the turn of events than anybody else in the crowd. Seeing the depressed state of his followers, he called out to his deflated flock as he walked to the fourteenth tee, "Come on, let's smile again!"

Patton recharged his supporters with a birdie at the fourteenth that partially offset his disaster at 13. He gambled once more at the par-five fifteenth and broke his followers' hearts again. Patton's attempt to reach that green in two came up short. His ball splashed into the pond in front of the green, and he made bogey. Patton parred in from there, and when the dust had settled, he was in second place, one stroke short of Hogan and Snead. Those two would play it off the next day for a green jacket that was almost Patton's.

In his postround comments, Patton maintained that he had no regrets about going for the green at 13. He said playing boldly is what had gotten him into contention in the tournament. Bobby Jones awarded Patton with a medal for being low amateur and said, "If anyone ever created a stir in golf, he did. He has no cause for regret because he finished one stroke behind the two greatest golfers in the world."

Two days following the Hogan-Snead playoff, Patton played his round with President Eisenhower. Seven months later, Sam Ervin was elected to the U.S. Senate from North Carolina. Eisenhower asked Ervin during their first meeting what city he was from. When

Ervin answered, "Morganton," Eisenhower exclaimed, "Morganton! That's Billy Joe Patton's hometown."

Patton would remain an amateur throughout his playing career and would be a fixture at the Masters for the next twelve years. He would later become a member of the club.

In that Snead-Hogan eighteen-hole playoff, the thirteenth was again center stage for some high drama. The match was seesawing back and forth when they reached the thirteenth hole. Snead had just bogeyed the twelfth to relinquish the lead he had taken with his chip-in birdie at the tenth.

Hogan's drive at the thirteenth drifted to the right and finished in no-man's-land. Snead got off a good drive that placed him in a position to go for it. Hogan was away, but before he decided whether he was going to go for it, he opted to walk over to Snead's ball and see what kind of lie he had. As he was inspecting the position of the ball, Snead told him what he was going to do. He said, "Ben, I am going for it!"

Hogan walked back to his ball and made the decision to lay up and count on a good third shot to put him in birdie position. After Hogan laid up, Snead lashed a three-wood to within twenty-five feet of the pin. Hogan hit a weak pitch to the green and two-putted for par. Snead two-putted for birdie and never relinquished the lead from that point.

Prior to Billy Joe Patton, the biggest stories about the thirteenth had centered around the play of Ralph Guldahl. In the final round in 1937 Guldahl's play at the twelfth and the thirteenth cost him the tournament.

At the twelfth tee Guldahl had a four-stroke lead over Byron Nelson. Instead of playing for the center of that green, he had fired at the right-side pin placement and had come up just a few feet short. His ball rolled back into Rae's Creek, and he made a double bogey.

At the thirteenth tee Guldahl appeared to have put his blunder at the twelfth behind him. He hit an excellent drive down the left side, which left him a four-iron's distance from the green. Guldahl elected to go with a three-iron just to be safe, but he did not get all of the shot. The ball landed in the creek, and he ended up with a bogey.

Nelson was playing several groups behind Guldahl. He drained a twenty-five-footer for birdie at the twelfth to cut Guldahl's lead to just one. At the thirteenth Nelson cleared the creek with his second shot, and his ball was sitting just a few feet off the green. From there Nelson chipped in for eagle to go to two ahead. He would maintain that margin the rest of the way home to claim the first of his two Masters titles.

Guldahl got a chance to redeem himself in the 1939 Masters. Because rain had canceled Saturday's third round, the players had to play the third and fourth rounds on Sunday. Guldahl, who had won two consecutive United States Opens after his collapse in the 1937 Masters, received word before he teed off at the thirteenth on his final eighteen that Sam Snead was in the clubhouse with a score of eight under par. Guldahl was at seven under.

Guldahl pushed his drive out to the right, and he had a nasty sidehill lie, to boot. Two years before, he had had a big drive and good lie and blew his chances with a poor second shot. This time he was forty yards farther back and had a bad lie from which to play the shot. Guldahl decided to take the big gamble and try to reach the green in two. He pulled out his three-wood and hit an absolutely marvelous shot. It easily carried the creek, landed on the green, and headed straight for the hole. It pulled up six inches away from the cup for an easy tap-in eagle. His bold gamble propelled him to a one-stroke victory.

To a deafening roar from the patrons, Phil Mickelson emerged from the pines on the right side of the fairway in the final round in 2010, holding his six-iron high in the air like it was a scepter. He had just hit what many believe was the shot of his career.

Mickelson, leading by one at that point, had been struggling with his driver for most of the day. Here at 13, his driver had really put him in a bad way, as it had strayed into the pines on the right side of the fairway. His ball was resting on pine straw between two of the pines, and he had a window-size opening through which to thread his next shot.

Bones Mackay, his caddie, wanted Phil to just pitch out. Phil said no. His thinking was his next effort would have to go through the same opening if it was a pitch or a full shot, and he was going with the latter.

Phil dug in the best he could on the pine straw and let it fly, splitting the 4-foot opening as it blasted off for its target 207 yards away. It came to rest just 4 feet below the hole.

If Phil made the short putt, it would easily have been the most spectacular eagle ever made at 13, but it wasn't to be. He settled for birdie and walked off the green with a two-shot lead. He would go on to win his third green jacket by three shots.

Two players have won the Masters thanks to some terrific luck with their attempts to reach the thirteenth in two. In 1982 Craig Stadler's wheels were already wobbling after a double bogey at the twelfth, which gave back two strokes of his six-stroke lead. His attempt to reach the thirteenth green in two was a mishit and landed on the fairway side of the creek. It ran down through the creek bed and somehow managed to crawl up almost to the top of the bank on the green side. Stadler was able to chip his third shot off the bank and then got down in two putts for a par. This break would be huge at the end of the day for Stadler. If his ball had not escaped the creek, it is unlikely that he could have saved par. Any additional strokes would have kept him from being in a tie at the end of the day with Dan Pohl, and he would not have had an opportunity to win the tournament in a playoff.

In the third round in 1985 Bernhard Langer had a similar experience at the thirteenth, but with a better result. Langer attempted to get home in two with a fairway wood from a sidehill lie from the right portion of the fairway. Langer's shot never had a chance of clearing the creek on the fly. His ball, like Stadler's, landed on the fairway side of the creek, but Langer's took a big hop and bounced over it, clearing the bank on the other side and rolling onto the green 18 feet from the hole. Langer then really cashed in on his good fortune and rolled in the putt for an eagle.

The next day in the final round, Curtis Strange appeared poised to write the final chapter in the story of the most remarkable turn-around in Masters history. Strange had overcome his horrendous opening round of 80. After rolling in a 20-foot birdie putt at the twelfth, he now had a three-stroke lead over his closest competitor, who was Langer.

At the thirteenth, Strange cranked out a pretty solid drive and had about 205 yards left to the hole, but he was dealt a sidehill lie. The year before, Ben Crenshaw had been in the same position. He had also birdied the twelfth to take a three-stroke lead and had hit a solid drive at 13 with a reasonable lie. Crenshaw decided against taking any unnecessary risks, and he laid up short of the creek with his second shot. He pitched onto the green and two-putted for par. Crenshaw would have one anxious moment at the fourteenth hole but would overcome it and ultimately win by two strokes.

Strange would have been well advised to follow Crenshaw's example. With a three-stroke lead and a difficult lie, the risk certainly outweighed the reward. Strange mulled it over and decided to go for the green. He then pulled out his four-metal. In a few seconds this decision would place Strange in the "Hall of Fame of Questionable Decisions" and start the unraveling of his green-jacket hopes. He did not connect solidly with the ball, and it fell short of the creek on the fairway side. Strange did not have either Stadler's or Langer's luck but did have Billy Joe Patton's. His ball ran down into the creek and stopped just inside the water line on the green side of the creek. Like Patton, Strange jumped down the bank to take a look at his ball's situation and then scrambled back out and yanked his rain suit out of his bag. He was going to play it out of the water.

After putting on the rain suit, Strange returned to his ball, but unlike Patton he did not reconsider his decision. He may have thought about it, though, because he stood over the shot for a long time. Finally, he swung, and his ball flew off to the right in a spray of water and muck. It almost cleared the bank, but then it fell back and rolled down toward the water. Thankfully for Strange, it stopped short of the water's edge. His next shot made it safely onto the green, and he two-putted for a bogey, but the damage had been done. Strange had opened the door for Langer, who was playing in the pairing directly in front of him and had birdied the thirteenth just minutes before. Strange would give Langer the lead on the par-five fifteenth, when he tried to reach that green in two. He came up short again and found the pond in front of that green, and made another bogey. Langer had birdied the hole and that two-shot swing put him in the lead for good.

Two Masters winners who fared better after final-round journeys into the creek are Claude Harmon and Tom Watson. In 1948 Harmon had a five-shot lead, but the back nine was giving him a pressure test. On the twelfth his tee shot had been so bad it didn't even make the creek. Harmon proceeded to line his next shot over the green, and it almost reached the thirteenth tee. He made a great pitch back onto the green and one-putted, being very fortunate to escape with a bogey.

At the thirteenth, Harmon's second shot found the creek. Earlier in the week at the fifteenth, Harmon had to take off his shoes and wade into that pond to play his ball, which was plugged in the muck at the water's edge. He blasted that one onto the green and saved his par. Harmon waded into the creek at the thirteenth, but this time he kept his shoes on. The results were the same, however. He splashed the ball up onto the green and two-putted for par. Harmon coasted home from that point to win by five strokes, which set a record at the time for the largest margin of victory in the tournament.

Tom Watson had a three-stroke lead over Jack Nicklaus in the final round in 1981. Nicklaus was in the pairing directly ahead of Watson. From the fairway Watson watched Nicklaus roll in a birdie putt at the thirteenth to cut his lead to two strokes. Watson then went for the green in two, but the creek swallowed up the shot. Watson did not go in after it. He elected to take a penalty stroke and take a drop behind the creek. Watson played a deft wedge shot to within five feet of the hole. He then calmly rolled in the putt to save his par and keep his lead at two strokes. Although there would be some more drama before the day concluded, Watson would ultimately win the tournament by two strokes.

Raymond Floyd got over the creek in a very unusual way in the first round in 1974. Floyd was experiencing a tough time on the hole. He was lying three off to the right of the green between the creek and the fourteenth tee. His ball was directly in line with the bridge the players use to walk from the thirteenth green to the fourteenth tee. Floyd elected to putt his ball across the bridge and onto the green. Amazingly, he almost holed it. The ball stopped just inches from the cup to give him an easy tap-in par.

In 1988 Masters officials decided to steepen the banks of the creek and make the entire hazard slightly wider. These changes raised the water level and made playing a shot out of the creek almost impossible. Eight years later, Masters officials decided they had had it right the first time and had the creek restored to its original state before the 1996 tournament.

Gary Player is the only Masters winner ever to survive a major disaster in the final round at the thirteenth. Player's happened in the 1961 Masters. He had started the day in first place, four strokes ahead of Arnold Palmer. When he reached the thirteenth tee, his lead had been reduced to three. Player drove his tee shot into the pines on the right side. He then pulled his second shot hard to the left, and the ball ran across the fairway into the creek. Player took a drop, and his next shot landed just off the green, thirty-five feet from the hole. He three-putted from there for a double-bogey seven. He continued to slide backward and was soon trailing Palmer by one stroke.

The only thing that saved Player was that Palmer experienced a similar meltdown when he double bogeyed the eighteenth hole to give Player the win by one shot.

After a 75 in the third round of the 2012 Masters, Sergio García told reporters he wasn't good enough to win a major, that he didn't have "the thing" he needs to win one, that he had reached a point in his career when he needed to play for "second or third place" in the game's four biggest tournaments.

Given his history, it was easy to understand why García had reached that conclusion. Beginning with his second major appearance, the 1999 PGA, which he lost in a duel with Tiger Woods by one stroke, Sergio had finished runner-up in a major four times. In the 2007 British Open his putt that would have won the tournament rimmed out from ten feet. He would go on to lose a playoff to Padraig Harrington. In the 2008 PGA Championship he had the lead down the stretch only to finish in a tie for second after going in the water at the sixteenth hole.

On the final day of the 2017 Masters, Sergio was the co-leader with Justin Rose when the fourth round began. When he walked off the fifth hole, Sergio had a two-stroke lead, but soon it began to look like he was going to have another painful experience to add to his record in majors. When he reached the thirteenth tee, he was three strokes behind Rose.

Rose's tee shot at 13 found the fairway and was close enough to easily reach the green in two. Sergio, faced with a now-or-never moment, made a bold attempt to cut his tee shot over the trees at the corner of the dogleg. His shot lacked a yard or two of carry and tangled with the top of a tall pine, dropping down into an azalea bush a few yards from the creek.

This should have been the point where Sergio's chances were declared legally dead, but his fortunes in major championships were about to undergo a major turnaround.

Sergio took an unplayable lie and pitched back into the fairway. Rose's second shot was just a little long and off the back of the green. From ninety-four yards, Sergio's fourth shot was stellar and checked up four feet from the hole. Rose's third left him with a five-foot birdie that he missed. He tapped in for a par. Sergio rolled in his par putt, and he walked off the green, having escaped the results of his tee shot and still with an outside chance.

Sergio would make the most of that outside chance; an eagle at 15 would propel him into a playoff with Rose that he would win on the first extra hole to claim the major title he once thought was out of reach.

As Sam Snead and Tony Jacklin found out, clearing the creek in two is no guarantee that one has avoided disaster. In the first round in 1955 Snead, the reigning champion, was off to a good start in defense of his title. He was two under through 12 and was in good position after his drive at 13 to get home in two.

He had a slight breeze in his face, but he decided that the risk was worth the reward, so he pulled out his three-wood and let it rip. The shot cleared the creek, but Snead had pulled it just a shade, and it missed the green. His ball slammed into the rear wall of a newly remodeled sand trap just off the left side of the green.

The shot buried itself in the sand, and Snead had to flick away a little sand with his fingers in order to make a positive identification of the ball. He then had to stand outside the bunker to play the shot with his feet approximately a foot or so above the ball. His first attempt at extraction succeeded only in driving the ball deeper into the sand. His next swing struck the top of the ball. This time it did not move at all. The force of the blow sliced open the cover of the ball, exposing its core. Snead brought the wounded condition of his ball to the attention of officials, and it was ruled unplayable. He was allowed to replace it without penalty. His third attempt did succeed in moving the ball, but it did not escape the bunker. It trickled off the wall down into the center of the trap. From that location, Snead was able to play a normal bunker shot. He got the ball onto the putting surface and two-putted for an eight. Snead would finish the tournament in third place, eight strokes off the lead.

It had to be pretty disheartening to travel four thousand miles to play in a major championship and see one's hopes go up in smoke on the first day, but that is what happened to England's Tony Jacklin at the thirteenth hole in the first round in 1974. He had already experienced a rough front nine due to two double bogeys and was trying to stop the bleeding with a birdie or an eagle at 13. His second shot cleared the creek, but then his misfortunes continued as his ball bounded across the green into one of the back bunkers. His explosion shot from the bunker ran back across the green into the creek. He dropped behind the creek and then chili-dipped his next shot back into the creek. Jacklin's next shot finally reached the putting surface, and he two-putted for a nine. He finished the day with an 81. In the second round the next day, Jacklin birdied the thirteenth and shot 71, but the damage inflicted by the hole on the day before was too great, and he failed to make the cut.

Tommy Nakajima set the Masters record, later tied by Tom Weiskopf and Sergio García, for highest score on a hole with a 13 in the second round in 1978. Nakajima, one of the top players on the Japanese tour, was playing in his first Masters. He had been roughed up by the course pretty good in the first round when he posted an eight-over-par 80. In the second round he appeared to be on the way to a respectable score and had an outside chance of making the cut.

Nakajima was one over par when he reached the thirteenth. He drove his tee shot into the woods on the left side (1). He had an unplayable lie and had to take a drop (2). He then laid up some ninety yards from the creek (3). He then dumped his wedge shot into the creek (4). He attempted to play his ball out of the creek, but the shot did not clear the bank (5). The ball rolled back down the bank and hit his shoe—a two-shot penalty (6 and 7). Nakajima swung again, and again the ball failed to clear the bank and rolled back toward him (8). Nakajima was able to get out of the way this time, but out of frustration, he swung his club in disgust. Ordinarily taking a practice swing or a swing in disgust is not a problem, but Nakajima was in a hazard, and his swing struck the ground, which was another two-stroke penalty (9 and 10). His next attempt cleared the bank and reached the green (11). Nakajima then two-putted for an unwanted place in the Masters record book (12 and 13).

Jeff Maggert recorded the best score ever at the thirteenth in the final round in 1994. Maggert holed a 225-yard second shot for the only double eagle ever made at the thirteenth. It was the third double eagle in Masters history. Maggert, who finished in fiftieth place that year, was one of the early starters that day, so few spectators were present to witness the shot.

The green at the thirteenth produces its share of drama. Those players who reach the green in two have their work cut out for them to make eagle, because this putting surface has more than its share of subtle breaks.

Bobby Jones almost made some big noise at this hole in the opening round of the first Masters in 1934. His second shot with a three-wood was a throwback to his glory days, and it came to rest just four feet from the hole. He missed the short putt, however, and had to settle for a tap-in birdie.

The amateur pairing of Billy Joe Patton and Ken Venturi did make some big noise at the thirteenth green in the first round in 1956 when they both made eagle putts. Venturi brought in a three-wood from no-man's-land to just about twenty feet to set up his three. Patton was about forty yards closer to the green than Venturi was, and he set up his eagle when his four-iron shot stopped fourteen feet from the flag.

Paired together in the final round in 1993, Bernhard Langer and Chip Beck had a shoot-out on the thirteenth green. Langer was in the lead, and Beck was two strokes behind. Both players elected to go for the green in two. Beck put his shot twenty-three feet from the flag, and Langer put his shot inside Beck's by three feet, practically on the same line to the hole. Beck's eagle putt failed to drop, but Langer's went right into the heart to put him up by three. Langer would ultimately win the tournament with a four-stroke margin.

The most difficult putt ever made at the thirteenth would have to be Cary Middlecoff's in the second round of the 1955 Masters.

Middlecoff reached the green in two, but his ball rolled to the back-right edge. The hole was cut eighty feet away on the left-hand side of the green. Middlecoff, one of the most deliberate players of that day, studied the putt from every conceivable angle before he stroked it. The ball took seven seconds to get to the hole and had only one or two revolutions left in it when it dropped in the cup for eagle. The putt would stand as the longest one ever made at the Masters until Nick Faldo made his one-hundred-footer at the second hole in 1989.

The putt propelled Middlecoff to a round of 65 and a four-stroke lead at the thirty-six-hole mark. He would stay in command of the tournament for the remaining two rounds and ultimately win by seven strokes, breaking the previous record for winning margin of five, which was coheld by Claude Harmon (1948) and Ben Hogan (1953).

The thirteenth hole has cost many a player their chance to have or to add to their collection of green jackets, but the strangest of these casualties has to be amateur Frank Stranahan. In 1947 Stranahan had shot closing rounds of 70 and 68 and finished tied for second place with Byron Nelson, two strokes behind winner Jimmy Demaret.

Needless to say, Stranahan had to be enthusiastic about his chances in 1948, and he arrived in Augusta a week before the tournament to begin practice. He was playing a practice round alone and was on the thirteenth when he was observed by the course superintendent ignoring a Cliff Roberts rule that prohibited players during a practice round from playing more than one ball. Stranahan knew the rule but thought it applied only to twosomes, threesomes, and foursomes, and not to someone playing alone. When he was confronted by the superintendent, he became agitated, and a first-class verbal brouhaha ensued, replete with expletives. As soon as Cliff Roberts was made aware of the incident, Stranahan's invitation to participate in the Masters that year was withdrawn.

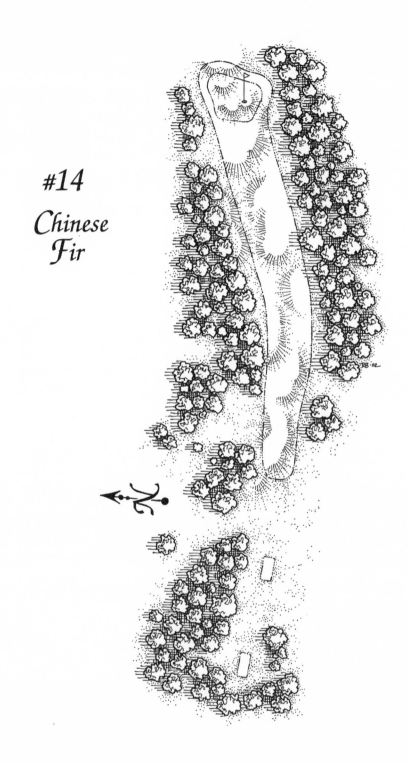

#14

*Chinese
Fir*

Hole No. 14

PAR FOUR—440 YARDS	CHINESE FIR

The fourteenth hole is another dogleg-left par four and the only hole on the course without a bunker. As part of the 2002 changes it was lengthened for the first time from its original distance of 405 yards to 440.

The fairway slopes from left to right, so players must guard against having their drives slip out of the fairway into the rough and the pines on the right side. The ideal play off the tee is a right-to-left draw around the dogleg. This usually leaves the player with a short-iron second shot to the largest green on the course. Although the largest, the green requires a very exacting approach. The green slopes significantly from right to left and features a very dramatic ridge running across it about one-third of the way on.

The experience of Tom Weiskopf in the third round in 1977 is a prime example of just how damaging not making it over the ridge on the green with one's approach can be. Weiskopf was battling for the lead when he reached the fourteenth hole. His approach shot made it only to the front of the green, and he was left with a 75-foot approach putt up over the steep ridge. He did not give the putt enough gas, and it failed to make it over the ridge. The ball trickled back toward the front of the green, and when it had stopped rolling, Weiskopf was left with a 60-foot putt for his par. His fourth stroke was a definite improvement over his third but still left him with a 12-foot putt for bogey. He put that effort 3 feet past the hole and then managed to drop that ultra-quick knee-knocker for a double bogey, which pushed him well down the leaderboard for the rest of the tournament.

During the third round in 1982 Dan Pohl struck the most famous approach shot to the fourteenth hole to that point. Pohl was making his first appearance in the tournament. He had gotten off to a very slow start on the tour that year and had won hardly any money at all. His first two rounds of the Masters indicated that his slow year was going to continue. He had started the tournament with a bogey at the first hole, and after thirty-six holes he was five over par. Pohl cut it down to four over after the front nine in the third round, and then it began to look as if it would be anything but a moving day for him. He bogeyed the tenth and the twelfth holes. Pohl, who was one of the longest hitters on the tour, unleashed a mammoth drive at the thirteenth and easily reached the green in two. He then rolled in a 15-footer for eagle to start an amazing run. At the fourteenth he cranked out another big drive and had 118 yards left to the hole. He hit a pitching wedge right at the flag. It carried just a few feet beyond the flag, and then it spun back right into the hole for two. It was the first time in Masters history back-to-back eagles had ever been made.

Going four under par over two holes shot Pohl from deep down in the pack up onto the leaderboard. But he was not finished yet. He made a tap-in birdie at the fifteenth hole and drilled in a 15-foot birdie putt at the sixteenth hole to complete his phenomenal run. Pohl finished his round with pars at 17 and 18 to end the day with a five-under-par 67.

Inasmuch as the fourteenth had been where Pohl had made his best swing in his round on Saturday, it was where he made his worst swing in the final round. He had crushed another big drive and had only 95 yards left to the flag. The day before, he had hit the perfect wedge to this hole, but twenty-four hours later his wedge shot was anything but perfect. The shot came up short of the green, and he took three more strokes to get down to post his only bogey of the day. Pohl's lone bogey would loom very large at the end of regulation play, because it put him into the playoff with Craig Stadler that he lost.

In 2009 Dustin Johnson was also making his Masters debut, and he matched Pohl's feat in the final round. Until he reached the thirteenth hole, he was in the throes of a dreadful round at six over. He dropped an eagle put there and then holed his 171-yard approach from the right rough at 14 for another. Johnson would finish the day in thirtieth place.

In the third round of his 2010 victory, Phil Mickelson matched the feats of Pohl and Dustin Johnson. Through twelve holes he was five shots off the lead. At thirteen he put his second shot 8 feet from the hole and made three. At fourteen he holed a wedge from 114 yards.

Phil almost made it three in a row at the par-five fifteenth. His third shot from 87 yards ended up a foot from the hole for a tap-in birdie that put him in the lead.

In the final round of the 1963 Masters, twenty-three-year-old Jack Nicklaus was leading the tournament by one stroke. He was about to tee off at the twelfth hole when a huge roar went up from the gallery at the fourteenth green. The young Nicklaus must have been a little rattled by the outburst because he hit a poor seven-iron tee shot that landed in the bunker in front of the twelfth green. His next shot from the sand flew across the green into the back fringe. Nicklaus chipped to within 8 feet and then ran in a clutch putt to save bogey.

The player responsible for all the noise at the fourteenth green was fifty-year-old Sam Snead. Before the tournament Snead had said in an interview that his long game was as strong as ever, but it was his putting that was killing his chances. He said it was all a question of nerves. If he could yank his current nerves out and replace them with a new set, his game would be as strong as anybody's.

Snead had played well up until he hit Amen Corner in the third round on Saturday. He double-bogeyed both the twelfth and the thirteenth, which should have killed Sam off for the rest of the tournament. But on the fourteenth green his putting nerve suddenly showed up. He drained a 10-footer for birdie and then made birdie putts at 15 and 16 to get back into the hunt.

Snead started the final round three strokes behind Nicklaus. When he reached the fourteenth green, he was trailing by two. Just where he found his putting nerve the day before, it showed up again in a big way. Snead dropped a curling 35-foot putt for a birdie, and the roar went up that spooked young Nicklaus back at the twelfth tee.

After Nicklaus's bogey at the twelfth, they were tied. Snead then made another birdie at the fifteenth to move atop the leaderboard for the last time on a Masters Sunday, but his stay there would be short-lived. Somewhere between the fifteenth and sixteenth greens, Snead's putting nerve clocked out for the day. He three-putted the sixteenth and the eighteenth, while Nicklaus played the rest of the back nine at one under par to win his first green jacket, finishing one stroke ahead of Tony Lema and two strokes ahead of Snead.

In the first round of the 1959 Masters, Art Wall immediately went into red numbers with a birdie at the first hole. A bogey at the seventh dropped him back to even par. Wall would not see red numbers again until the fourteenth hole on Sunday. Wall put his approach shot just off the back of the green and then snaked in a 22-foot putt for his birdie to go one under par. Wall would stay hot the rest of the way in, birdieing 15, 17, and 18 to get to four under par and win the tournament by one stroke.

After his gigantic birdie putt at 10 and a sensational tee shot at the twelfth that set up another birdie, Ben Crenshaw's final-round charge in 1984 was almost halted at the fourteenth green. Crenshaw's approach shot to the green was a disaster. The pin was cut above the ridge on the right side, and Crenshaw's ball barely held the green on the back left side. He was faced with a very long 90-foot down-hill putt. Crenshaw misjudged the pace of that putt miserably, and the ball stopped 20 feet short of the hole.

Crenshaw collected himself and obviously regained contact with his putting stroke in the process. His downhill putt was perfectly played, and it dropped softly into the cup. The par-saving putt kept the door shut on Crenshaw's pursuers, and he would go on to post a two-stroke victory.

In the final round in 1990 Raymond Floyd's quest to become the first player ever to win a major in four different decades was dealt a huge blow at the fourteenth green as the result of a bad decision on his part. Floyd had just missed the green to the left but had a very makeable chip of approximately 25 feet. John Huston, his playing partner, had hit his approach shot stiff, just a few feet from the hole but on practically the same line as Floyd's chip. Huston marked his ball's spot with a coin. Huston then checked with Floyd to see if he wanted him to move the coin either to the left or the right. Floyd told Huston that the mark was fine where it was. That decision by Floyd may have kept him from becoming a four-decade wonder. Floyd perhaps never hit a better chip. It had the ideal pace and the perfect line until it rolled over the edge of Huston's coin. The little bump threw the ball just enough off line that it barely missed dropping into the hole. When it came to a stop, Floyd's ball was practically hanging on the right lip of the cup. When the day was over, Floyd could have used that birdie. It would have kept him from the playoff that he lost to Nick Faldo. Many would say it wouldn't have really mattered, because Floyd had sealed his fate on Wednesday, when he won the Par 3 Contest.

Don Cherry was a singer by profession and one of the country's top amateur players in the 1950s and early 1960s. He played in nine Masters from 1953 through 1962. Cherry was used to seeing his name on the marquee of the places where he performed. In the second round of the 1957 Masters, Cherry rolled in a crucial birdie putt at the fourteenth hole that resulted in one of golf's most noted marquee players, Ben Hogan, being knocked out of the tournament.

The 1957 Masters was the first year the field was cut down after thirty-six holes. At present the top forty-four players and all players within ten strokes of the lead qualify to play the last two rounds. That first year the cut was adopted, the top forty players and ties made the field.

The new cut policy was not enthusiastically received by the players. One of its biggest critics was 1935 champion Gene Sarazen. He thought it would hurt attendance on the weekend if some of the game's big names had been eliminated. Cherry opened with a 78, and his chances for being around for the weekend were not looking good, but he played much better in the second round. His birdie at the fourteenth hole resulted in his posting an even-par 72 for a two-day total of 150. If Cherry had finished one stroke higher, he and Hogan would have been tied for the fortieth spot, and both players would have made the field for the weekend.

In the early years of the Masters, Cliff Roberts worked hard at making the field an international one. As previously described in chapter 1, concerning Gary Player's first invitation, the selection process for international players was practically as loose as the criteria for U.S. players were rigid.

In 1952 a French invitee named Albert Pelissier did not play up to his billing. This was five years before the thirty-six-hole cut was implemented, so the entire field played all four rounds. At least they were supposed to; Pelissier decided to withdraw during the course of his third round.

At the time General Eisenhower was in Paris commanding the North Atlantic Treaty Organization. Roberts sent him a letter filling him in on the tournament and advising the eighteen-handicap Eisenhower of a possible match for him: "We declared a 100% bonus to the players across the board, meaning the first 24 professionals got $20,000 [allocated among them based on finishing position], instead of $10,000, and the also-ran professionals got $200.00 [each] instead of $100.00, The French entry . . . struggled manfully to uphold the honor of his country but he required far two many blows to finish three rounds and then withdrew. Messr. Pelissier collects his $200 just the same. You can play him for it when he gets back to France—starting him, I would say, about one up a side."

The competitiveness of foreign players remained weak until Gary Player broke through with a win in 1961. Player won again in 1974 and in 1978. The international players really stepped forward in the 1980s, with Spain's Seve Ballesteros winning in 1980 and 1983, Germany's Bernhard Langer winning in 1985, Scotland's Sandy Lyle in 1988, and then England's Nick Faldo taking back-to-back titles in 1989 and 1990.

Bobby Jones would have been pleased that the foreign players were making their mark on the Masters. Jones was the winner of the British Amateur once and the British Open three times during his career, and the outpouring of support he received from the very knowledgeable and courteous golf fans of Great Britain was something to behold.

Jones was a gentleman's gentleman. He loved golf and the rules of conduct the game required. He expected the gallery at the Masters to adhere to a high standard as well. In the mid-1960s Jones became concerned about some in the gallery cheering after a player played a poor shot. He addressed these concerns by penning the following message, which was prominently featured in a guide to the course that was provided to spectators:

> In golf, customs of etiquette and decorum are just as important as rules governing play. It is appropriate for spectators to applaud successful strokes in proportion to difficulty, but excessive demonstrations by a player or partisans are not proper because of the possible effect on other competitors.
>
> Most distressing to those who love the game of golf is the applauding or cheering of misplays or misfortunes of a player. Such occurrences have been rare at the Masters, but we must eliminate them entirely if the patrons are to continue to merit their reputation as the most knowledgeable and considerate in the world.

The wave of foreign winners had been hard for some Masters fans to take, and some of this bitterness spilled out at the fourteenth tee in the 1991 Masters in the final round. Ian Woosnam from Wales and the epitome of the all-American golfer, Tom Watson, were paired in the last group and battling it out for the green jacket.

Woosnam had started the day three in front of Watson and moved to four with a birdie at the ninth. It was beginning to look like it was going to be a long day for those in the gallery who wanted a U.S. victory. This contingent showed its colors when Woosnam's approach to the tenth green was a little hot. As the ball was rolling across the green, there were pleas and cheers for it to keep rolling and go off the back of the green, which it did. Woosnam made bogey, Watson parred, and the margin was again three strokes.

At the twelfth hole some of the wind was taken out of the pro-USA crowd when Watson dumped his tee shot in Rae's Creek and took a double bogey to fall five strokes behind. The situation changed radically, however, at the thirteenth hole. Woosnam's attempt to reach the green in two found the creek in front of the green, and, again, huge cheers went up. Watson did reach the green in two, and when he drained his fifteen-foot putt for eagle, the roar that went up from the gallery sent the noise meter off the scale. Woosnam finished the hole with a bogey for a three-stroke swing, and his lead was now just two strokes.

It was now one of those "Sunday afternoons on the back nine at Augusta" where you can almost feel the electricity in the air. While the two combatants were walking to the fourteenth tee, a man in the gallery couldn't resist mouthing off at Woosnam. Implying that Woosnam was out of his accustomed element, he yelled out, "This ain't a links course. This is Augusta National."

The taunt really got under Woosnam's skin. Sensing that Woosnam was about to lose his cool, Watson took him aside for a quick conference at the fourteenth tee. Watson may have been triggered to act by an incident that occurred with him during the 1977 Masters. In the same supercharged atmosphere, he had acted in a manner that would later have him apologizing during the awards ceremony on television.

That year in the final round Watson had been locked in a back-nine struggle with Jack Nicklaus, who was playing in the pairing directly ahead of Watson. Nicklaus birdied the thirteenth and was exiting the green headed for the fourteenth tee when he made a gesture. Watson was standing in the fairway waiting to hit his second shot to the thirteenth and interpreted Nicklaus's gesture as a taunt directed at him.

Watson stayed charged up about the gesture for the rest of the final round. He ended up defeating Nicklaus by two strokes. When Nicklaus congratulated Watson at the eighteenth green, he was surprised to learn that Watson had been upset by his gesture. He told Watson that he was simply acknowledging the applause of the crowd, and he was shocked to think that Watson thought he would do something like that in the first place. Watson immediately apologized and apologized again during his post-tournament television interview.

Now Watson, older and wiser, took his fellow competitor aside and told the young Welshman to cool it and to concentrate on the golf in front of him. He then told him how Don January, a top professional in the 1950s and 1960s, had instructed him on handling comments from behind the gallery ropes: tell the person "Thank you very much," but then add an expletive to it for emphasis.

Woosnam then drove his ball down the fairway and turned to his friend in the gallery and said, "Thank you very much," and then put an expletive on the end that would make Tommy Bolt proud. Woosnam would end up needing all his composure before the round was completed to squeeze out a one-stroke victory.

Anthony Kim's approach shot to the fourteenth in the second round in 2009 was his best shot in a record-setting performance. It came to rest just eight inches from the cup for a tap-in birdie.

The birdie was one of eleven Kim would make during the day to break the record of ten birdies in one round, set by Nick Price in 1986.

Kim, twenty-three, whose earned his PGA Tour card in 2007, was being heralded as the next Tiger Woods. He was playing in his first Masters, and he was paired with fellow Masters rookies Rory McIlroy, nineteen, and Ryo Ishikawa, seventeen, for the first two rounds.

In the first round played in ideal conditions, Rory shot an even-par 72, Ryo a 73, and Anthony a very disappointing 75.

Kim's second round had an inauspicious start. He was in trouble before he reached the first tee, incurring the wrath of Masters officials on the practice tee for not observing the club's ban on cell phones. Anthony's drive from the first tee found a fairway bunker.

With his next swing Kim's fortunes changed. He dropped a nine-iron fifteen feet from the pin and rolled it in for birdie number one. His next birdie would come at number 3. He stumbled at number 4 and made a bogey. At 5 he began a string of four consecutive birdies by canning a twenty-footer.

Kim stumbled again at nine with a bogey and then fell hard at the tenth with a double bogey. It looked like his front-nine birdie barrage would soon be wiped out. But he caught fire again at the twelfth and went on another tear with four straight birdies, highlighted by his wedge shot into 14. His record-breaking eleventh birdie would come at the eighteenth when he rolled in a twelve-footer for a seven-under 65.

Afterward, Kim revealed what had sparked his amazing round. It was a newspaper story he had read that morning about Nick Adenhart, the twenty-two-year-old Los Angeles Angels pitcher who had died two days before in a car crash. The story had closed with this line: "You never know what can happen, even at 22. You have to live every moment of every day like it's your last." That closing line inspired Kim to play more aggressively and enjoy the moment, the fulfillment of one of his top golfing goals: to play in the Masters.

Kim followed up his record-breaking birdie performance with rounds of 72 and 74 and finished twentieth. He would appear in only the next two Masters, finishing third in 2010 and missing the cut in 2011.

In 2012 Kim had surgery after injuring the Achilles' tendon in his left leg and has failed to play a single tournament since. At the time of this writing, it was unknown if Anthony would ever return to competitive golf.

The biggest moment in the history of the fourteenth hole came in the final round of the 1997 Masters when Tiger Woods made the birdie that took him to a record-breaking total of eighteen under par for the tournament. Of course, the bigger story of the day was that Woods's victory made him the first black player to win the Masters.

Since Woods's first appearance as an amateur at the Masters two years earlier, many had predicted he would win a closet full of green jackets over his career. Few expected, however, that he would claim his first win the first time he played in the Masters as a professional and break the record for lowest total score in the process.

One special fan of Woods's broke something in trying to reach Augusta that day—the speed limit. Driving from Atlanta to Augusta via I-20, Lee Elder, the first black player to play in the Masters, was stopped by the Georgia Highway Patrol when he was clocked at a speed of eighty-five miles per hour. Elder tried to explain that he was on the way to watch history in the making at the Masters, but the trooper was not moved and wrote him a ticket.

Elder did eventually reach Augusta, and he had a chance to speak to Woods and wish him well as he was heading for the first tee in his historic final round.

In the history of the Masters, no one has ever teed off in the final round with victory so seemingly assured. After his opening round of 70, Woods had scorched the course in the second and third rounds with scores of 66 and 65, respectively. The big uncertainty for the final round day was whether Woods would break the tournament record for low score, seventeen-under-par 271. Jack Nicklaus had established the mark in 1965, and Raymond Floyd had equaled it in 1976.

Woods opened the day needing a three-under-par 69 to break the record. He had an up-and-down front nine, picking up two birdies but canceling them out with two bogeys to post an even-par 36. Woods parred the tenth hole but then birdied the eleventh hole. He picked up another birdie at the thirteenth hole to tie the record.

When Woods stepped on the fourteenth tee, one of the largest television audiences ever to view a golf tournament was following his quest for the record. Woods went with a three-wood, and those present in the gallery and those millions watching on television witnessed what may have been the most perfect drive ever hit on the fourteenth hole. The shot took off like a bullet, and it had the perfect draw for the dogleg of the hole. When the shot hit the ground, it ran like a rabbit, and when it finally stopped, it was only 70 yards from the hole. Even Woods was surprised at how far the ball had gone, and his face broke out in a big sheepish grin.

The pin was cut in the back of the green right of center. Woods's approach landed about 2 feet to the right of the flag, bounced back to the edge of the fringe at the rear of the green, and then spun back. The green's slope took it to the left, and it stopped eight feet to the right of the hole. Woods then ran his putt into the hole to reach eighteen under par. He parred the last four holes to preserve his record-breaking score.

Tiger added another notch on his Masters holster at the fourteenth in the first round in 2006 when his eight-iron approach from 162 yards disappeared into the hole for a two. It was Tiger's first eagle on a par four at the Masters.

#15
Firethorn

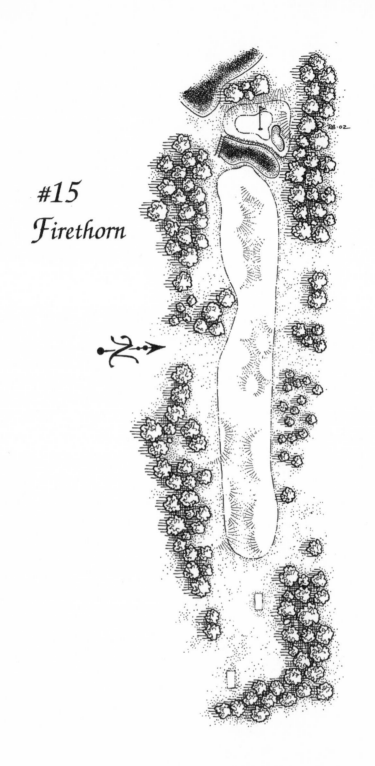

Hole No. 15

PAR FIVE—530 YARDS	FIRETHORN

The most spectacular shot in golf history was struck at this hole: Gene Sarazen's unforgettable double eagle in the final round of the second Masters in 1935, which became known as "the shot heard 'round the world." The crowd noise the shot created that day was described by a sportswriter who was covering the action at the eighteenth green as "a commotion down at 15." From those whoops and hollers that were generated by a scant few, the crowd roars that have become such a special part of the Masters were born.

Just minutes before, there had not been any kind of indication that the day was about to become one of the most historic in golf. The weather was mirroring Sarazen's prospects: cold and bleak. He walked to where his drive had come to rest on the right side of the fifteenth fairway, knowing he had to attempt to reach the green in two shots to have the slightest chance of catching the leader, Craig Wood, in the clubhouse with a three-stroke lead.

When he reached his ball, he found it in a disheartening lie, nestled down in the grass. The green was guarded in the front by a small pond, and the distance to the flag—230 yards—called for a three-wood, but the close lie dictated the greater loft of a four-wood. It was, indeed, a problem.

It had been a week of problems for Sarazen. He had missed the first Masters because he had been on an exhibition tour in South America and was having to get familiar with a course that most of the field had already played one tournament on. Also, he was breaking in a new putter because the one he had used to win three major titles had recently been stolen. If learning a new course and getting comfortable with a new putter weren't enough, Sarazen was deprived of a good night's sleep on the eve of the first round. A female had entered his room in the wee hours of the morning and stood at the foot of his bed, calling out another man's name. An irate Sarazen bolted out of bed and grabbed his driver, and the woman took off out of the room.

Those putting money down on who would win the second Masters at the "Calcutta" at the Bonn Air Hotel picked Bobby Jones as the favorite, despite his lackluster play in the first Masters. Sarazen was right behind him in the bidding. By the time the third round ended, it appeared the oddsmakers had known what they were doing. Sarazen's problems seemed to be behind him. He was trailing the leader, Craig Wood, by just three strokes.

It turned out Sarazen would have one more problem to deal with in the final round. Much to his dismay, he had been paired in the last round with Walter Hagen, for whom he had a great deal of respect but whose habits and personality Sarazen had found from previous experience difficult to deal with for eighteen holes. The two had often resorted to snarling at each other during a round. Hagen had Sarazen snarling even before they had hit their first drives. Hagen was famous for being late for his tee time, and he was true to form on this day. Sarazen quickly became miffed when the appointed time came and Hagen was still lingering on the practice green. Sarazen angrily yelled out for someone to get "Grandpa" (Hagen was ten years his senior) to come on.

This was decades before the practice of having the leader play in the last group of the day was adopted, and the leader, Craig Wood, was actually playing some four holes ahead of Sarazen and Hagen. Wood stumbled coming out of the gate and shot a 39 on the front side. Through the eighth hole Sarazen was at even par and briefly held the lead when Wood started the back nine with a bogey. Sarazen then made back-to-back bogeys at the ninth and the tenth to drop back to one behind.

Wood caught fire midway through the back nine. He posted three consecutive birdies at 13, 14, and 15. He made a very costly bogey at 16, but then birdied the eighteenth to go six under par.

Sarazen was back to even for the day at this point, after birdieing the thirteenth. He had hooked his drive out of the fairway on 14. He was preparing to play his second shot when word reached him that Wood had completed his round at six under, which still left Sarazen three strokes behind.

Sarazen's approach shot to 14 was off line. It barely caught the putting surface and was one hundred feet from the hole. His first putt came up six feet short of the hole, but he made that character test to hold on to just scant hope.

As Sarazen teed off on 15, Wood and his wife were in the clubhouse accepting congratulations. Wood believed his lead was safe and that there would not be a repeat of the year before, when he had been the leader in the clubhouse only to be edged out by a stroke by late-finisher Horton Smith. It also happened to be the couple's first wedding anniversary, and it looked as if Wood had given his wife quite an anniversary present. The press corps, too, thought the tournament was over and coaxed the couple into posing for a picture with the winner's check.

Meanwhile, back at 15, Hagen was the shorter of the two drives and hit a layup shot short of the pond in front of the green. While Hagen was playing his shot, Sarazen huddled with his caddie, who was called "Stovepipe" because of the battered tall silk hat he always wore. They both concurred that there was no way to hit a three-wood out of that lie and have it carry the pond to the flag.

Sarazen had been one of the poorest bunker players on the circuit until he personally invented a club to allow him to overcome the problem: the sand wedge. Now to overcome the problem of the lie of his ball at 15, he was going to have to invent a shot on the spot that would allow him to get enough force on the ball to carry it 230 yards and enough height to clear the pond in front of the green.

Sarazen decided to go with his four-wood. It was a new model called Turfrider, which had a hollow-back sole that enabled the club to go down after a ball that was in a tight lie. Sarazen addressed the shot with the ball slightly back in his stance and toed the clubhead in slightly. As he came down into the shot, he cut slightly across the ball to give the shot some additional loft.

Bobby Jones, who had finished his own round, had walked down from the clubhouse to follow Sarazen and Hagen in. Jones was standing on a mound about 50 yards away from Sarazen. He later wrote, "His swing into the ball was so perfect and so free, one knew immediately that it was a gorgeous shot."

The moment he hit the shot, Sarazen knew he had caught it purely. The ball was on line with the flag on a very low trajectory, but it would carry the pond. Sarazen began running toward the green. He saw the ball hit the front of the green and bound slightly to the left, directly toward the hole. Sarazen was straining to see how close it had finished when the gallery behind the green began to scream and yell, and he knew then that the ball had gone into the hole. When Sarazen reached the green, the young man reporting the scores to the master scoreboard at the clubhouse via telephone was trying to make it clear that Sarazen had made a two on the fifteenth. The scorer on the other end of the line thought the young man was confused and obviously meant to report a two on the par-three sixteenth, but the young man kept repeating that he didn't mean the sixteenth; he meant the fifteenth.

Legendary sportswriter Grantland Rice, an Augusta National member, described the shot in his nationally syndicated column the next day: "A gallery of more than 2,000 was banked back of Sarazen and packed back of the green.... [T]he ball left the face of his spoon—like a rifle shot. It never wavered from a direct line to the pin. As it struck the green, a loud shout went up, then suddenly turned into a deafening reverberating roar as the ball spun along the way and finally disappeared into the cup for a double eagle."

Rice's account can best be described as highly embellished. He missed the number of people who saw the shot by 1,978. Over the years Sarazen developed a little comedic routine he liked to use when he was being interviewed about the double eagle. He would have a friend ask him, "How many people actually saw the double eagle, Gene?" "Twenty-two," Sarazen would answer, deadpan. Then the friend would ask, "How many people say they saw it, Gene?" Sarazen would answer, "Twenty-two thousand," and his face would break into a wide grin.

After they heard the commotion down at 15 and then received the official word via the scoreboard, most of the gallery, which was clustered around the eighteenth hole, did stream down the hill to see Sarazen finish his round. Sarazen could have won the tournament outright at the par-three sixteenth. He put his tee shot just 10 feet from the hole, but after making a two from 690 feet minutes earlier, he could not make a putt for a two from ten feet. He made a routine par at 17 and had to work for a four at 18 to complete his round tied with Wood.

In cold and damp conditions, Sarazen played like a machine the next day in a thirty-six-hole playoff with Wood. He carded thirty pars, three birdies, and three bogeys for a total of 144 and defeated Wood by five strokes.

Twenty years later, in 1955, a new bridge across the pond at 15 was dedicated on Wednesday of tournament week and named the Sarazen Bridge in Sarazen's honor. As part of the ceremony, forty-three golfers from the field tried to duplicate Sarazen's shot from the fairway. No one came close.

The fifteenth has gone through a few changes since Sarazen's double eagle. The hole began at 485 yards; it now plays at 530 yards. In the late 1960s mounds were placed in the landing area on the right side of the fairway to diminish the amount of roll players hitting a hook could receive. These mounds became obsolete when the driving distance of the players increased to the point that they could easily carry them with their tee shots.

In 1999 most of the mounds were graded flat, and several clusters of mature pines were spread along the right side of the fairway to make the drive a more exacting shot.

The area to the right side of the green has always been a safe play for players to bail out to when they were trying to get across the pond in two. They played it like the "Hoganism" at 11, but instead of trying to get up and down for par, they now are trying to get up and down for birdie. A bunker was placed on the right side in 1957 (at Ben Hogan's suggestion) to make that approach a little more interesting.

Arnold Palmer received a much-needed spark from winding up in this area in the final round in 1960. The spark wasn't from a good shot but rather the look on his caddie's face. His approach shot had drifted well to the right, and he was under a TV tower. Palmer made a poor chip and lost his composure briefly. He tossed his club back to his caddie, Iron Man, at a velocity that was not appreciated. Iron Man glared back at his superstar employer. The expression on Iron Man's face was the same kind of stern look Palmer's father had given him as a child when he threw a club after a bad shot. The look and the memories it triggered prompted Palmer to make a major attitude adjustment and regain his focus. He played brilliantly over the next three holes, almost holing a fifty-foot putt for birdie at 16 and then birdieing 17 and 18 to win by one stroke.

This area of the fifteenth was the deciding hole for Peter Oosterhuis in 1973. He was in a battle with Tommy Aaron for the lead when he reached the fifteenth. He had chosen to lay up with his second shot in the second and third rounds on the hole and had birdie and par to show for it. This time he was going to try to get over the pond in two. His shot was way right of the bunker and went deep into the gallery. When Oosterhuis reached his ball, he found it was resting in a dreadful lie. It was sitting on dried and stomped-down mud. His chip shot from that lie did not even make the green. His next chip did reach the putting surface, but it still took him two more strokes to get down, and he carded a bogey six.

He would ultimately finish in third place, two strokes behind the winner, Tommy Aaron.

In what could have turned around the worst day he ever spent on the golf course, Greg Norman almost made eagle from this area in the final round in 1996. He had seen a six-stroke lead at the start of the day wiped out, and he was now two strokes behind playing partner Nick Faldo. Norman's approach shot landed just short of the bunker and rolled back toward the water about ten feet. He had a sixty-foot chip to the pin that he almost holed. His ball burned the right side of the cup as it trickled by. Norman fell to the ground and rolled over on his back in anguish. He had just missed a chance to resuscitate his chances and put some much-needed pressure on Faldo. Faldo made birdie as well, and Norman went into the water at 16 with his tee shot to drown any remaining hopes he had.

The gallery used to be allowed to stand behind the green, and some mounds were subsequently built to accommodate them further. Herman Keiser, the 1946 winner, got a lucky break in the final round. His third shot was flying over the green and possibly into big trouble when it struck a spectator and bounced back onto the green. Keiser made a par and went on to edge out Ben Hogan by one shot.

In the third round in 1961, Gary Player, on his way to winning his first green jacket by one stroke, launched his second shot, a towering four-wood for the green. The ball landed deep into the green and took a huge bounce. The bounce was so high that it was going to go above the heads of the spectators, who were standing five to six deep behind the green. Suddenly, a set of arms shot high into the air and batted the ball back onto the green.

Tournament officials responded to the green like an emergency 911 call. They immediately had the guilty party hauled out of the crowd and taken away. They then huddled on the green for a lengthy period of time to make a ruling. While they were in these deliberations, Player approached the group and proposed that he drop a ball in the area where the officials thought it would have ended up.

His recommendation was ultimately turned down for one that he certainly found more to his liking. The officials ruled that the incident was a rub-of-the-green and that he would play the ball from the spot that it had ended up after the interference. Player almost holed his next shot from 40 feet for eagle. His putt came to rest just inches from the hole. He had to be very happy, however, to make a birdie, given the direction his second shot appeared to have been heading before it was diverted. In a postround press conference, Player stated, "I realize that was not actually fair, and I certainly don't approve of it." He then added wryly, "But I'd like to give the fellow who did it a dozen balls."

Augusta National seems to have a way of doling out its own justice, and one would think that might have been the case in the final round, when Player missed a 2-foot putt for par at the fifteenth. After the 1961 tournament Cliff Roberts exiled spectators from that area, and the mounds were removed. This increased the chances that a shot that was long would run into the back pond, and from the fairway made the green look almost like an island.

Before the 2006 Masters the tee was shifted to the left and moved back to its current distance of 530 yards. But the strategy for the tee shot essentially remains the same as it was in the first Masters. Since the fairway slopes to the left, one must guard against landing on the left side because the shot can easily run into the pines that line that side of the fairway. The ideal play is to aim down the right side of the fairway with a slight draw, and one will be in a position that he can reasonably expect to get home in two. There are two factors that can work against a player, however: he is usually faced with a less than ideal downhill lie and the presence of wind. If the wind is against the player, he must guard against coming up short and splashing in the pond in the front. If there is a following wind, he runs the risk of not being able to hold the green and running into the pond on the backside of the green.

The pond in front has produced a number of great Masters moments, when players have chosen to play their shots out of the water instead of taking a penalty stroke. In the first round in 1940, after shooting 37 on the front, Jimmy Demaret (the ultimate winner) was four under on the back nine when his second shot just missed carrying the edge of the pond, and the ball ended up half buried in mud and water. Demaret, one of the most colorful dressers ever in golf, removed his red-and-blue suede shoes and rolled his chartreuse pants up to his knees and then stood in two feet of water to address the shot. He then hit an explosion shot to within 6 feet and made the putt for birdie. Demaret would record his sixth birdie of the nine on 16 and would par in to establish a backside record of 30.

In 1973 Jack Nicklaus's chances of winning two consecutive green jackets for the second time were drowned at the fifteenth in the third round. He put his second shot in the pond fronting the green. He took a drop and then dumped his next pitch shot in the middle of the same pond. When he finally walked off the green, he had made an eight.

It looked as if 15 was going to do another number on Nicklaus in 1974. He was trying to overtake Gary Player in the final round and was just one shot behind when he got to the fifteenth. His second shot fell short of the green and rolled back into the edge of the pond. The ball was lying in heavy grass and muck at the water's edge. Nicklaus took off his right shoe and sock and rolled up his pants leg and then put his right shoe back on and stepped into the pond. With his right foot under water and his left foot on the bank, he took a powerful swing at the ball and exploded it out of the bog. It came to rest only 6 inches from the hole for an easy birdie. Bogeys on two of the last three holes coupled with Player's own fine birdie up-and-down from the greenside bunker at 15 ended the Golden Bear's hopes that year.

There is more pressure playing the fifteenth than the other par fives because it is the last opportunity for a player to make the big move with an eagle. During the first three rounds, it can turn a ho-hum round into a good one. And in the final round on Sunday, it can mean the difference between winning and losing.

The fifteenth hole is where Doug Ford said he won the Masters in 1957, but he almost had to fight with his caddie to pull it off. He was in the same position with his drive in the final round as he had been in the third round. The day before, he had gone for the green. The shot carried the pond, but it hit the bank and rolled back into the water, and he made a bogey six. When Ford finished the round, he was three strokes out of the lead. In the clubhouse a couple of old pros told him that on Sunday at 15 he should not try for the green in two and to lay up.

On Sunday, when he reached 15, Ford had surged into the lead by one stroke over Sam Snead. He drove his tee shot to almost the exact spot as it had been on Saturday and was some 240 yards from the hole. His caddie, Fireball (George Franklin), wouldn't let him take the three-wood out of the bag. He wanted him to take an iron and lay up. They were tussling over the club and arguing so much that the gallery began laughing at them.

Finally, Ford told Fireball that Snead was right behind them, and he would easily be able to reach the green in two and that nobody remembers you unless you go for it and win. He then took the three-wood from Fireball. The shot barely cleared the bank and made the green. Ford two-putted for birdie and ended up defeating Snead by three strokes.

In 1993 Chip Beck was three shots off the lead and in a position to go for the green, but he decided to lay up instead. He was widely criticized for not playing to win. He got support for the decision, however, from Gene Sarazen, who told Beck later that when he went for the pin in 1935, second prize was $700, and if he was playing for the big money of the 1990s, he would have laid up, too.

It is hard to second-guess Beck from the financial angle. He finished alone in second place, four strokes behind Bernhard Langer, and collected a check for $183,600. Two strokes back, there was a four-way tie for third, and each of those four players received $81,600.

The award for attempting to reach the fifteenth in two in the final round, while carrying the most mental baggage, would have to go to Craig Wood in the 1941 Masters. As he stood near the crest of the hill looking down at the green, Wood had most of the gallery pulling for him. He had become golf's symbol for misfortune and missed opportunities. Wood had lost in a playoff or in a final match in the United States Open, the British Open, and the PGA. At Augusta he had almost won the first two Masters, but they had both been snatched away, by Horton Smith in 1934 and Gene Sarazen in 1935.

Wood had to be fearing that things were about to unravel on him again. He had just bogeyed 14 and was clinging to a one-stroke lead over Byron Nelson, who was in the group behind him. To add pressure to a situation that didn't need any more, it had been Nelson who had beaten him in a playoff for the 1939 United States Open.

Wood must have decided that if he was going down, he was going down swinging. He took out a three-wood and gave it a ride from 225 yards. The shot easily carried the pond, and he two-putted for birdie. The momentum Wood picked up at 15 carried over to 16. He picked up another birdie there while Nelson had to settle for a par at the fifteenth, and Wood was suddenly ahead by three strokes. He parred in to win by that number. Wood's good fortune continued through the summer, when he also claimed the 1941 United States Open.

In sharp contrast to Craig Wood, Fuzzy Zoeller was sizing up his second shot to the fifteenth in the final round in the 1979 tournament with absolutely no mental baggage from the past. It was his first Masters, and the fact that he was four shots behind the leader meant only one thing to Zoeller: "I had to go for it."

Zoeller was 235 yards from the flag, which under normal conditions was the maximum distance he could get from his three-wood, but a fairly strong breeze was blowing straight at him. Fuzzy gave the shot all the power he could muster. There were a few anxious moments as his ball fought through the wind. It cleared the pond by just a few yards and stopped on the front left edge of the green. Zoeller would later say, "I don't know how it got there." Zoeller missed his 35-foot eagle putt by inches and then tapped in for birdie. Reaching the fifteenth green in two and making birdie helped put Zoeller in the playoff that he would win with that great approach shot and putt at the eleventh hole.

While Zoeller had watched anxiously as his second shot made its dangerous flight over the pond, Tommy Jacobs took a different approach in his three-way eighteen-hole playoff with Jack Nicklaus and Gay Brewer in 1966. Jacobs saw 15 as his last chance. Brewer had already shot himself out of contention. Jacobs was two strokes behind Nicklaus at this point, and he knew he had to go for the green in two and try to make an eagle. He launched a towering shot for the green, but Jacobs didn't know how the shot was looking; he couldn't bear to watch. Once he struck the shot, he turned away and looked at the gallery to await their response. In a few seconds he got the kind of response he was hoping for when the gallery broke into cheers as the shot landed safely on the green. His eagle putt from 30 feet lipped out of the cup, and he had to settle for a birdie. Nicklaus ran in a clutch 15-foot birdie of his own to keep Jacobs two strokes behind, and that is how they finished.

Locked in a four-way dogfight for the lead in the final round in 1969, George Archer decided it was now or never and went for the green with his second shot, but it splashed into the pond. Fortunately, Archer was able to recover from that misfire. His pitch from the drop area ran 10 feet by the hole, but he calmly stroked his putt in, to save par. He would go on to win, finishing one stroke ahead of Tom Weiskopf, George Knudson, and Charles Coody.

If one chooses to lay up, however, he can still get into plenty of trouble. The shot from the layup area to the green has been called one of the toughest pitch shots in golf, because the player faces a very delicate pitch from a downhill lie, over water, to an elevated green.

Mike Reid was tied for the lead in the final round in 1989 at five under par. He laid up with his second shot, and his ball stopped 45 yards short of the pond. Reid's pitch shot was weak and landed just on the other side of the sloped bank and trickled back into the pond to smash his chances.

In the first round in 1994, with the pin just five paces from the front edge, Nolan Henke, who had made fourteen straight pars to that point, ran up a ten from the layup area. His first pitch shot landed just a few feet from the flag and spun back into the water. He chunked his next shot directly into the middle of the pond and understandably flew his next shot, which was his seventh, over the back of the green. He then chipped back and two-putted for his ten. Henke parred the last three holes, giving him seventeen pars and a quintuple bogey for the round.

Henke was not the only player to find 15 a tad difficult that day. Payne Stewart and Constantino Rocca had nines, and Steve Elkington and Tom Watson both took eights.

Jordan Spieth, having blown the 2016 Masters with a quadruple bogey in the final round, picked up another one here at 15 in the first round in 2017.

Spieth had laid up to 100 yards for his second shot. His third landed on the front of the green and spun back into the pond. He took a drop for stroke four and then was too strong with his fifth shot. He sent it 60 feet over the green on the left side. His chip also was too strong, and it rolled well past the pin to the front of the green. He faced a 50-footer for double bogey and left it 6 feet short of the hole. His next putt missed to the left, and he tapped in for a nine.

That same year (2017), Sergio García experienced one of the finest moments of his career in the final round at 15. Using an eight-iron from 180 yards, his second shot nicked the pin and then bounded 12 feet to the right of the hole. Sergio's eagle dropped into the cup with one rotation to spare.

Sergio had teed off one behind his playing companion, Justin Rose. Rose birdied the fifteenth, and the two left the green tied. Sergio would win in a playoff that will be detailed in chapter 18. He was the first player since 1994 to register an eagle in the final round at 15 and go on to win. Sergio had a strong connection to that player. He was one of his idols and a fellow Spaniard, José María Olazábal.

A year after that exhilarating experience at 15, Sergio experienced his most embarrassing moment in golf when he tied the record of highest score ever on a hole in the Masters when he ran up a thirteen in the first round in 2018, joining Tom Weiskopf and Tommy Nakajima as holders of that dubious distinction.

Sergio was one over through 14 and had 206 yards to the flag for his second shot. His six-iron second shot did not carry deep enough into the green and spun back into the water. He went to the drop area and proceeded to hit four more into the water. Each landed on the green, but they were either short or pin high and spun back into the pond.

Sergio's fifth effort landed beyond the flag and then bounded to the right. It came to rest approximately the same distance from the hole as his eagle putt the year before, and he one-putted for his record-tying thirteen. He finished the round with an 81, which placed the defending champion in a tie for eighty-fifth place.

One of the loudest eagle roars ever heard at 15 came in the final round in 1991. Tom Watson was battling it out with José María Olazábal and Ian Woosnam on the back nine in the final round. Watson had fallen four strokes behind when he double-bogeyed 12. He roared back into the fight with an eagle at 13, and when he put his 200-yard five-iron 8 feet from the hole at 15, the crowd went wild. Near bedlam broke out when he stroked in his putt for three. Watson would carry the fight to the eighteenth hole, where an errant tee shot would doom his chances.

The loudest roar ever at 15 had come five years before Watson's heroics. The 1986 tournament has been called the best Masters ever, and few could argue with that statement. The main stage for this unforgettable show was the fifteenth hole in the final round.

Late that afternoon, Jack Nicklaus stood at the crest of the hill at 15 with his son Jackie, who was his caddie. He had unleashed a drive of almost 300 yards and was in prime position to go for the green.

The Golden Bear had started the week sluggishly, but on Saturday he posted a 69 that put him at two under par for the tournament and four strokes behind the leader, Greg Norman. Between Norman and Nicklaus were Seve Ballesteros, Donnie Hammond, and Nick Price at five under and Tom Kite, Tom Watson, and Tommy Nakajima at four under.

After an up-and-down first eight holes, which featured a great recovery shot from the woods but two missed 4-foot putts, Nicklaus caught fire and had the gallery buzzing with birdies at the ninth, tenth, and eleventh. The bogey at 12 appeared to douse Nicklaus's hopes severely and put him three shots off the pace of Ballesteros, who had been on a tear and had taken the lead.

Nicklaus birdied 13 to trail by just two and then parred 14. While he was walking to his drive at 15, a huge roar went up from 13. Ballesteros had made his second eagle of the day, and Nicklaus was now four strokes behind.

When Nicklaus reached his ball, he surveyed the situation; then he and Jackie did the math and concluded that they were 202 yards from the flag. Nicklaus asked Jackie for a four-iron, and Jackie thought, "That's a big four-iron."

Nicklaus then asked Jackie, "How far do you think a three on this hole would go here?" He wasn't talking about changing clubs; he was referring to the score, and Jackie answered, "Let's see it."

Nicklaus put a great swing on the ball. The shot never left the flag and came within a few feet of going into the cup on the fly. It came to rest 12 feet away from the hole. Nicklaus couldn't tell how close it was. Jackie saw it, all right, but Nicklaus didn't. He had always been colorblind, and over the previous few years, his vision had dimmed to the point where he could no longer see a shot of that length finish. He could tell, however, from the cheers of the crowd that the shot was close, and he pumped his fists into the air.

Nicklaus strode to the hole acknowledging the cheers of the crowd, but with a look on his face that seemed to say, "Is this really happening?" On the green he took his time in studying the putt.

Although Nicklaus's eyesight was not what it used to be, his memory was as sharp as ever. He was somehow able, under such immense pressure, to recall that he had had virtually the same putt before in a previous Masters and had left it short. He backed away from the putt once because of applause at the sixteenth green. After recollecting his thoughts, he addressed the ball again. He took a practice stroke and then went into the go mode. Ten seconds went by, and then he stroked the ball. It had the line, it had the speed, and it dropped into the hole.

When the ball disappeared into the cup, the roar from the gallery was so deafening that the ponds seemed to ripple and the Georgia pines seemed to sway. Gallery members at other parts of the course immediately began to stream toward 15 as fast as they could get there; they could tell by the roar something truly special was occurring.

Some ten minutes later, Seve Ballesteros was waiting to go for 15 in two as the pairing ahead of him, Tom Watson and Tommy Nakajima, putted out and cleared the green, when another deafening roar erupted. Nicklaus had birdied the sixteenth, and Ballesteros's lead was now only one stroke.

Ballesteros then watched his playing partner, Tom Kite, put his second shot safely on the green. It was his turn now. He had birdied the hole on Saturday and eagled it on Friday and was in a position to reach the green easily. He had to be thinking that a two-putt birdie was practically a given, and his lead over Nicklaus would then be two strokes. Ballesteros was having trouble deciding between a hard five-iron and an easy four-iron for the shot. He chose the four-iron and moved confidently into his address position, but when he went into his swing, something went terribly wrong. Instead of making his classic graceful swing, he turned his body much too quickly and made a lurching, slapping, ugly swing. He appeared to throw the clubhead at the ball, hitting it fat and with the clubface closed. This produced a weak hook that seconds later was at the bottom of the pond in front of the green.

Ballesteros then took his drop, pitched onto the green, and two-putted for a bogey six. Kite made birdie, and briefly he, Ballesteros, and Nicklaus were tied for the lead. Nicklaus would take the lead at the seventeenth hole with another stellar birdie to secure his sixth green jacket.

#16
Redbud

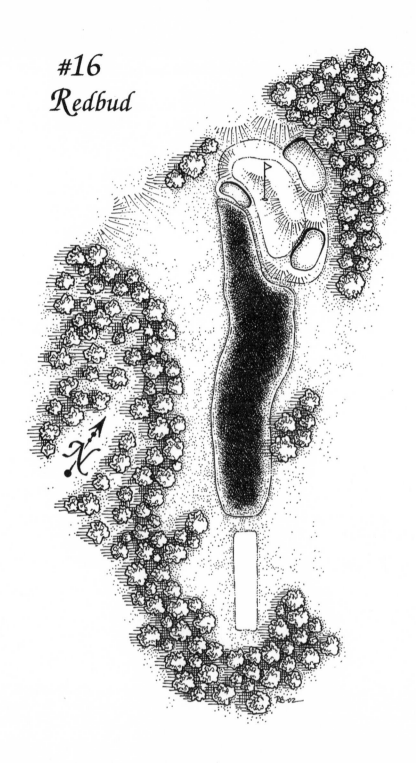

Hole No. 16

PAR THREE—170 YARDS	REDBUD

On his way to his one-stroke victory in the final round in 1967, Gay Brewer arrived at the sixteenth tee. He was handed a cup of water, but his hands were shaking so badly he could barely hold on to it. Eventually, he was able to get the cup to his lips, and he ultimately got his ball into the cup for a par on the hole.

This hole did not start out causing this type of reaction from the players. It was originally a very "plain Jane" hole. It was only 145 yards in length with a shallow stream curled in front of a narrow green, which featured a sizable mound in its middle. The primary tee was located to the right of the fifteenth green. A few years after the first Masters, an alternate tee was added to the left of that green.

The hole's early claim to fame was its holes in one. Canadian Ross Sommerville, a former United States Amateur champion, recorded the first hole in one in Masters history at the sixteenth in the 1934 inaugural, when he one-hopped an eight-iron into the cup in the second round. In the second Masters in 1935, Willie Goggin, from San Francisco, aced the hole with a six-iron in the first round, and in 1940 Ray Billows, out of Poughkeepsie, New York, did it the hard way, when he aced it on the fly in the third round.

The sixteenth's most decisive moment in the early Masters came in the seesaw playoff round between Byron Nelson and Ben Hogan in 1942. Nelson had overcome his near-disastrous start and had surged to a three-stroke lead, but Hogan's birdies at 14 and 15 had cut the margin to just one. Hogan's tee shot at 16 was weak and landed in a greenside bunker. He could not get up and down, and Nelson parred to ease back into a two-stroke lead, which allowed him to play the last two holes cautiously and take a one-stroke victory.

In 1947 Bobby Jones decided that the hole needed a makeover. He drew up plans that called for a new tee to be built farther back on the left side of the fifteenth green and for a new green. His plan also called for the stream to be dammed and a pond created between the tee and the green. Jones hired famed golf course architect Robert Trent Jones to carry out his plans.

When the makeover was completed, the hole had been transformed into one of the most elegant stages in golf. The tee shot was now played almost entirely over water, and it played 170 yards in length. The new green was protected by three bunkers: one on the right; one on the back right, which would become the one most feared by the players; and one on the left side, between the green and the pond.

The new green became one of the most adventurous on the course because of the ridge that divides it into two sections. The upper tier extends across the green, on a line starting at approximately the halfway point of the first bunker on the right side and running across the green until it nearly reaches the top left-hand corner.

This ridge provides the green with an arsenal of difficult pin placements. The most difficult location is the right rear, because it is extremely difficult to get a shot onto the ridge and have it hold the green. The second most difficult is the front right. Either of these locations brings the right-side bunkers into play. If a shot from these bunkers is the least bit strong, the ball can reach the ridge and run practically off the other side of the green. A shot hit thin can easily end up in the pond, which extends partially up the left side of the green as well.

The other pin locations are front left and back left, with the latter being the traditional final-round position for approximately the past thirty-five years. Both bring into play the water that extends up the left side of the green and the left-side bunker. The shot of choice to the traditional back-left pin placement on Sunday is to play a slight draw into the center of the green and then let the ridge feed the ball down to the hole. If the shot stays on the other side of the ridge, however, the player is left with a putt straight down the ridge, which is nearly impossible to get close to the hole. Another problem is that if the player overcooks his draw and turns it into a hook, he can end up in the left-side bunker or, worse, the water.

As before its makeover, the sixteenth remains the most aced par three in the Masters, giving up a total of twenty, which is eleven more than the combined total of holes in one for the other three par threes. Two of the twenty holes in one at 16 came within ten minutes of each other in the final round of the 2004 Masters. Padraig Harrington's seven-iron found the bottom of the cup first that day. The gallery had barely caught its breath when Kirk Triplett, playing in the next pairing, aced the hole with a six-iron shot.

In the 2016 Masters there were three holes in one at 16 in the final round. Shane Lowry did it first. Shortly after, Davis Love III did it. A few groups later, Louis Oosthuizen made one with an assist from his playing partner, J. B. Holmes. Holmes had hit an excellent tee shot that was sitting three feet above the hole. Oosthuizen followed Holmes, and his shot was a good one. Once it landed it was on a track that would send it a few feet above hole. On this path was Holmes's ball. Louis's ball bumped into it, and it redirected into the hole.

As at Augusta National other par-three holes, club selection and being committed to one's shot are critical. In the 1969 Masters Charles Coody had a one-stroke lead when he arrived at the sixteenth tee in the final round. He wanted to hit a six-iron, and then he observed his playing partner, George Knudson, hit a four-iron. Knudson's shot did not reach the back level of the green where the pin was located. Coody then decided to go with a five-iron, but he never got rid of the notion that the six-iron was the club for the shot. As one would expect, the shot came off miserably. Coody hooked it into the left bunker and then took three shots to get down for bogey. He then bogeyed 17 and 18 and finished in a tie for fifth.

Two years later in the final round in 1971, Coody had a chance for redemption. He arrived at the sixteenth locked in a tie for first with Johnny Miller. Jack Nicklaus was bearing down as well, and the monkey was firmly affixed to Coody's back from his collapse that began at the sixteenth in 1969. The pin was set on the right side, and this time Coody took his six-iron out of the bag and stuck with it. He stuck his shot fifteen feet from the pin and then drained the putt to take the lead for good. He would ultimately finish two strokes ahead of both Nicklaus and Miller, who tied for second.

Coody credits his caddie for keeping him loose in the third and fourth rounds. He was on the center stage of the golf world for the last two rounds; his caddie, Walter Pritchard, nicknamed "Cricket," was acting as though he were on the Federal Bureau of Investigation's Ten Most Wanted list. It seems that Cricket, one of the experienced caddies the Augusta National had brought in from out of town to augment its own caddie corps for the tournament, had told his boss at his regular job as a bus driver in Atlanta that he was going to visit a sick relative in Texas. He had not expected to be in the highly visible leader's group, and when he and Coody reached the holes that were being televised, it looked as if Coody had a sheikh caddying for him. Cricket had taken a towel and draped it over his head to hide his face from the TV cameras. When Cricket went back to work on Monday, he quickly learned that his attempts to cloak his identity had not worked, but the only penalty he incurred was some good-natured ribbing.

The sixteenth can be a feast-or-famine hole. In 1986 Corey Pavin moved into contention on Saturday when he eagled the fifteenth. He immediately negated the two strokes under par he had picked up when he put his tee shot in the pond and took a double bogey. Pavin had a strong round going Sunday and had an opportunity to post a low number early to put some pressure on the leaders. He again eagled the fifteenth and then five minutes later went into the water again at the sixteenth. He took another double bogey to drown his hopes.

On the other side of the coin, Bert Yancey's third-place finish in 1968 was built around the sixteenth, as he birdied in all four rounds. In 1969 he birdied the hole in three of the four rounds and finished thirteenth.

Unlike the par-three twelfth, where one has two reachable par fives to attempt to recover from a bad hole, the sixteenth is where it can all end for a player in the final round. Losing a stroke here, this close to the finish, is often fatal. A player's fortitude and his ability to overcome adversity are often put to an extreme test here.

Arnold Palmer found himself in just that kind of situation in 1962. He had started the day two strokes in the lead but was two strokes off the lead when he reached the sixteenth tee. A few moments later, his prospects looked even bleaker. Palmer's tee shot was long and ran off the green, leaving him with a very difficult forty-five-foot downhill chip back to the hole. As the gallery was being moved out of the way, Palmer overheard Jimmy Demaret, who was the commentator for the hole for CBS's television coverage, tell the viewing audience essentially that Palmer's goose was cooked.

Palmer had been out of focus all day, and like the look that Iron Man had given in 1960 at 15 and Hogan's locker-room comments in 1958, Demaret's negative comments got Palmer's competitive engine really fired up and his mind focused for the first time all day. Since the green slanted toward the pin, Palmer played an ultra-soft chip with his pitching wedge. The ball landed on the green like a marshmallow and headed for the hole with just enough speed to get to the cup. It trickled up to the hole and bumped into the flagstick and then wedged itself gingerly between the stick and the cup. "Arnie's Army," which had been in virtual retreat all day, exploded; another patented charge by their leader was under way. While the thunderous roar was taking place, Palmer made his birdie official. He strode up to the hole and shifted the flagstick, and the ball dropped into the bottom of the cup. Palmer would birdie 17 and par 18 to force an eighteen-hole playoff the following day with Dow Finsterwald and Gary

Player, which he would win by three strokes over Player and nine over Finsterwald.

Ángel Cabrera displayed Arnold Palmer–like fortitude at 16 in the final round in 2009. In the last pairing with the leader, Kenny Perry, he was two back and really needed a birdie.

Ángel's tee shot was pretty good but hardly the stellar one he was hoping for. It was 15 feet beyond the hole and left him a real tester for birdie. His putt got a lot tougher when Perry hit his tee shot. It was the shot Ángel had been hoping to deliver. Perry had stiffed it for a sure birdie. His ball was less than a foot below the hole. Verne Lundquist, covering the hole for the CBS Television broadcast, described it as "the shot of his life."

Ángel was facing some really long odds now. But the Argentinean elementary school dropout had faced long odds all of his life and could handle the pressure. He read the putt from all angles. It was a big left-to-right breaker, and he rolled it right into the heart of the cup to stay two behind.

Perry, after hitting the shot of his life, would self-destruct over the last two holes to fall into a three-way playoff that Cabrera would win.

Trailing Louis Oosthuizen by one stroke in the final round in 2012, Bubba Watson pulled even with the South African at 16. He used an eight-iron from 182 yards for his tee shot. It checked up 8 feet from the hole. Louis's tee shot with a seven-iron was 30 feet short, and he two-putted. Bubba canned his. There would be plenty of drama between the two before it would finally be settled in their playoff by Watson's miraculous shot at number 10.

In 1960 Ken Venturi was leading Palmer by one stroke in the final round. His tee shot had left him only about 20 feet from the cup, but it had also left him in an almost impossible situation. The shot had followed a great line for the pin, but it had been just a touch strong and had run into the back bunker. Venturi had very little green to work with, and what he did have was running away from him down the ridge. If he was the least bit strong with the shot, he could be laying two, 60 feet from the hole in three-putt territory.

During his long career with CBS as a golf analyst, Venturi did a popular feature called "Stroke Savers" in which he would give tips, often very creative, on how to play shots from difficult situations. On this Masters Sunday, he showed where all that creativity had been fostered. He had to get up and down to stay in the lead. Under the excruciating pressure of that moment, Venturi concocted a shot that he thought would work and executed it with near perfection. It was a half-explosion, half-pinched shot that nestled up to within 6 inches of the hole. He would later say it was the greatest bunker shot he had ever played in his life. Palmer would defeat Venturi by one stroke, but his sand save would force Palmer to do it the hard way with a birdie-birdie finish on the last two holes.

In the final round in 1999, Davis Love and his caddie, his brother Mark, were pointing to the spot on the sixteenth green where most of the field would hope their tee shots would reach. It was just to the left of the crest of the ridge, that ideal spot where the ball will trickle down to that Sunday traditional pin placement at the back-left portion of the green. The problem was Love wasn't getting ready to play his tee shot; he was preparing for his second shot. He had, as it is really easy to do in the pressure of the final round, pulled his tee shot left of the green. He managed to stay out of the water and had cleared the left-side bunker, but he was in one of the toughest spots one could be in at 16. He was above the hole and in nearly an impossible position. The green was running away from him, and any little pitch aimed at the pin was going to take off and run well past the hole. It would be like rolling a ball down from the top of a sliding board. The best he could hope for with that shot would be a 25- to 30-foot putt back up the green to save par.

In the last round in 1995, Love shot a blistering 66 and came within one stroke of forcing a playoff with Ben Crenshaw, but his tee shot at 16 with a seven-iron was just about 4 or 5 feet off target and stayed up on the ridge. He three-putted for his only bogey of the day. Unless he could produce a miracle, it looked as if 16 was going to do him in again. He trailed José María Olazábal by two shots, and a bogey here would kill his chances. It was time to be bold. It was time to dig deep. Love did dig deep, and he came up with one of the most imaginative and creative shots in Masters history. He decided he would pitch his ball, instead of at the pin, at the spot where he should have gotten to with his tee shot: up to the left of the crest of the ridge where an ideal shot from the tee would reach and then turn left and trickle down to the hole. The patrons around Love had to be thinking that he had come unglued from the Sunday back-nine pressure when they saw him pointing at that spot some 75 feet away and some 30 feet above and to the left of the hole.

Love had a look of intense determination. He fixed his eyes on the spot and then made a low pitch at the target with his wedge. The ball appeared to be laser guided. It landed softly, rolled up the ridge a bit, drifted to the right, and then gradually turned around in a well-executed U-turn fashion and began to trickle down the 30 feet to the hole. It was in no hurry; one could practically count the dimples on it as it made its way down to the hole. At this point, the throng of patrons who were packed around the green and across the pond rose to their feet almost in unison. It was like being at a college or pro football game and the home-team quarterback had just let loose with a 50-yard "Hail Mary" pass for the end zone and everyone stood up and held his or her breath. At the 10-foot mark, it looked as if it was dead on line for the hole, but at the 5-foot mark, as it was going through a heavily spiked marked area, it began to wobble. It appeared to have wobbled its way off line to the right, but in the last 6 inches it wobbled back to the left ever so slightly and caught the right corner of the cup and disappeared.

Another classic, thunderous Augusta roar exploded out of the low little valley. Olazábal was approaching the fifteenth green and had a clear view of the sixteenth green. He could see Love walking onto the green and then retrieving the ball from the cup. He could not fathom how anyone could have holed a shot from that location. Olazábal's lead was now just one stroke. He parred 15 and then answered Love's shot. Although it was not as dramatic and spectacular as Love's, it did secure Olazábal's second green jacket. He hit a six-iron almost perfectly for the pin location. It landed slightly to the left of the ridge and ran perhaps a foot or so by the spot where Love's ball had made its U-turn and began to trickle down to the hole. It was about 3 feet off line all the way, but it came to rest almost hole high. Olazábal then made that lighting-quick putt for a birdie and moved his lead back to two strokes.

Love had to settle for second place. But he had provided Masters lore with a shot that ranked just behind Sarazen's double eagle and Mize's chip in to beat Greg Norman, as one of the most miraculous shots in the tournament's history. Love's shot would drop a notch in 2005, however, when Tiger Woods played almost the same shot in the final round and achieved the same miraculous result. Tiger's phenomenal chip proved to be crucial in his finishing in a first place tie with Chris DiMarco, whom he would go on to defeat in a playoff.

Tiger and DiMarco were the final pairing of the day. When they arrived at 16, Tiger had a one-stroke lead, but after they hit their tee shots, it looked like DiMarco was going to leave the hole at least tied or very possibly in the lead. His ball was 15 feet below the pin, which was in its traditional final round location of back left, while Tiger had missed the green long and left with his eight iron. His ball was in a position close to Davis's location back in 1999, but higher up from the pin, and his ball was resting against the collar of the rough.

Because of the severe slope he was facing, Tiger knew it would be impossible to get his next shot close if he aimed right at the hole. Remembering what Davis had done, he decided that course of attack would be his best option. He wasn't thinking about duplicating Davis's heroics, however; he just wanted to get his ball inside of DiMarco's.

Tiger took aim at a spot some 25 feet left of the pin. He took a couple of practice swings and then chipped away. Because of the lie, he had been concerned that he might chunk it. But he hit it cleanly and dead to the spot he had been aiming for. His ball then checked up and took a right-hand turn for the hole. It was a virtual carbon copy of Davis's shot, as it took a slow roll right for the hole, with one exception: Tiger's ball paused on the lip for a moment but then tumbled into the hole. Tiger would later give his take on his anxious moments while his shot was on its journey to the bottom of the hole: "All of a sudden, it looked pretty good, and all of a sudden it looked like really good and it looked like how could it not go in and how did it not go in and all of a sudden it went in. . . . It was pretty sweet."

Quite naturally, the crowd at sixteenth went wild. It took several minutes for things to calm down. DiMarco then missed his birdie putt, and Tiger left the sixteenth with a two-stroke lead, which proved to huge because he would bogey 17 and 18 to fall into a playoff with DiMarco. He would claim his fourth green jacket, however, with a birdie on the first playoff hole.

The proximity of the fifteenth and sixteenth greens can add another ingredient to the Masters drama, especially on Sunday. Jack Nicklaus's tee shot in 1986 landed about 8 feet to the right of the pin and then bounced almost dead left and stopped no more than 4 feet below the hole. This, of course, sent another roar across the course. A few minutes later, Tom Watson was looking at a putt for an eagle from 20 feet at 15. If he made it, he would move to within two strokes of the lead. He saw Nicklaus getting ready to putt for birdie at 16. He knew another deafening roar was about to be let loose, because Nicklaus wasn't going to miss that putt. Watson may have wanted to give Nicklaus something to think about with an eagle roar of his own, or he may have been just wanting to ensure that he was not in the middle of his putting stroke when the roar let loose from 16. In any event, Watson sized up his putt in a real hurry and quickly putted. It was not a good stroke. The ball missed by a wide margin. He made his birdie, but his haste appeared to have cost him a critical opportunity to pick up another stroke.

Nicklaus, of course, didn't miss, and another deafening roar went up. It turned out it would not be the last reverberation from the sixteenth. Approximately thirty minutes later, someone finally got off a roar for Nicklaus to hear. Greg Norman had started the day in the lead but had run into trouble; by this point he was two strokes behind Nicklaus. His tee shot settled down about 5 feet below the hole. He drilled his putt into the hole, and another roar shot across the back nine of Augusta.

Sixteen gave Seve Ballesteros back-to-back blows in the final round in 1989. The first was as Ballesteros, who had birdied eight of the first fourteen holes and had moved to within one stroke of the lead, was lying two just off the green at 15. He was about to pull the trigger on his chip shot for eagle when a roar went up from 16. Norman had canned a 35-foot birdie putt to also move within one stroke of the lead. Ballesteros was visibly rattled and had to back off the stroke. When things finally calmed down, he hit a poor chip that left the ball 10 feet short. His putt for birdie slid by the hole, and he ended up with a par when only moments before it looked as if he could do no worse than birdie.

The second blow came moments later with his tee shot to 16. The pin was set back in the left corner. Ballesteros launched a six-iron that was dead on line, but the distance was just a few feet short. The ball landed on the bank between the pond and the green and rolled back down into the water; Ballesteros's hopes for the day went down with it.

The players typically welcome the patrons' shouts around the sixteenth green after their strokes, but there was an occasion in the 1954 playoff between Ben Hogan and Sam Snead when one patron's partisan shout was unwelcome because it occurred during a stroke. Snead had taken the lead at the thirteenth. The pin was set in the back-right location, and both Snead and Hogan came up short with their tee shots and had lengthy putts from the front of the green. Snead was away, and his putt stopped just a foot away from the hole. He elected to go ahead and putt out, and as he was starting his stroke, a patron yelled out, "Miss it!" Luckily, Snead's stroke was not affected by the outburst, and he made the putt. Hogan then made his approach and got within about 3 feet, but he stroked his next putt as if someone had yelled out. He put a rapid short jab stroke on the ball and missed it to the right. Snead was now up by two strokes and would go on to win by one.

The 1975 Masters will be talked about as long as golf is played. It is considered by many to be one of the greatest Masters ever played, and what proved to be the deciding stroke of this epic contest between Jack Nicklaus, Tom Weiskopf, and Johnny Miller would come at the sixteenth hole.

The final round was played under warm and bright Georgia sunshine and with just enough wind present to test a golfer's ability. The day had started with Weiskopf in the lead at nine under, Nicklaus one stroke back at eight under, and Miller four off the lead at five under. Weiskopf was paired with Miller in the last group of the day, with Nicklaus and Tom Watson just ahead of them in the next-to-last pairing. Through fifteen holes, the trio stroked one splendid shot after the other in one of the most sustained give-and-take battles ever witnessed on the final day. The poise, concentration, and grit each displayed were truly something to behold as each of the three was able to summon his most stellar golf when it counted the most.

Nicklaus turned the front in 33 and made up a stroke on Weiskopf, who had a 34. Miller had five birdies and a bogey on the first nine for a 32 to close within two. Weiskopf bogeyed the eleventh to fall one behind Nicklaus. Miller bogeyed as well, and he fell three back. Miller picked a stroke back up at 13 with a birdie. Nicklaus bogeyed 14, and Weiskopf made birdie there to move back into the lead by one stroke over Nicklaus and two over Miller.

At the fifteenth Nicklaus birdied, and as he walked off the green, he could see on the leaderboard that Miller had birdied 13 and Weiskopf 14, so he knew exactly where he stood as he headed for the sixteenth tee. Ironically, each player in this trio had had a problem at this hole in the recent past.

In the final round in 1971 Miller was trying to become the second-youngest player ever to win a green jacket, but his tee shot to a back-right pin location needed to draw to the left just a bit. It didn't, and he caught the right-side bunker. His explosion shot from the sand got him to within six feet. His putt looked as if were going in the hole and then spun out, giving him a bogey. Charles Coody, as earlier described in this chapter, birdied the hole and took the victory. Miller finished two strokes back in second.

Nicklaus's and Weiskopf's problems at 16 had occurred a year earlier in the final round of 1974. Nicklaus was on a back-nine tear in an effort to run down the eventual winner, Gary Player. He had eagled 13 and had made birdie at 15, despite playing his third shot with his right foot under water. Nicklaus's charge was ended abruptly at the sixteenth, however. The pin was on the back left, and Nicklaus hooked his tee shot. The left bunker saved it from going in the pond. His sand shot barely cleared the lip of the bunker and left him with a twenty-foot par putt that failed to drop and that ended his chances. Weiskopf birdied 15 to move into a tie with Player, but then his tee shot landed in the last yard of the pond, drowning his hopes and earning him second place for the third time in his career.

Both Miller and Weiskopf had cleared the pond at the fifteenth with their second shots and were walking toward the green as Nicklaus was preparing for his tee shot at the sixteenth. The pin was set on the front of the ridge on the back right of the green. Nicklaus selected a five-iron for the shot and fired away. He did not strike the shot solidly, and he began to plead with the ball to get up, but it plopped down onto the front of the green, rolled down the left side, and stopped on the lower tier some forty feet from the hole. From that spot, par was anything but assured.

Fate then selected Nicklaus's playing partner, Watson, for a train wreck at 16. His tee shot landed in the edge of the pond, and after inspecting the lie, Watson chose to declare it unplayable and returned to the tee to play another shot.

While Watson was going back to the tee, Nicklaus was afforded an opportunity to watch the action on the fifteenth green. He got to see more than he probably wanted to, since he was held up for a longer period of time than he would have liked, because Watson had more problems. Watson put his next shot from the tee in the water as well and then had to regroup and tee up a third ball. Nicklaus first saw Miller two-putt for birdie and then witnessed Weiskopf can a pressure-packed fifteen-footer for his birdie to stay in the lead. The gallery roared, and the CBS cameras went to a shot of a seemingly emotionless Nicklaus watching the action. Ben Wright, who was doing the commentary at 15, remarked, "That will be evil music ringing in Nicklaus's ears."

Watson's third shot from the tee did reach the green and provided Nicklaus with a big break. Watson's ball was outside of Nicklaus's ball and practically on the same line. Nicklaus watched Watson's putt carefully and observed how the ball curled off to the left after cresting the ridge.

Nicklaus then studied his own putt. By this time Miller and Weiskopf had reached the sixteenth tee and were watching the action on the green intently. Initially, Nicklaus's thoughts were just on getting it close, so he could make three. He wanted no part of a four-foot knee-knocker for par, but as he stood over the putt, his thought process switched from "get it close" to "make it."

Nicklaus struck the putt solidly. The speed looked perfect, and it was dead on the intended line. It climbed up the ridge, onto the plateau, then curled slightly to the right, and down it went. In a reaction that will be part of highlight films forever, Nicklaus raced around the green with his putter held high, probably in just as much disbelief as celebration. His caddie, Willie Peterson, already the premier green dancer, gave a footwork performance that would have gotten him a Tony Award on Broadway.

Back on the tee, Weiskopf and Miller looked on in stunned disbelief. For Weiskopf, it would turn out to be another huge blow administered by the man in whose shadow he had played throughout his career. His frustrations boiled over, and he looked over at his caddie and said, "That [expletive] has done it to me again!"

Weiskopf appeared to have trouble in club selection for his tee shot, and he hit a weak five-iron that came up just short of the green, some one hundred feet from the hole. It took three strokes to get down from there, and he left the hole after the two-stroke swing in Nicklaus's favor, one down. Miller put his tee shot on the green and two-putted for par. He then birdied 17 to move into a tie with Weiskopf in second place. They both had realistic birdie opportunities at 18 to tie, but they each missed to give Nicklaus the victory.

It has been said that losing at Augusta is like experiencing a death in the family. To Weiskopf, his Masters dreams died that Sunday. Years later, he would say, "The 1975 Masters, that was the end of me. It was just so disheartening. It was very deflating, very humbling. I don't think I ever really recovered."

#17
Nandina

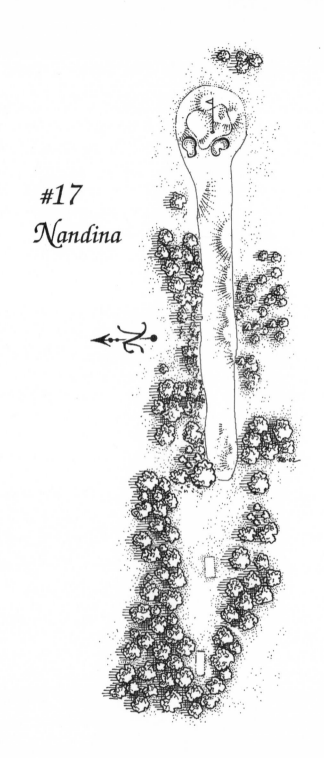

Hole No. 17

PAR FOUR—440 YARDS	NANDINA

The walk from the sixteenth green to the seventeenth tee at Augusta in the final round of the Masters can be quite an experience. In 1986, after picking up a birdie at 16 to grab a share of the lead, Jack Nicklaus had to fight back the tears in his eyes. In 1998 Mark O'Meara was trailing Fred Couples by one shot. O'Meara's eyes had a different kind of look to them according to his caddie, Jerry Higginbotham. O'Meara, who had just had a twelve-foot uphill birdie putt at 16 bend away from the hole at the last instant, looked at Higginbotham and said, "I'm going to birdie the last two holes and win." Higginbotham noted a faraway look in his employer's eyes. He would later say, "He was like, stoned, man." Many other Master contenders who have been in that situation would love to know what forces were at work with O'Meara that afternoon, because he, in fact, did birdie the last two holes to win.

This hole is an uphill par four. It played at four hundred yards in length until 1999 when it was lengthened by twenty-five yards and the tee repositioned slightly to the left. Before the 2006 Masters, the tee was moved back fifteen more yards.

The fairway runs uphill all the way from the tee to the green. The ideal shot off the tee is a draw. The best angle to attack the green is from the right side of the fairway. The players will typically play their second shots with short irons.

The green is large and protected by two bunkers, one on the left side and one in front. The front bunker covers roughly 70 percent of the front of the green. The unprotected area is on the left front between the two bunkers and is approximately thirty feet in width. The putting surface is very undulating and seems to slope in all directions. Being long on the right side can be very punishing because there is a steep slope, which can take a shot twenty to twenty-five yards farther from the green.

The lengthening of the hole in 1999 and 2006 brought the most famous tree in golf, the "Eisenhower Tree," much more into play. This giant loblolly pine protruded into the fairway on the left side approximately two hundred yards from the tee, and it caused President Eisenhower more trouble than the Russians ever did.

The event that would put this stately Georgia pine and the president of the United States at odds occurred on the football field while Eisenhower was a cadet at the U.S. Military Academy at West Point. In his sophomore year Eisenhower was heralded as one of the most promising collegiate backs in the country. In a game against Tufts University, however, his promising career was ended when he injured his left knee.

Years later, when Eisenhower took up golf with a passion, this injury would always be an impediment to his game. The bad left knee prohibited him from making the proper transfer of his weight to his left side on the downswing. Typically, this caused his shots to start out to the left and bend back to the right. The pine's position was just before the distance at which Eisenhower's ball would start to bend back to the right. Countless times, his back-nine score was inflated when his tee shot tangled with that tree. The regularity of this occurrence caused his playing partners to begin referring to the tree as "Ike's Tree," which over the years was changed to the more formal designation, the Eisenhower Tree.

During his presidency, Eisenhower served on the Board of Governors of Augusta National twice. It was during one of these stints on the board that he moved that his "favorite" pine at the seventeenth hole be cut down. Cliff Roberts quickly adjourned the meeting before Ike could obtain a second for his motion.

What a president of the United States could not get done was taken care of by Mother Nature six weeks before the 2014 Masters.

A severe ice storm hit the Augusta area, and the Eisenhower Tree suffered major damage and had to be taken down. A cross-section from it was preserved and later sent to the Eisenhower Museum in Abilene, Kansas, for public display.

The famous tree might have been renamed the "Palmer Pine," if not for a lucky break. In the final round of his first Masters victory in 1958, Arnold Palmer was leading by one stroke when he arrived at the seventeenth tee. While on the tee at the fifteenth hole, thirty minutes or so earlier, Palmer had glanced over at the seventeenth green to get a read on the pin location. He had decided he would need to play a draw around the Eisenhower Tree, to have the best angle for his approach shot. It was a good plan, but Palmer over-cooked the draw, and it became a snap hook. Instead of going around the Eisenhower Tree, the shot turned left much too soon and headed right for it. The ball struck the trunk of the tree, but fortunately for Palmer, it ricocheted back to the right and rolled out into the center of the fairway. Although the approach was much longer than Palmer had planned, he was able to reach the green with a four-iron. He two-putted for his par to maintain a one-stroke lead.

Ben Crenshaw had a similar experience in the final round in 1989. There was a steady light rain falling, and the wet conditions made it difficult for the players to keep their hands from slipping on the club. Crenshaw's hands slipped on his drive at the seventeenth, and he pulled it left. The ball tangled with the Eisenhower Tree but got beyond it and was just off the fairway. Crenshaw had to use a four-wood to reach the green, and he hit a good one. It stopped about thirty feet from the hole, and Crenshaw rolled that one into the hole for a birdie to move within one stroke of the lead. A birdie at the eighteenth would have gotten him in the playoff with Nick Faldo and Scott Hoch, but he hit his approach into a bunker and made a bogey.

José María Olazábal had a two-stroke lead in the final round in 1999 when he teed off at 17. He gave himself some anxious moments when he pulled his tee shot into the Eisenhower Tree. But like Crenshaw's shot, his ball got through and landed off the fairway on the left side. Olazábal was faced with a blind five-iron shot from two hundred yards, and he would have to keep the ball low enough to get under the branches of another pine tree that was in his line. He hit a textbook shot hard and low. The ball flew under the branches of the pine. It landed well short of the green, but it still had plenty of steam and rolled through the narrow opening between the two bunkers and onto the green. Olazábal two-putted to keep his two-stroke lead, which turned out to be his final margin of victory.

Players who successfully drew the ball around the Eisenhower Tree often had their ball miss the fairway on the left side.

Jordan Spieth established a new Masters record for lowest fifty-four-hole score after a two-under-par round placed him at sixteen under par in 2015. This total broke the previous record of fifteen under shared by Raymond Floyd and Tiger Woods.

Spieth's mark could have been even lower if it had not been for his double bogey that day at the seventeenth. Jordan pulled his drive into the pines down the left side of the fairway. His wedge carried the pines but came up short of the green. He then duffed a short pitch that just made the green and left him a fifty-footer for par. He left his par putt five feet short and then made a weak effort for bogey that stayed out on the left side of the hole, leaving him a tap-in for his six.

Jordan would end the day with a four-shot lead. In the final round he would post another 70, bringing his score to eighteen under par. This tied Tiger Woods's record for lowest seventy-two-hole, which he set in 1997.

The most extreme example of a missed drive to the left at 17 belongs to Seve Ballesteros in his 1980 win. In the second round Ballesteros hooked it so badly that the ball landed on the seventh green, which was like aiming for Kansas City but hitting Dallas.

Ballesteros took his second visit of the day to the seventh green in stride. He was given a free drop off the putting surface. He could not actually see the seventeenth green from where he was, so he took a few moments to get his bearings and chart a flight path that would get him to the green. Ballesteros then launched a seven-iron that stopped 15 feet from the hole. His next stroke dropped into the hole for a quite remarkable birdie.

Jack Nicklaus may still have had a problem keeping his emotions in check in the final round of 1986. After fighting back tears on his walk to the tee, his tee shot may have brought them right back. His shot easily got by the Eisenhower Tree, but it had too much draw on it and ran out of the fairway. It stopped between two pine trees on a section of very hard ground 120 yards from the hole.

Nicklaus recovered beautifully. He artfully directed his wedge under a low-hanging branch. The ball hit the green very hard, but Nicklaus had applied plenty of backspin to the shot. When the ball landed on the green, it checked up quickly and stopped 11 feet from the hole. Nicklaus ran that putt into the hole to take the lead alone for the first time. He parred 18 and then had to wait in the Jones Cabin for the remaining contenders to finish.

One of those contenders was Greg Norman. He ran into trouble on the left side as well when his drive stopped in a divot. Norman then played a shot that would have made Bobby Jones smile. He hit a classic run-on shot, hitting his ball on a low trajectory and having it land short of the green and run between the bunkers onto it. The ball came to a stop 12 feet below the hole. Norman then made that putt to move into a tie with Nicklaus for the lead. His great shot at 17 would be washed out by a poor approach at 18 that would lead to a bogey and allow Nicklaus to claim the win by one stroke.

You would think that all these birdies resulting from trouble on the left would mean that any player who was in good shape in the fairway with his drive would have a fairly easy time with this hole, but that is certainly not the case. In the final round in 1942, Byron Nelson was in fine shape in the fairway, but he couldn't make up his mind about which club to hit. He was torn between a seven-iron and the eight-iron and finally decided to go with the eight. He should have hit the seven, as his eight-iron came up short and landed in the bunker on the front right. He made bogey and finished the round tied with Ben Hogan. He then had to endure a night of stomach problems and an eighteen-hole playoff the next day to earn the win.

A similar decision by Ben Crenshaw in the final round in 1987 kept him out of a playoff. Crenshaw was in excellent shape in the fairway, but he was also having trouble with club selection. He wanted to hit a nine-iron, but his caddie, Carl Jackson, wanted him to go with a pitching wedge. Crenshaw's selection won out. An hour or so later during press interviews, he would be saying, "I should have listened to Carl." He hit what he described as a soft nine, but it was still too much club, and it ran over the green. It took three more strokes for him to get in the hole. This bogey kept him from joining Larry Mize, Seve Ballesteros, and Greg Norman in a playoff.

In the final round in 1990, Raymond Floyd's decision not to have John Huston move the coin he had marked his ball with from his line at the fourteenth green had cost him a critical stroke. Now at the seventeenth hole, a bad swing was going to cause him to lose another. Floyd was in good position in the fairway and had 140 yards left to the hole. He had a one-shot lead over Nick Faldo and was thinking that a par here and another one at the eighteenth would give him the win. He would later state that he should have been thinking birdie instead of par.

The hole was cut on the right side. Floyd, electing to play safe, was aiming more for the center of the green with his eight-iron shot. Floyd pulled the shot, and it landed on the left side of the green and ran all the way to the back fringe. He was left with a treacherous 60-foot downhill putt to the hole that he ran 6 feet past the hole. He missed that putt coming back, and he dropped into a tie with Faldo. An hour later, Floyd would pull another approach shot to give Faldo the win in a playoff.

Scott Hoch would have never had the opportunity to miss that two-and-a-half-foot putt in his playoff with Nick Faldo in 1989 if it had not been for his ever so slightly misplaced approach to the seventeenth in the final round. The pin was on the right side. Hoch had an uphill lie in the fairway. His nine-iron was just a little long and a little right. It carried the green on the back right by a couple of feet, hit the down slope, and rolled about 20 yards beyond and slightly to the right of the green. Hoch had an uphill pitch to a green that was running away from him. His pitch was marvelously played, and it almost went in the hole, passing within an inch or two of the right lip. It went about 6 feet by the hole, and Hoch missed that putt to fall into a tie with Faldo.

During their final-round duel in 2012, Bubba Watson and Louis Oosthuizen both avoided bogeys at 17 after less than desirable drives to stay locked in a tie.

Bubba's drive was to the left and in the pines, not yet in the dire straits he would be in later in the playoff at 10. He had a stand of pines in front of him but was able to go up and over them and land his ball 35 feet from the hole. Bubba two-putted from there to save his par.

Oosthuizen, who had been superaccurate from the tee to this point, lost his drive well right but caught a break. His ball struck a pine and ended in the first cut of rough with a clear path to green, but he had a lot of distance to cover—220 yards. His second shot was short and landed in the front bunker. With the pin back right, Louis faced a difficult long bunker shot that he played superbly. It stopped 3 feet below the hole and he made that putt to save his par.

There have been some great approach shots hit to the seventeenth green. Bob Toski thought he had made the first eagle ever at the seventeenth in the second round in 1955 when a huge roar went up at the green after his second shot landed very near the pin. Toski celebrated by doing a somersault in the fairway, but when he reached a point near the green and could see the hole, he discovered his ball was just a few inches from it.

The seventeenth did not give up its first eagle until fourteen years later in the fourth round in 1969, when Takaaki Kono holed his second shot.

The best approach to the seventeenth under pressure would have to belong to Gary Player in the 1974 Masters. After ripping his drive into good position, Player was a little pumped up. He had a one-stroke lead over Tom Weiskopf and Dave Stockton. While walking to his ball, Player told his caddie, Eddie McCoy, "This is where I won the Masters in 1961, and this is where it's going to happen again." The pressure of the moment may have been getting to Player just a little bit because his memory was a little off. Player had won the Masters in 1961, when Arnold Palmer had gone into a greenside bunker with his approach at the eighteenth hole and then made double bogey to give him a one-stroke victory. Player may have had the past wrong, but he was dead on target for the future.

When Player reached his ball, he went with a nine-iron approach. He hit the shot and then immediately pitched his club to his caddie and said, "We won't have to putt this one, matie." Player was wrong about not having to putt, but not by very much. His ball came to rest eight inches from the hole. The tap-in birdie would seal his second Masters win.

The seventeenth green has certainly had its share of big moments, such as Horton Smith's experience in the final round in 1936. For poor weather conditions during a Masters, it would be hard to beat that year's tournament. The opening round was postponed a day because of rain. When the tournament started on Friday, the temperature was hovering around the freezing mark. The weather improved on Saturday for the second round. The third and fourth rounds were to be played on Sunday, but the rains returned and forced those two rounds to be postponed until Monday. The first eighteen holes that Monday were played under very soggy conditions, and things got worse for the final eighteen that afternoon. The rains returned, accompanied by very blustery winds. There were calls from the players for the round to be canceled, but Masters officials declined to stop play. Harry "Hard Luck" Cooper had been the leader after rounds one and two and had maintained that position with a one-under-par 71 in the third round. Horton Smith, winner of the inaugural Masters in 1934, was in second place, three strokes behind.

Cooper was playing approximately an hour ahead of Smith and caught much tougher weather. He slipped a bit on the front nine, shooting a 39. Cooper reeled off seven straight pars on the back, but he pushed his drive to the right at the seventeenth and made bogey, then parred the eighteenth for a 76. Smith shaved two strokes off Cooper's lead on the front nine and caught a break on the back nine when the rain stopped and the winds calmed. A birdie at the fifteenth gave him the lead, but he found himself in a tough spot on the seventeenth green. His approach shot left him forty feet from the cup. Smith misjudged how much effect the wet green would have on the pace of his ball, and he hit the putt much too hard. The ball did not stop rolling until it was seventeen feet past the hole. Smith regrouped and stroked his next putt. The ball kicked up a rooster tail of water all the way to the hole and then dropped into the cup for truly a par the hard way. Smith then parred 18 to become the first player to win two Masters.

One of the key strokes in Arnold Palmer's charge to victory in the final round in 1960 took place on the seventeenth green. He was trailing Ken Venturi by one stroke. Palmer hit an eight-iron approach to the green, but it checked up quickly when it landed and left him a twenty-seven-foot putt for birdie. One year earlier in 1959, Palmer had a chance at a birdie on the seventeenth in the final round, but had missed it, which he attributed to movement in the gallery. Twice as he was standing over this putt, he backed away because there was movement in the crowd. Finally, he stroked the putt. It was on line all the way, but it appeared that its speed might cause it to come up a hair short. The ball made it to the lip of the cup, paused for a moment, and then toppled in. The birdie pulled Palmer even with Venturi and would set up one of the most dramatic finishes ever on the eighteenth hole.

In 1977 Jack Nicklaus was standing in the eighteenth fairway about to hit his approach to the green. He was tied with Tom Watson for the lead and was hoping to hit his second shot close so he would have a chance to take the lead with a birdie. As he was getting ready to play the shot, a huge roar went up behind him at the seventeenth green. Watson had a few minutes before dropped his approach fifteen feet above the hole at 17. The roar had gone up because he had drained the wicked downhill putt for birdie to take the lead.

Nicklaus now needed a birdie just to tie. He did not respond in a way you would expect of Nicklaus. He dumped his approach in the bunker in front of the green. His bunker shot got him only to about twelve feet from the hole, and he missed that putt to take a bogey. Watson made a par at 18 to win by two strokes.

In his second Masters win in 1981, Watson had a tough time with the seventeenth hole. In the second round, he hit his approach shot into the front bunker and made bogey. In the third round Watson was threatening to pull away from the field. He had birdied the thirteenth, fourteenth, and fifteenth and had a four-shot lead. But he had a reversal of fortune at the seventeenth, when his approach shot again landed in the front bunker. He blasted out of the bunker to within six feet of the hole. His putt for par went two feet by the hole, and he missed again on his next effort and tapped in for a double-bogey six. The round ended with Watson just one ahead of Nicklaus, who had putting problems of his own at 18 when he missed a two-footer.

In the final round Johnny Miller joined Nicklaus in trying to overtake Watson. Late in the round, it was becoming apparent that they were going to need some help from Watson to have a chance. At the seventeenth, it looked as if Watson was about to cooperate. He had hit an excellent drive and had only a pitching wedge left to the green. The shot was about six inches from being perfect. It barely missed clearing the far edge of his favorite front bunker and rolled back down to its center.

Watson had a good lie in the bunker and hit an excellent shot that stopped four feet from the cup. Given Watson's putting experience from the day before, anything could happen, but he all but sealed the victory when he smoothly stroked his ball into the hole for par. Watson played the eighteenth solidly and made a par to win by two strokes over Nicklaus and Miller.

In 1966 a missed putt at the seventeenth hole actually helped Jack Nicklaus become the first player to win back-to-back green jackets. Nicklaus missed a three-foot birdie putt on the seventeenth hole in the final round. The miss proved crucial because when the day was over, Nicklaus was in a three-way tie with Tommy Jacobs and Gay Brewer. Shortly after Nicklaus had concluded his round, he saw a replay of his miss at the seventeenth green. In watching the replay he detected a flaw in his putting stance. His head was too far out over the ball. He immediately went to the practice green and worked on keeping his head in the proper position.

The next day Nicklaus won the playoff by shooting a 70 to Jacobs's 72 and Brewer's 78. The key strokes for him in the playoff were two big birdie putts that he made: a downhill eighteen-footer at the sixth hole and a twenty-five-footer at the eleventh hole.

In 1956 an amateur, a journeyman pro, and the defending champion were the three principals in a battle for that year's green jacket. The seventeenth hole in the final round was the key in determining the winner.

Ken Venturi had been the story of the tournament. Venturi was recently discharged from the army and was making his second appearance in the Masters as an amateur. His previous appearance at Augusta had been in the 1954 Masters, and he had finished in sixteenth place.

Much like Billy Joe Patton in the 1954 tournament, Venturi had grabbed all the media attention from practically his opening tee shot. He had received an invitation to Augusta thanks to the previous Masters champions. At that time, they were allowed to select one player from a list of players who had not met any of the other qualifying criteria, and they chose Venturi. His starting the first round with four straight birdies certainly proved the former champions had made a sound choice.

Venturi finished the first round with a six-under-par 66 to lead by one stroke over defending champion Cary Middlecoff. In the second round, an unwelcome guest arrived in the form of a brutally fierce wind that would be present for the remainder of the tournament. No tournament old-timer could remember the wind being so brutal at Augusta. It was described as making the fairways seem like wind tunnels. Venturi handled the wind better than anyone else in the field. He shot a three-under-par 69 to move out to a four-stroke lead over Middlecoff.

In the third round Venturi stumbled on the front nine and shot 40. Middlecoff was shooting a 35 on the front nine and very briefly took the lead by one stroke. This was the day, however, that Middlecoff made that quick trip to the locker room after completing the front nine to take his allergy medication, only to find it missing. Without the medication, he suffered through a difficult back nine, shooting a 40, while Venturi righted himself on the back and shot a 35 to go again into the lead by four after three rounds. Middlecoff retained second place.

Jackie Burke, thirty-three, had qualified for the United States Open at age sixteen. Burke had turned pro at the age of eighteen and had won five PGA events in his career. His best finish at Augusta had been in the 1952 Masters, when he finished second to Sam Snead. When the final round started in 1956, Burke was eight strokes off Venturi's pace. He did not think he realistically had a chance at winning and was hoping just for a top-four finish.

Burke teed off almost two hours ahead of Venturi and Middlecoff. He parred the first hole and made birdie at the second. He ran off seven more pars to post a very solid 35 on the front nine, which was a very good score, given the brutal wind conditions. On the back nine, he parred the tenth and then dropped a shot when he bogeyed the eleventh. He got the stroke right back with a birdie at the twelfth. He ran into problems at the fourteenth and made another bogey to fall back to even par for the day. When he arrived at the seventeenth tee, the wind was at his back, and it pushed his drive well up the fairway. Burke gauged the wind's effect nicely on his approach shot. He dropped his ball onto the green just beyond the bunker, and it stopped fifteen feet from the hole. His putt for birdie on a calm day would have never reached the hole, but on this day the stiff wind gave it the last revolution it needed to topple into the hole.

Burke would have some anxious moments at the eighteenth green. His approach shot landed in the front bunker, but he hit a superb sand shot to within a few feet of the hole and then one-putted to save his par. His score of one-over-par 289 was looking really good. Burke would not know exactly how good it would turn out to be for a while, because the other contenders still had plenty of golf left to play.

Approximately an hour and a half later, Cary Middlecoff came to the seventeenth hole. He was quite possibly playing the most inconsistent final round ever by a contender. On the positive side, he had opened with birdies at the first and second. On the negative side, he had that four-putt green at the fifth for a double bogey. On the par-three sixth, he missed a two-footer for a birdie. At the seventh, he had flubbed that little chip from behind a greenside bunker right into it and picked up his second double bogey. Middlecoff went back to the positive side on the ninth. He made a birdie when his second shot stopped two inches short of going into the hole.

On the back nine Middlecoff started with a bogey at the tenth and then ran off six straight pars. When he reached the seventeenth hole, amazingly, he still had a great shot to win or at least force a playoff. Venturi, playing a couple of groups behind him, had developed a case of the three-putts and had not made any birdies. If Middlecoff parred in, he would tie Burke and then have to wait and see what Venturi did down the stretch. Middlecoff's hopes began to dim, however, when he missed the green with his approach. His chip still left him nine feet from the hole. He desperately needed a one-putt, but once again his putting stroke betrayed him. Middlecoff took three strokes to get down for another double bogey, and his chances for repeating as champion were ended.

When Venturi came to the seventeenth tee, he was pretty battered since he was seven over par for the round and now in a tie with Burke. His drive was a good one. On his approach shot, he took dead aim at the pin, but the shot was long and ran over the green down the slope on the right rear. His pitch onto the green left him with a ten-foot putt, which he missed. He was now one stroke behind Burke.

Venturi had one last shot at the eighteenth. His approach left him with an eighteen-foot birdie putt for a tie. The putt, like so many for him that day, would not drop, and Burke was the winner.

In 1968 the seventeenth hole was the stage for one of the most classic moments in the history of the Masters. Roberto De Vicenzo was on the seventeenth green putting for birdie, and Bob Goalby, who was one stoke behind De Vicenzo, was putting for eagle at 15. Minutes before, the two had generated some major noise. Goalby had struck a big drive. He then hit an absolutely classic three-iron that settled softly on the green just eight feet from the hole, and a huge roar went up from the gallery at 15. While that roar was still going on, an answering roar went up from the seventeenth green. De Vicenzo had hit his approach shot to within eight feet of the pin.

While Goalby was preparing to putt for eagle, another roar went up at 17. De Vicenzo had drained his birdie putt and now held a two-stroke lead, but only for a moment. In mere seconds, an answering roar went up from 15, the loudest of the four roars—a definite eagle roar. Goalby had drained his putt as well, and he was now tied with De Vicenzo for the lead.

The two would end up tied at the end of seventy-two holes, but Goalby would be declared the winner because of the mistake on De Vicenzo's card. After all that noise at the seventeenth hole, the deciding stroke was made off the green with Tommy Aaron's pencil, when he wrote down a four instead of a three on De Vicenzo's scorecard.

#18
Holly

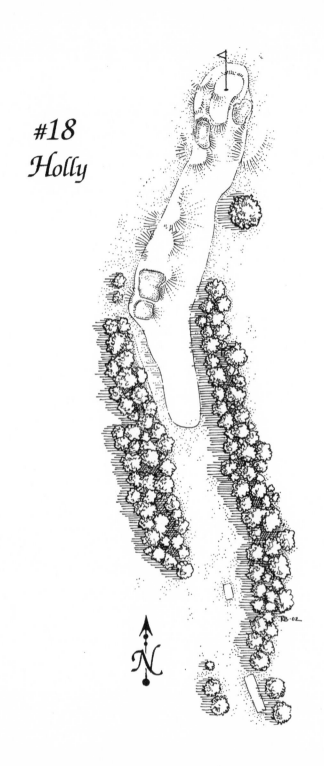

Hole No. 18

PAR FOUR—465 YARDS	HOLLY

The finishing hole at Augusta National is an uphill par four. It is the second hole on the course (number one is the other) that doglegs to the right. Prior to 2002, the eighteenth hole drew mixed reviews. Some players believed it was a great finishing hole, while others had quite a different opinion. This latter group believed that it was just an average golf hole, and most of the difficulty players experienced there was from the mental pressure of its being the last hole, not from its design.

From 1934 to 2001, only one significant change was made at the hole, and that was the addition of the two-section fairway bunker on the left side in 1967. This bunker was added because of the increased driving distance the players, particularly one named Jack Nicklaus, were achieving on the hole.

The drive is played from out of a chute of pines that run until the bend of the dogleg. The trees on the right side follow the fairway almost to the green. The left-side trees thin out as the fairway on that side makes a right turn toward the green. The fairway bunker is positioned just up the way and becomes the chief threat to avoid on the hole.

Prior to the bunker's construction, players could bomb away at the hole, and even if they ran out of fairway on the left side, they still had a relatively easy shot to the green. The addition of the bunker required that players take less club off the tee to avoid reaching the bunker or attempt to shape their shots left to right, which has often produced misfires that ended up in the pines on both sides.

The second shot is played to a two-tier green that is 50 feet wide and 107 feet deep. It is protected by a bunker on the front left side and a bunker on the right side of the green.

The easiest pin locations are on the front tier. Players will often use the slope that runs from the first tier to the second level as a backstop, playing their approach shot beyond the flag and letting the slope bring the ball back down to the hole. When the pin is cut on the back tier, there is a full club to a club-and-a-half difference on the approach shot. Also, it can be very difficult to get a shot all the way back to the flagstick and have it hold the green. Another problem with top-tier pin positions is the slope that is so friendly for low-tier pin locations turns into an enemy when the pin is on the upper level. A second shot that doesn't make it all the way back to the top tier can roll back some twenty-five to thirty feet, which will leave a very lengthy and difficult uphill putt.

Reaching the eighteenth tee in the final round with a chance to win the Masters has to be every golfer's dream, and when it actually happens, deciding how to play the tee shot and then executing the swing to produce the desired shot has to be one of the most pressure-packed moments a player will ever experience.

When Tom Watson teed off at the eighteenth hole in the final round in 1978, he needed a birdie to take the lead or a par to remain tied with Gary Player, who had already finished his round. Watson wanted to make sure his drive landed safely in the fairway, so he dropped back to a four-wood for his tee shot. He pulled the shot, however, and it ended up in some small pines on the left side of the fairway.

Watson did not have a clear shot to the green and attempted to hit a fade, but he again pulled the ball to the left. It missed the green, and Watson took three more shots to get down for a bogey, which dropped him into second place.

Thirteen years later in 1991, Watson was involved in a three-way battle in the final round, and the drives of the trio at the eighteenth tee would play a huge part in determining who would be the winner. The other two players were Ian Woosnam, who was paired with Watson in the last group, and José María Olazábal, who was playing in the next-to-last pairing.

Olazábal's drive had just a shade too much roll and was just a few feet too much to the left as it ran into the right end of the fairway bunker. His second shot landed in the greenside bunker on the left side, and he failed to get up and down and dropped a stroke behind Woosnam and Watson.

Watson decided to play a three-wood off the tee. This time his drive strayed into the pines on the right side of the fairway. Woosnam then fired off his drive, and he couldn't find the fairway either, but the outcome was better than those of his two rivals. He crushed the shot, and it sailed over the fairway bunker into the gallery beyond it.

Watson was forced to play a low three-iron to keep his ball under the branches that were between him and the fairway. The shot escaped the woods but ran into the same bunker that Olazábal had found minutes before. Woosnam had a decent lie in the rough, and his approach cleared the left front bunker but missed the green by just a few feet.

The hole was cut on the top tier of the green, and Watson's long bunker shot almost hit the pin. If it had, he might have had a short putt for his par; instead, it went 12 feet past the cup. Woosnam had approximately 40 feet to the pin, and he putted his ball to within 6 feet. Watson missed his par effort, and then Woosnam rolled his putt in to win by one stroke.

In the final round in 1986, Greg Norman could have denied Jack Nicklaus his sixth green jacket with a birdie at the eighteenth hole or forced him into a playoff with a par. Norman elected to go with a one-iron off the tee to keep the ball in play and short of the fairway bunkers. His drive found the fairway, but he was left with a long second shot of 185 yards. Norman would have to go with his four-iron to get the ball to the pin. This was the same four-iron that he had hooked into the woods at the tenth to start his back nine with a double bogey. He pushed the shot way to the right and deep into the gallery. Norman could not get up and down, and Nicklaus won by a stroke.

One year later in the final round, Norman was again tied for the lead when he reached the eighteenth tee, this time with Larry Mize and Seve Ballesteros. Norman decided not to lay back this time and unleashed a huge drive. When the ball came to rest, it was less than 90 yards from the green. Norman used a sand wedge for his second shot but did not get as close to the pin as he would have hoped from that distance. He had a 25-foot putt for a birdie that he appeared to stroke perfectly. A foot from the hole, it looked as if Norman had won the Masters, but then his ball turned ever so slightly. It rolled by the left lip of the cup as close as it possibly could without contacting it, and Norman was then on his way to the playoff with Mize and Ballesteros that Mize would win.

In 1989 Norman came to the eighteenth tee on Sunday, again needing a birdie to win and par for a playoff. Norman decided to lay back with a one-iron, as he had done in 1986. His distance this time was a little better, and he had a five-iron to the green, or at least he thought he was at five-iron distance. The shot came up well short of the green, and again he could not get up and down and lost a chance to be in a playoff with Nick Faldo and Scott Hoch.

In 1997 Tiger Woods stood on the eighteenth tee in the final round with a twelve-stroke lead, the biggest in Masters history, and he was on his way to setting a new record for low score. He had already surpassed Jack Nicklaus's record of seventeen under par by one stroke and was looking to add to it, but his efforts were affected by a photographer who was too quick to click his camera. The photographer pulled the trigger while Woods was in the middle of his swing and caused him to hit the shot off line into the left rough. Fortunately, he had a decent lie and put his next shot on the green and two-putted for par to preserve his record-setting performance.

Getting into trouble off the tee at the eighteenth has been the end of the line for a number of competitors, but several have pulled off great recoveries that saved the day for them.

Byron Nelson pulled a Houdini-like approach in the final round in 1942. He was coming off a disastrous bogey at the seventeenth hole that had dropped him into a tie with Ben Hogan. His misfortunes continued at the eighteenth tee when his drive found the pines on the right side of the fairway.

It didn't appear that Nelson would have any hope of reaching the green in two because of the number of low-hanging branches between him and the fairway. But he played one of the most splendid shots of his career, as he hit the shot hard and still managed to keep it below the branches. The shot rocketed out into the clear and headed toward the green. It landed well short of the putting surface, but had enough juice left on it to roll up onto the green. Nelson got down in two putts to keep a share of the lead and force the eighteen-hole playoff the next day with Hogan, which Nelson took by one stroke.

Tommy Jacobs was one of the tournament long shots in 1966. Since 1952 he had made it to the Masters five times and had finishes of sixtieth, forty-third, twenty-eighth, fifty-seventh, and fifteenth. This year, however, the scoring was unusually high, and Jacobs stood a chance when he reached the eighteenth hole to win it all. He was at even par for the tournament and tied for the lead with Jack Nicklaus, who was in a pairing behind him, and Gay Brewer, who was already in the clubhouse.

A par stood a good chance of putting him into a playoff with Nicklaus and Brewer the next day, but if you were Tommy Jacobs, the last thing you want to do is take on Nicklaus in a playoff. Jacobs needed a birdie to win it all. The most important tee shot he ever hit in his life, however, turned out to be a dud. Jacobs hit the shot off the toe of his driver, and it sputtered down to the bend in the dog-leg and left him with a four-wood shot to the green instead of the six- or seven-iron approach a good drive would have provided him.

Where his drive had made him look like a weekend duffer, his shot with the four-wood made him look like he belonged at Augusta. In a classic example of the golfing axiom "It's not how you drive but how you arrive," the shot landed just to the right of the flag, skipped up the slope that runs up to the back tier, and then rolled back toward the flag, stopping fifteen feet above the hole. Jacobs then had the opportunity to win it all, but his birdie putt missed, and he had to make a three-footer coming back for his par. Nicklaus almost made a forty-foot birdie putt to win in regulation, but he did win the playoff with Jacobs and Brewer the following day.

In 1988, Sandy Lyle pulled his drive slightly on the eighteenth hole in the final round and it ran into the fairway bunker. The shot appeared to be the finishing blow in what had been a devastating back nine for Lyle. He had started the final nine holes with a four-shot lead, but he had been cut to pieces at Amen Corner by a bogey at the eleventh hole and a double bogey at the twelfth hole. Lyle had appeared to have bounced back by birdieing the sixteenth to pull himself back into a tie with Mark Calcavecchia for the lead. When Lyle saw his drive disappear into the bunker, he thought it was all over.

In the "every cloud has a silver lining" category, Lyle did catch a break: his ball had a decent lie in the bunker. Lyle decided to go with his seven-iron for his second shot. He had had a good day with that club. He reached the par-five second hole with it on his second shot, which led to a tap-in birdie. At the ninth hole he hit it stiff to set up another birdie. And at the par-three sixteenth, he had hit his tee shot to within ten feet, which put him in position for another birdie.

It turned out there was one more good shot left in the club. Lyle was dangerously close to the front lip of the bunker and had to hoist the shot really high to get it out safely. He launched the shot skyward, clearing the lip, and it had some carry to it, almost too much carry. The ball flew right over the flag, which was on the lower tier on the left-hand side. It landed about twenty-five feet beyond the hole and missed making the top tier by about eighteen inches, which would have been disastrous for Lyle. The ball was then captured by the slope, and it rolled backward and stopped ten feet above the hole.

Thousands in the gallery began making their way to the tenth hole in anticipation of a playoff, while thousands more squeezed in on the spectators who had been entrenched at the eighteenth green all day. Lyle's putt was straight downhill and wickedly fast, but he had caught another break: the putt's line was the straightest he'd had all day. He admitted his knees were knocking a little as he stood over the putt, but he managed to put a nice stroke on the ball. It rolled straight down the slope and into the hole, and Lyle was the champion.

Even if a player is in the fairway with his drive in the final round, the pressure of the approach shot can be just as excruciating as the tee shot. In 1957 Doug Ford looked as if he had the tournament locked up after his drive found the center of the fairway. He had a three-stroke lead over Snead, who was playing several groups behind him, and a par at the eighteenth would probably have sewn up his victory. Ford's seven-iron approach shot, however, was short and plunged into the bunker on the front left side.

Ford, one of the fastest players in the game, wasted no time once he reached the bunker. He charged down into it, took a quick look at the flagstick that was about thirty-five feet away from him, and fired away. His ball landed a few feet short of the cup and rolled in for a birdie, assuring Ford's victory. Ford threw his sand wedge high into the air after the shot. He then exclaimed that it was the greatest shot he had ever played.

The approach shots of Roberto De Vicenzo in 1968 and Ed Sneed in 1979 at the eighteenth hole did not have the happy ending that Ford's had.

De Vicenzo needed a par to win, while bogey would place him in a playoff with Bob Goalby. His approach shots had been excellent all day. He had holed his approach at the first hole for an eagle and had came within inches of doing the same thing at the third hole. De Vicenzo's approach at the seventeenth hole had also been outstanding; however, his approach to the eighteenth was anything but out-standing. He hooked his four-iron shot. The ball carried the left-front bunker but ran off the green on the left side down into the gallery.

De Vicenzo had to play his next shot from grass that had been matted down by the gallery. He elected to use his putter but came up eight feet short of the hole and then missed his next effort to record his only bogey of the day. He walked off the green in a tie with Bob Goalby. A few minutes later, De Vicenzo would make that crucial miss at the scorers' table. He failed to detect the error his playing partner, Tommy Aaron, had made recording his score on the seventeenth hole that cost him a stroke and made Bob Goalby the winner.

Ed Sneed was reeling after bogeys at the sixteenth and seven-teenth holes, but he was still clinging to a one-stroke lead when he teed off at the eighteenth. Sneed's drive was solid, and he chose to go with a seven-iron for his second shot. He left that shot out to the right and missed the green, and his ball stopped just an inch or so from the edge of the right-side bunker. Sneed chipped onto the green to within six feet of the hole. His putt to win stopped on the right lip of the cup and refused to drop. The bogey forced Sneed into a sudden-death playoff with Tom Watson and Fuzzy Zoeller that Zoeller would win.

The year before in the final round in 1978, Hubert Green had started the day three strokes in the lead but had slipped on the back nine, and Gary Player had surged from out of the pack with a record-tying round of 64 to take the lead. Green came to the eigh-teenth hole needing a birdie to force a playoff.

Green's drive from the eighteenth tee split the fairway. He then hit a beautiful six-iron shot that came to rest just three feet from the hole to make prospects of a playoff very likely; all Green had to do was hole the three-footer. He addressed his ball and was just about to putt, but then he suddenly backed away. A CBS radio sportscaster, whose description of the action had found his ear, had distracted him.

After taking a few moments to regroup, Green addressed the putt again. Gary Player had won his first Masters in 1961 when Arnold Palmer had self-destructed at the eighteenth hole, and good fortune was about to smile on him at the finishing green. Green pushed his putt to the right, and his ball slid by the hole to give Player the victory.

One of the best approach shots ever in the final round at the Masters occurred in the 1955 tournament. Cary Middlecoff had the tournament won when he teed off at the eighteenth with a commanding six-stroke lead. He hit a near-perfect drive and then followed that up with a near-perfect approach. His six-iron second shot struck the pin and dropped down a foot from the hole for an easy closing birdie and a record for victory margin of seven strokes.

In the final round in 1946, Herman Keiser had a tough time writing the last chapter of his Cinderella story. Keiser had started the day with a five-stroke lead over Ben Hogan, who had gone on a tear on the back nine, birdieing 12, 13, and 15. Keiser had been hearing the roars and had heard chatter in the gallery that Hogan was on fire. Before he teed off at 18, his playing partner, Byron Nelson, told him that Hogan was three under for the day. Herman was one over for the round. The five-stroke lead he had had over Hogan, who was still looking for that first Masters win when the day started, was now down to just one stroke.

Things did not start off well for Keiser at the eighteenth tee, and they would go downhill from there. He missed the fairway with his drive and had to play his second shot from the left rough, which he fired straight at the pin with a midiron. His ball struck the flagstick, but instead of dropping down by the hole, it caromed twenty-five feet away and left Keiser with a treacherous downhill putt. His birdie effort got away from him, and he was left with a five-footer coming back to save par, which he missed. "I've lost it," Keiser muttered as he headed for the clubhouse.

Hogan drove off the eighteenth tee needing a birdie to win and a par to remain tied with Keiser. His drive was in the fairway, and his six-iron approach shot to the eighteenth was on line with the flag, just a little long, and stopped twelve feet above the hole.

Keiser by this time was in the clubhouse. Craig Wood, who had been caught by Sarazen's double eagle in 1935, sat down beside Keiser to give him some much-needed company. Hogan studied his potentially winning putt for a considerable amount of time. When he finally addressed his ball, he never looked comfortable over the putt. The stroke he executed was not a good one. Hogan immediately knew he had made a bad stroke and looked away after he had struck his ball. When he looked back at the outcome of the shot, expecting to see that he had a tap-in for a par and a playoff, he was surprised to see it was an even worse putt than he had imagined. His ball had run three feet by the hole. Hogan then made it two bad strokes in a row, missing the par putt to giver Keiser the win.

Hogan came to the eighteenth tee in the final round in 1951 needing just a bogey to secure for what had been for him a very elusive first Masters win. He did not want a repeat of his 1946 experience, and to make sure, he kept his ball below the hole on the green. He chose to play his approach shot just short of the putting surface. On his third shot, Hogan chipped his ball almost stone dead and tapped in for a par and a two-stroke win.

Hogan did make a putt for the ages at the eighteenth green in the third round in 1967. Playing in what would be his last Masters, at age fifty-four, Hogan had a back nine like he had never had before. When he reached the eighteenth tee, he was at five under par on the back nine after an even-par performance on the front nine. Hogan struck a stellar drive and then hit his approach shot to about twenty-five feet above the hole.

Hogan walking to the eighteenth green that day was truly a "Masters Moment" for the ages. There were hoops and hollers and an abundance of moist eyes as Hogan slowly walked up the steep slope to the green.

A Hollywood scriptwriter could not have come up with a better ending for the day. Hogan studied the putt carefully and then gave it a good stroke, and the ball made a big curling journey to the cup and fell into the hole to give Hogan a 30 on the back nine and a 66 for his round. Needless to say, the throng at 18 made so much noise, one would have thought Hogan had holed his tee shot rather than sunk a twenty-five-footer.

Making the putt put Hogan just three shots off the lead going into the final round. The magic that was in his stroke did not return for an encore that Sunday, as he shot a 77. His reception at the eighteenth green that day, however, was as if he was shooting a 67.

When Byron Nelson handed Sam Snead his scorecard after Snead had putted out at the eighteenth hole in the final round in 1954, one can bet Sam paid a great deal of attention to the numbers Nelson had recorded. In the first round of the Masters the year before, Nelson and Snead had also been paired together. At the eighteenth green, Snead had closed out his round by making a very fast thirty-foot downhill putt for birdie and an opening score of two-under-par 70. Sam gave a quick look to his scorecard and signed it. He then hurried off to get in a little fishing. When Snead returned to the club that evening for a dinner function, he was told that he had signed an incorrect score card and had been credited with a 71 instead of a 70. Nelson had written down a four for the eighteenth hole instead of a three, and when Snead signed his card, he made that score official.

Snead was naturally upset about the error, and a friend tried to console him by telling him to go out and birdie number one the next day to make up the stroke. Snead replied, "I can go out and birdie number one, all right, but I will never get that stroke back." Snead never quite got back in sync for the rest of the tournament and finished in sixteenth place.

Nelson's record keeping was flawless in 1954, and after all the scores were in, Snead and Ben Hogan were tied, and their classic eighteen-hole playoff was held the next day, which Snead won by one stroke. At the eighteenth green that day, Snead didn't take any chances. He needed to get down from five feet in two to win, so he bunted his first putt to inside a foot and then tapped in for the win.

Art Wall, Mark O'Meara, Phil Mickelson, and Tiger Woods have all experienced the ultimate golf high of draining a green jacket–clinching birdie putt at the eighteenth. Art Wall seemingly had the tournament wrapped up when he reached the eighteenth tee in 1959. He had birdied four of his last five holes and had a two-shot lead over Cary Middlecoff, who was playing several groups behind him.

Things looked even better for Wall after he uncorked what he would later call the drive of his life from the tee. He had an eight-iron left to the green and put that shot in the heart of the green, twelve feet above the hole. Wall calculated at that point that all he needed to win was to finish with a par. When he was walking to the green, an explosive roar occurred in the vicinity of the fifteenth hole. Wall knew by the sound what had happened: Middlecoff had eagled the fifteenth, and his two-stroke lead was history.

When he reached the green, Wall studied his putt for several moments and decided to play it straight at the hole and hope for the best. It stayed on a straight line all the way and fell into the cup, and Wall had recaptured the lead. There were some anxious moments as Middlecoff finished his remaining holes, but he could not come up with a birdie, and Wall's incredible five birdies over the last six holes had won him the Masters.

In 1998 Mark O'Meara put it all together on the eighteenth hole. O'Meara was tied for the lead with his playing partner, Fred Couples, at eight under par. O'Meara was the holder of a golf distinction that he wanted to shed. He had won more tournaments than any other player on tour without a win in a professional major. O'Meara had pulled even with a birdie at the seventeenth, and on the eighteenth hole he displayed the confidence of a multimajor winner. His drive was solid and down the middle. His approach shot put him in good position, leaving him hole high and twenty feet to the right of the pin, which was cut on the front-left side.

Couples had driven into the fairway bunker off the tee and then had placed his approach shot in the right-side bunker. His third shot from the sand left him with a short putt for par. It was then

O'Meara's opportunity to win it all, and he seized the moment at hand. He played the right-to-left breaking putt perfectly, and a Masters title was now on his résumé.

In 2004 Phil Mickelson had the same monkey on his back O'Meara had shed in 1998. He had won twenty-two golf tournaments in twelve season as a pro but never a major. Mickelson had come oh so close a number of times, and it appeared the 2004 Masters was going to be another near miss. He had started the day tied for the lead but had dropped out of the lead thanks to a two-over-par 38 on the front nine. With a 0-for-46 record in major championships, to say he was the Masters' gallery sentimental favorite was beyond question. This fact was accentuated by the huge roar that went up when Mickelson snaked in a fifteen-footer at the sixteenth to tie Ernie Els for the lead.

Mickelson parred the seventeenth, and while he was headed for the eighteenth tee, Els's twenty-five-foot birdie for the outright lead at the eighteenth green curled away from the hole at the last moment.

Mickelson's approach shot at 18 came to rest twenty feet above the hole. A few minutes later, Phil received a sign that it might just be his day when Chris DiMarco, his playing partner, blasted out of the front bunker and the shot came to rest just three inches behind his ball.

Phil studied every inch of DiMarco's par putt, which just fell off to the left. Phil's putt for birdie proved to be a real heart-stopper. As it appeared, it too was going to just barely miss on the left side. But it caught a piece of the lip of the cup and then circled around the hole and fell in, and Mickelson did a jump that has been best described as a low-altitude jumping jack. Years later, he would make the image of that jump his logo.

In 2005 Tiger Woods added another first to his long list of accomplishments at the Masters when he became the first player to win at the eighteenth in a playoff. Tiger and Chris DiMarco had battled it out all day. Tiger clearly had the momentum after his miracle chip-in at sixteenth, but back-to-back bogeys at 17 and 18 by him had left the twosome tied at twelve under par at the end of regulation. The change in playoff format, which had been announced the year before, put them back on the eighteenth tee for the first playoff hole.

DiMarco's approach failed to reach the green, while Tiger stuck his fifteen feet above the hole. DiMarco's chip left him with a five-foot par saving putt that he never got to attempt, as Tiger ran in his birdie putt for his fourth green jacket.

The only other playoff to end at 18 came in 2017, when Sergio García ended his long quest for a major title in his playoff against Justin Rose.

The two had pulled away from the other contenders and were tied at nine under when they reached the eighteenth tee in the final round. Both had makeable birdie putts to win, but they were both off line and they went back to the eighteenth tee to begin the playoff.

Rose missed his drive to the right, and ended up in the trees and he was forced to play his next shot well short of the green.

García's drive found the right side of the fairway, and he hit his approach to twelve feet, while Rose's third shot stopped fourteen feet right of the hole. Rose missed his putt, giving García two putts to win the championship. He only needed one, claiming his first major by dropping his birdie putt.

The most special moment for Tiger Woods at the eighteenth green had to be in 2001 when he claimed his second green jacket and in the process became the only player to hold all four of golf's major titles at one time. He played his approach perfectly into the green, using the slope as a backstop and having his ball roll back to within twenty feet of the hole. He had left the tee with a one-stroke lead over David Duval, who had concluded his round fifteen minutes earlier. Woods needed a two-putt par to complete his slam of the majors, but he punctuated his tremendous accomplishment by knocking in a smooth birdie putt instead.

Having Woods conclude his amazing run with a birdie at the eighteenth at Augusta National was truly a sight to behold. Wood's drive on the eighteenth that day, however, was a sight Augusta National officials probably hoped they would never see again. His drive would have to be the longest ever at the hole and left Woods with a seventy yard lob wedge shot to the green.

In 2002 the tee at the eighteenth was moved back sixty yards and over to the right five yards. The fairway bunker was expanded, and additional pine trees were added to the left side. The changes definitely had an effect on the scoring, particularly the increased distance. In 2001 the hole had played as the thirteenth toughest on the course. In 2002 it shot up to the number-one position, giving up only fifteen birdies, compared to fifty-five the year before.

Arnold Palmer's emergence on the Augusta scene at the same time the Masters was being exposed to millions, thanks to television, was a perfect match. Palmer's charisma and his playing style quickly put him in the top tier of American sports heroes.

Palmer certainly had a flair for the dramatic at the Masters. From 1958 through 1962, he reached the eighteenth tee in the final round with a shot at winning the tournament.

In 1958 he appeared to have it won when he teed off at the eighteenth with a two-stroke lead. His drive was good, but his second shot with a seven-iron may have been the victim of an adrenaline rush. Palmer ended up on the very back of the green, and he three-putted for a bogey. He then had to endure watching Doug Ford and Fred Hawkins both miss makeable birdie putts before he could put on his first green jacket.

In 1959 Palmer was an early starter in the final round and got to the clubhouse with the lead at two under par; however, it should have been three under par. Palmer had hit a splendid approach shot to just three feet from the pin at the finishing hole. The area around the eighteenth green in the last round on Sunday can get so quiet, one can hear a pin drop. The crowd was hushed as Palmer addressed his ball, so much so that Palmer was distracted by the hum of a news camera and missed the putt.

Palmer's lead would not hold up; Art Wall would overtake him by two strokes with his four birdies in the last five holes to post the winning score of four under par. Palmer would be knocked down one more spot to third place by Cary Middlecoff, thanks to Middlecoff's eagle at the fifteenth hole that got him to three under par.

In the 1960 Masters Palmer needed a par at the eighteenth for a playoff and a birdie to win. His drive was in the center of the fairway, and he had a six-iron left to the green. The shot was almost as good as his approach in the final round in 1959; this one stopped six feet from the hole.

The tremendous hush again fell over the eighteenth green. Palmer addressed the putt, and again he was distracted, this time by some noise behind him. He stepped away and regrouped and then drilled it into the hole for his second win.

Palmer arrived at the eighteenth the following year with a one-stroke lead over Gary Player, who was already in the clubhouse. One would have reasonably expected that the worse thing that could happen to Palmer was that he make a bogey and end up in a playoff, but one would have been wrong. Palmer crushed his drive right down the center of the fairway and was left with just a seven-iron to the green. His ball settled down into the grass, and Palmer did not catch his approach shot cleanly, and it hung out to the right, ending up in the greenside bunker.

Palmer was now facing having to get up and down from the bunker for the win. His bunker shot, however, could have reasonably qualified for federal disaster aid. He caught it thin, and the ball raced across the green and deep into the gallery on the other side. Palmer was too strong with his fourth shot, and it went pass the hole by some fifteen feet. He was then faced with making that putt to force a playoff, but the stroke was off line, and Gary Player became the first foreign player ever to win the Masters.

In 1962's final round, Palmer played an absolutely dismal round. He had started the day in the lead but was about to be counted out until he made that miraculous chip-in birdie at the sixteenth hole and followed that up with a birdie at 17. Palmer needed a birdie at the eighteenth to win outright, but his approach shot left him sixty feet from the hole. There were no heroics or blunders this time; he made a two-putt par, which put him in an eighteen-hole playoff with Dow Finsterwald and Gary Player the next day. Palmer would win that playoff when he surged ahead by birdieing four of the first five holes on the back nine to defeat Player by three strokes and Finsterwald by nine.

Palmer finished the 1963 Masters five strokes behind Jack Nicklaus, but in 1964 he finally got to experience the great feeling of reaching the eighteenth tee in the final round and having the Masters won. Palmer teed off at the hole with a five-stroke lead and capped his fourth and final Masters win by rolling in a twenty-foot putt for birdie.

Zach Johnson's approach in the final round in 2007 just missed that bunker on the right side. He made a great chip to save his par and finish with a two-shot lead. There were two pairings behind him, but only Tiger Woods in the next group had a chance to catch him. Woods's chance was slim. He needed to hole his approach to tie. He missed by twenty-five feet. Johnson's win marked the first time in seventeen years that the Masters champion had not come out of the final pairing.

In 2009 that right-side bunker did claim another green-jacket hopeful, Chad Campbell. The eighteenth was the first hole in the three-way playoff between Campbell, Kenny Perry, and Ángel Cabrera.

Cabrera, who would be the eventual winner at number 10 in about twenty-five minutes, had gone deep into the woods on the right side with his tee shot. Trying for a valiant shot through the trees to the green, his ball ricocheted sharply left off a tree and back into the fairway.

Kenny Perry had 156 yards for his approach and chose an eight-iron for his second shot, a club he had hit stiff on three occasions during the week. This time it let him down. He pushed it out to the right, just short of that infamous bunker.

With both Perry and Cabrera in some difficulty, all Chad Campbell needed to do was to hit the green from 151 yards. He didn't do it. His shot, like Perry's, drifted to the right and came down just inside the bunker's left edge.

Cabrera played an excellent third shot to about 8 feet and saved his par. Perry almost chipped in and saved his par as well. Campbell couldn't get up and down from the bunker and was eliminated from the playoff.

Perhaps no other venue in sports has produced so many moving and eye-moistening moments than the eighteenth green at Augusta: the climax of Hogan's sensational Saturday in 1967; Jack and Jackie Nicklaus walking off the green arm in arm after Jack's amazing performance in 1986; caddie Carl Jackson in 1995 gently consoling Ben Crenshaw, who, after stroking in the winning putt, bent over and let all the emotions that had been penned up during the week drain from his body; the following year Nick Faldo consoling Greg Norman after Norman had endured perhaps the longest day anyone had ever spent on Augusta National; Tiger Woods and his father, Earl, embracing after Woods's first win in 1997.

Another very moving moment at 18 occurred after Phil Mickelson's last putt fell to give him a three-stroke win in the 2010 Masters. Phil caught sight of his wife, Amy, waiting behind the eighteenth green. He hastened to her, and the two shared a long and emotional embrace.

Amy had been diagnosed with breast cancer in May 2009. This was the first time she had been in attendance at a tournament since receiving her diagnosis. His voice breaking with emotion, Phil spoke later to the press about how much Amy's being there meant. "For my wife and I, it means a lot to share some joy together. She's an incredible wife, an incredible mother, and she has been an inspiration for me."

Standing just behind just them when they were embracing behind the eighteenth green was Phil's mother, Mary. She was also battling breast cancer, having been diagnosed several months after Amy's diagnosis. Both Amy and Mary would go on to be breast cancer survivors.

There was a very special moment in the final round of the 1948 Masters that none of the huge throng around the eighteenth green were aware they were witnessing. If they had known, the applause would have boomed.

Claude Harmon, an unheralded professional, closed out his final round with a two-putt par at the eighteenth green to win the tournament by five strokes, and he received a very loud ovation from the crowd.

Harmon spent the early part of his life in Atlanta. When he was seven years old in 1924, Harmon walked to the train station to be in the throng that was going to welcome home twenty-two-year-old Bobby Jones from the United States Open, where he had finished in second place. Jones became Harmon's idol; twenty-four years later, it had to have been a very special feeling for him to win his idol's tournament.

Regrettably, it turned out to be a special moment for Jones that day at the eighteenth green as well. Playing almost an hour and a half ahead of Harmon, Jones holed out his last putt for par and received a warm round of applause from the gallery. The putt would turn out to be Jones's last stroke in competitive golf. A few months later, he would be diagnosed with the spinal condition that would slowly rob him of his mobility and eventually lead to his death.

On behalf of the thousands by the green that day who surely would have seized the opportunity had they known it was his farewell appearance and given him a very long and rousing ovation of tribute, and for the millions who have enjoyed his course and his tournament over the years, I say—Thank you very much, Mr. Bobby Jones!

Masters Champions

2018	Patrick Reed	1992	Fred Couples
2017	Sergio García*	1991	Ian Woosnam
2016	Danny Willett	1990	Nick Faldo*
2015	Jordan Spieth	1989	Nick Faldo*
2014	Bubba Watson	1988	Sandy Lyle
2013	Adam Scott*	1987	Larry Mize*
2012	Bubba Watson*	1986	Jack Nicklaus
2011	Charl Schwartzel	1985	Bernhard Langer
2010	Phil Mickelson	1984	Ben Crenshaw
2009	Ángel Cabrera	1983	Seve Ballesteros
2008	Trevor Immelman	1982	Craig Stadler*
2007	Zach Johnson	1981	Tom Watson
2006	Phil Mickelson	1980	Seve Ballesteros
2005	Tiger Woods*	1979	Fuzzy Zoeller*
2004	Phil Mickelson	1978	Gary Player
2003	Mike Weir*	1977	Tom Watson
2002	Tiger Woods	1976	Raymond Floyd
2001	Tiger Woods	1975	Jack Nicklaus
2000	V. J. Singh	1974	Gary Player
1999	José María Olazábal	1973	Tommy Aaron
1998	Mark O'Meara	1972	Jack Nicklaus
1997	Tiger Woods	1971	Charles Coody
1996	Nick Faldo	1970	Billy Casper*
1995	Ben Crenshaw	1969	George Archer
1994	José María Olazábal	1968	Bob Goalby
1993	Bernhard Langer	1967	Gay Brewer Jr.

1966	Jack Nicklaus*	1950	Jimmy Demaret
1965	Jack Nicklaus	1949	Sam Snead
1964	Arnold Palmer	1948	Claude Harmon
1963	Jack Nicklaus	1947	Jimmy Demaret
1962	Arnold Palmer*	1946	Herman Keiser
1961	Gary Player	1943–45	*No tournament due to World War II*
1960	Arnold Palmer		
1959	Art Wall	1942	Byron Nelson*
1958	Arnold Palmer	1941	Craig Wood
1957	Doug Ford	1940	Jimmy Demaret
1956	Jack Burke Jr.	1939	Ralph Guldahl
1955	Cary Middlecoff	1938	Henry Picard
1954	Sam Snead*	1937	Byron Nelson
1953	Ben Hogan	1936	Horton Smith
1952	Sam Snead	1935	Gene Sarazen*
1951	Ben Hogan	1934	Horton Smith

* Won in playoff.

2018 *Qualifications for Invitation*

› Masters Tournament champions (lifetime)
› U.S. Open champions (honorary, noncompeting after five years)
› British Open champions (honorary, noncompeting after five years)
› PGA champions (honorary, noncompeting after five years)
› Winners of the Players Championship (three years)
› Current Olympic gold medalist (one year)
› Current U.S. Amateur champion (honorary, noncompeting after one year) and the runner-up to the current U.S. Amateur champion
› Current British Amateur champion (honorary, noncompeting after one year)
› Current Asia-Pacific Amateur champion
› Current Latin America Amateur champion
› Current U.S. Mid-Amateur champion
› The first twelve players, including ties, in the previous year's Masters Tournament
› The first four players, including ties, in the previous year's U.S. Open Championship
› The first four players, including ties, in the previous year's British Open Championship
› The first four players, including ties, in the previous year's PGA Championship
› Winners of PGA Tour events that award a full-point allocation for the season-ending Tour Championship, from previous Masters to current Masters

› Those qualifying for the previous year's season-ending Tour
  Championship
› The fifty leaders on the Final Official World Golf Ranking for
  the previous calendar year
› The fifty leaders on the Official World Golf Ranking published
  during the week prior to the current Masters Tournament

The Masters Committee, at its discretion, also invites international
players not otherwise qualified.